kamera
BOOKS

www.kamerabooks.com

STEVEN PAUL DAVIES
Foreword by Simon Callow

OUT AT THE MOVIES
A HISTORY OF GAY CINEMA

kamera
BOOKS

First edition published in 2008 by Kamera Books
P.O.Box 394, Harpenden, Herts, AL5 1XJ
www.kamerabooks.com

© Steven Paul Davies, 2008

The right of Steven Paul Davies to be identified as the author of this work has been asserted in accordance with the Copyright, Designs and Patents Act 1988.

All rights reserved. No part of this book may be reproduced, stored in or introduced into a retrieval system, or transmitted, in any form or by any means (electronic, mechanical, photocopying, recording or otherwise) without the written permission of the publishers.

Any person who does any unauthorised act in relation to this publication may be liable to criminal prosecution and civil claims for damages.

A CIP catalogue record for this book is available from the British Library.

ISBN-13: 978-1-84243-291-4

2 4 6 8 10 9 7 5 3 1

Typeset by Elsa Mathern
Printed in China

CONTENTS

Acknowledgements	7
Foreword by Simon Callow	8
Introduction	13
In the Closet – Pre-60s	17
Victims, Villains and Sissies – The 60s	45
Post-Stonewall Cinema – The 70s	65
The Indie Years – The 80s	93
Life After AIDS – The 90s	121
Hollywood Goes Gay – 2000s	153
And the Winner Is... The Gay Oscars	201
Index	206

ACKNOWLEDGEMENTS

With much love and thanks to Mum, Dad and Kate, for their support and encouragement. Special thanks to Simon Callow for his kind support and interest. I am grateful to Hannah Patterson and Ion Mills at Kamera who made this book possible. My thanks also go out to everyone who has supported me, but especially to Luke Conod, Mike Deakin, Martyn Green, Peter Houghton, Lynsey Radmore, Mark Ruck, Stephen Rabbitts, Alex Russell, Tom Sheckleston, Phil Watts and Jonathan Welford.

Pictures used by kind permission from: DiscoDog, Millivres Multimedia, Picture This, TLA Releasing and Wolfe Video.

FOREWORD BY SIMON CALLOW

As Steven Paul Davies notes in the fascinating volume you have in your hands, we live in interesting times as far as the gay presence in cinema is concerned. For him, *Brokeback Mountain* is the great breakthrough into the mainstream, and though some of us may quarrel with his interpretation of the movie itself, there can be no doubting the enormity of the leap it represented. It stands in the long and by no means dishonourable homosexuality-as-problem tradition in the movies; indeed, it is arguably a film about the difficulties of bisexuality. But the fact that in a mainstream film two highly bankable and impeccably butch actors are shown making passionate love to each other, that no moral judgement is made on this, and that the actors' careers were greatly advanced by appearing in it (one of them, of course, tragically curtailed) is a quite remarkable development; inconceivable to me 35 years ago when I started acting, much less so when I started going to films 15 years before that.

In those distant days, every homosexual was an expert decoder, as skilled as any to be found at Bletchley Park. Messages were being sent to us, and we learned to read the signs, to infer the hidden communications, to sniff out the double meaning. This was not without its thrills, but it's no way for grown men and women to experience their lives. Little by little, things began to change. It had started already in the theatre, where illicit kisses had been exchanged, tortured psyches examined and what was now known as gay humour freely flaunted. The movies, as well documented by Davies, began to deal with the troublesome matter of same-sex attraction with increasing subtlety and truthfulness to life: it is hard to describe how powerful was the impact on the gay community of films such as Schlesinger's great *Sunday, Bloody Sunday* and *Midnight Cowboy*. Nonetheless, the prevailing mood was summed up by a line from Mart Crowley's seminal – if I may so express myself – play then film, *The Boys in the Band*: 'Show me a happy homosexual and I'll show you a gay corpse.' The notion of depicting the normal homosexual man or woman (as, by definition, most homosexual men and women are) was still thought of as dangerously radical. It must be said that perhaps homosexuals themselves contributed to this: the drama of being gay is central to many gay people's identities. And indeed it took major social changes before gay lives could in any way be described as normal.

One of the great debates of the 1970s and 1980s was about the desirability of normalcy for gay people. Was homosexuality inherently radical? Was it of the essence of being gay that one was consciously distancing oneself from heterosexual norms? Were gay people born crusaders against conventional society, glorying in their otherness? Or was it our demand, indeed our right, to be accepted as part of society, just another strand of human existence, different in orientation but not in emotional experience, equal in the right freely to express our loves and desires, but not in any way superior? Militantly gay films are few, but many of the films described in this book fall naturally into one or other of two camps: those of a specifically gay sensibility, and those which attempt to depict gays as part of the general human situation. The specifically gay ones by no means necessarily advocate a separatist gay position, but they do insist on a viewpoint that sees the world differently, with homosexual eyes. The other kind of film seeks to integrate gays into the world at large. I appeared in what I suppose is one of the most important films of this kind, *Four Weddings and a Funeral*. Gareth, the character I played, was flamboyant but not camp; he belonged to no stereotypical category; and he died not of AIDS, which was at that time ravaging the gay community, but of Scottish dancing.

When I read the script, it was immediately evident that this was a new kind of gay character in films: not sensitive, not intuitive, kind and somehow Deeply Sad, nor hilarious, bitchy and outrageous, but masculine, exuberant, occasionally offensive, generous and passionate. He was also deeply involved with his partner, the handsome, shy, witty, understated Matthew. In the original screenplay, they were glimpsed at the beginning of the film asleep in bed. In the final cut, the filmmakers removed this sequence, in order to allow their relationship to creep up on the audience. They were right to do so: before they knew it, viewers had come to know and love them individually, and were hit very hard, first by Gareth's death and then by

Matthew's oration (with a little help from another splendid bugger, WH Auden). Perhaps the most important moment in the film from a gay perspective was Hugh Grant's remark after the eponymous funeral that while the group of friends whose amatory fortunes the film follows talked incessantly about marriage, they had never noticed that all along they had had in their midst an ideal marriage, that of Gareth and Matthew. It almost defies belief, but in the months after the release of the film, I received a number of letters from apparently intelligent, articulate members of the public saying that they had never realised, until seeing the film, that gay people had emotions like normal people. (I also had a letter from Sir Ian McKellen saying how much more important *Four Weddings* was in gay terms than the simultaneously released *Philadelphia*, with its welter of chaste histrionics.)

Gay men and women have now entered the mainstream of cinema, losing their exoticness on the way. They are, increasingly, just a part of life, though still generally a somewhat marginal part. Sexual roles are less fixed, not in a 1960s androgynous way, but in the sense that it might be possible to have sex or even an affair with someone of the same gender and not compromise one's masculinity or femininity. Rose Troche's *Bedrooms and Hallways* played most entertainingly with this idea: a gay man joins a men's group, whose sexiest, most rampantly heterosexual member falls for him; the gay man himself later has a fling with the straight guy's girlfriend. A highlight of this film about sexual musical chairs is the speech by the hunk (James Purefoy) hymning the unexpected delights of being anally penetrated. I played the co-ordinator of the group – straight. In fact, not a single gay character in the film was played by a gay actor. One of the ironic side effects of the new dispensation in movies was that straight actors were queuing up to play gay, and it became increasingly hard for gay actors to get the parts for which they were uniquely qualified. This issue, though scarcely a subject of deep concern, raises interesting questions about authenticity. It is striking that not a single gay person had anything to do with *Brokeback Mountain*, from the author of the original novella, to the director, to the actors. (Perhaps someone in make-up slipped through? Who can tell?) Would it have been different had gay artists been involved? Better? Or perhaps, to return to my earlier point, it isn't really a film about being gay at all, simply about deep friendship which, under certain circumstances, turns sexual.

What, if anything, is missing from the gay cinematic scene? In fact, the single most significant piece of gay celluloid was a television series, *Queer as Folk*, which in telling it like it is (at least for the young and pretty), broke so many taboos that almost everything else was left looking pretty silly. Russell T Davies's stunningly witty and truthful script was an account of what it is to be part of the scene today. But, of course, many – perhaps most – gay people aren't part of that scene. There is a gay world elsewhere. Early in the 1970s, as part of a theatre company called Gay Sweatshop, I appeared in a little play by Martin Sherman called *Passing By* which I still regard as one of the most radical gay plays ever written. It showed two men meeting, falling in love with each other, falling out of love and then parting. At no point did they ever mention the word gay or homosexual, there was no reference to mothers or even Judy Garland. They simply found each other highly attractive and one thing led to another. It was amusing, touching, sexy and entirely normal. This little play has had few successors, on stage or screen. Jonathan Harvey's *Beautiful Thing*, the film version of which Steven Paul Davies describes very well in these pages, was a sort of 1980s version of the same thing, though the youthfulness of the characters lent it a special poignancy; *My Beautiful Launderette* showed another sort of tender relationship which defied race and class in the most spontaneous, natural, innocent fashion. Ferzan Ozpetek's exquisite *Hammam*, a film I think SPD is somewhat inclined to under-rate, showed the gradual, delicate development of feelings between a heterosexual Italian and a young Turk, a story which conveyed the gentle seduction of one culture by another. These are all quietly persuasive, lifelike accounts of the birth of homosexual desire.

What I personally would like to see is a story of overwhelming passion, a gay *Antony and Cleopatra* or *Romeo and Juliet*, on a grand scale. For that I suppose we need a gay Shakespeare. The gay directors who might have told that story – Zeffirelli, Visconti, Schlesinger – didn't. Let's hope that their successors will take the plunge. And let's hope that two huge box-office stars who fully acknowledge their own gayness will play the leads. Meanwhile, Steven Paul Davies's book describes the astonishing, moving, witty (and sometimes blissfully silly) things that have been achieved so far.

INTRODUCTION

'Without homosexuals there would be no Hollywood, no theatre, no Arts.'
– Elizabeth Taylor

Gay cinema is attracting a huge amount of mainstream attention, following recent hits such as *Capote* and *Brokeback Mountain*. In fact, further to the amazing success of Ang Lee's 'gay cowboy movie', as it was dubbed by many critics, most major studios have been clamouring to get behind new, gay-themed projects.

This acceptance and willingness by studios to back pictures focusing on gays is, of course, wonderful. But it's been a long time coming.

Hollywood has featured homosexuality since the movies were born but it was always as something to laugh at, or pity, or even fear. Throughout the 1930s and 1940s, gay characters were usually cast as the leading man's effeminate buddy or as the sissy, with their orientation understood, but never discussed. Later, especially from the late 1950s through to the 1970s, gay characters always seemed to be portrayed as emotional wrecks, many of them suicidal. These images of tormented individuals left a lasting legacy, as they not only told straight people what to think about gay people but also gay people what to think about themselves.

Throughout the decades, however, there were always a handful of films that broke new ground – *Victim* (1961), *Making Love* (1982) and *And the Band Played On* (1993) to name just a few. On the whole, films with a homosexual theme were full of anguish. From psycho-thrillers like the Al Pacino movie *Cruising* (1980), to bitchy melodramas such as *The Killing of Sister George* (1964) and films full of self-pity like *The Boys in the Band* (1970), the industry was notorious for churning out limited, stereotypical images of gays and lesbians.

Nevertheless, faced with negative images, many gay men still managed to glean something positive from the silver screen. In the 50s, James Dean played it straight but most knew the score and before Ellen DeGeneres and

Clifton Collins Jr (left) as Perry Smith and Philip Seymour Hoffman (right) as Truman Capote

Will and Grace made coming out acceptable, many gay men lived vicariously through Hollywood's women. Strong women like Joan Crawford embodied the in-your-face assertiveness that gay men longed to express, while in Judy Garland's drugs and multiple comebacks, they saw their own closeted battle between loneliness and survival. Revealing a love for these women was often a code for expressing a love for men.

Gay singles scenes grew up around film revivals, and phrases like 'friend of Dorothy' were code, a way to come out, but only to someone who was also in the know. Later, Cher, Bette Midler, Barbra Streisand and then Madonna also offered gay men real-life versions of Davis's and Crawford's wonderfully bitchy characters.

Today, diva worship isn't as focused as it was in the 50s and 60s. In this millennium, the gay population don't need to remain closeted, although some still do, and no longer need to set up a diva as some kind of unifying force against oppression and discrimination. Yes, gay men still respect people like Madonna and Cher but the real need for a connection is no longer there. Today it's more likely to be the diva's hunky male co-stars who draw the stares.

Gay and lesbian characters are now out and proud. Real progress was made with the rise of independent cinema in the 1980s – films such as *Parting Glances* (1986) and *Poison* (1991). Then, soon after these indie achievements, big Hollywood studios began embracing gay-themed movies with films such as *Philadelphia* (1993), which had Tom Hanks dying of AIDS; *Too Wong Foo* (1995), which had Wesley Snipes in tights; and *The Birdcage* (1996), United Artists' remake of the 1978 French comedy, *La Cage aux Folles*.

More recently, with the explosion of gay images on mainstream TV – *Queer as Folk*, *Queer Eye for the Straight Guy*, *Will & Grace* etc – filmmakers suddenly found it easier to break out from the gay, indie-film subculture and get their films high-profile releases and better distribution deals. A whole host of gay and lesbian film festivals began to crop up all around the world and, by the late 1990s, more gay movies were being made than ever before. Some great, some good, some really not so good. As the gay underground quickly became obscured by the gay mainstream, plenty of film companies rushed to produce as many cheesy gay dramas and camp comedies as they possibly could.

In a world where gay identity is being scrubbed clean so that it can be marketed as 'acceptable' to the masses who watch *Will & Grace*, much of the cinematic dross that wouldn't have made it past financiers eyes were the stories based around straight characters. Nevertheless, as documented in the final chapter, despite the rubbish, gay cinema continues to move forward with movies like *L.I.E.* (2001), *Capote* (2005) and, of course, *Brokeback Mountain* (2005), a total triumph and monumental moment in gay film history.

After *Brokeback*, more high-quality, thought-provoking, gay-interest films followed – *Breakfast on Pluto* (2005), *Transamerica* (2005), *Shortbus* (2006) – and by the time this book was going to print, most Hollywood studios had even more projects in pre-production. In 2008, Gus Van Sant made *Milk* starring Sean Penn, while Glen Ficarra teamed up with John Requa to direct *I Love You Phillip Morris*, starring Ewan McGregor and Jim Carrey. Both of these high-profile pictures are discussed later in this book. So perhaps, thanks to *Brokeback*, film financiers will continue to back scripts that don't simply rely on gay stereotypes to entertain and pull in a crowd – and that will certainly be progress.

So times have changed and this book tells the story of how we got here. From the early fleeting images of screen sissies to mainstream gay movies and beyond, the aim of *Out at the Movies* is to fascinate, even educate. Each chapter has an overview of the decade, reviews of all the main films, memorable dialogue and profiles of key players in the industry – all adding up to what is, hopefully, the complete guide to both mainstream and independent gay and lesbian movies.

Of course, not every gay reference in the movies is covered. After all, if I'd decided to include the homoerotic subtext of almost every American buddy movie, war movie, cop movie and western, this History of Gay Cinema would have been a huge tome. Instead, the book delves deepest into gay films that have really pushed the boundaries – those which have politically or emotionally reached out to gay people from London to LA and from Kettering to Kansas.

So, enjoy reading and happy viewing!

IN THE CLOSET – PRE-60s

'Hey, you wanna come home with me? ... If you wanna come, we could talk and then in the morning we could have breakfast...'

Plato (Sal Mineo) to Jim (James Dean) in ***Rebel Without a Cause***

From the days of Chaplin-era silents, through the early talkies, into the changing – though not always progressively so – standards of the 1930s, 40s, and 50s, gay characters were stereotypically portrayed as stock sissy caricatures, humorous swishy sidekicks and tragic figures to be pitied.

Welcome to one very large pre-60s closet...

Homosexual imagery can be traced back to the very start of American cinema, with the Thomas Edison film *The Gay Brothers* (1895), directed by William Dickson, in which two men dance together while a third plays the fiddle. In fact, this primitive test is one of the earliest surviving motion picture images.

Female impersonators and women playing male roles began appearing in films of the early 1900s, such as the Vitagraph release *The Spy* (1907), the feminist satire *When Women Win* (1909), or DW Griffith's *Getting Even* (1909). However, looking at this work today, the imagery can seem more overtly gay or lesbian than it did in its time, when the notion of homosexual desire was more strictly taboo.

By the teens, American silent comedies began relying on the audience's recognition of homosexual types and filmmakers began to feature the 'sissy'. One of Hollywood's original stock characters, the sissy was the one who everyone laughed at. So in the films of the teens and 20s, homosexuality was, quite literally, a joke.

In *The Florida Enchantment* (1914), two women dance off together, leaving their bewildered men folk to shrug their shoulders and dance off together themselves. Meanwhile, even one of cinema's greatest stars was facing a challenge to his masculinity. In *Behind the Screen* (1916), Charlie Chaplin is seen kissing Edna Purviance passionately when she's disguised as a boy;

Teen rebels get close: Sal Mineo (left) with James Dean

that is until bully Eric Campbell spots them and starts mocking the pair as two gay lovers.

In the spoof westerns of the 1920s, the limp-wristed sissy was dropped into the macho cowboy world for comic effect. In *The Soilers* (1923), a parody of the rugged western *The Spoilers*, made in the same year, the laughs come from a gay cowboy who adores the macho men around him. Later, Stan Laurel played the pansy creating consternation in *With Love and Hisses* (1927), and together with Oliver Hardy starred in *Liberty* (1929), as escaped prisoners who shed their prison uniforms but inadvertently slip on each other's trousers. The farce involves the duo trying to hide and swap pants, but whatever they do and wherever they go to do this, they are constantly caught with their pants down by shocked passers-by.

Lesbian references in film also began in the late 20s and into the 30s. Step forward Countess Geschwitz (Alice Roberts), the first movie lesbian in *Pandora's Box* (1929), although this character was deleted from British and American versions of the German film. Later, in 1931, also from Germany, came *Maedchen in Uniform*, in which a young girl's crush on her female schoolteacher becomes public knowledge at a boarding school. Probably the most famous early lesbian film, *Maedchen in Uniform* was the first to be seen publicly in America and the UK and was the first in a long line of lesbian-themed films set in boarding schools.

Meanwhile, back in America, a tuxedoed Marlene Dietrich caused a storm when, in the 1930 film *Morocco*, she finished a song in a nightclub by kissing a young woman in the audience full on the lips. And Greta Garbo raised eyebrows with her portrayal of *Queen Christina* (1933), based around the inner conflicts of a Swedish lesbian ruler. While the film invented a hetero romance with John Gilbert, hints of lesbianism remained, most notably in her affectionate relationship with her lady-in-waiting. Christina kisses Elizabeth Young, and claims she'll die not an old maid but 'a bachelor'. Hollywood glanced again at lesbianism with the women's-prison film *Caged* (1950); and in the same year came *All About Eve*, whose title character's lesbianism was obvious to those in the know.

As for the men, the first years of sound saw – and heard – the same sissy characters of the silent era, with more clichéd images in such films as *The Gay Divorcee* (1934), *Call Her Savage* (1932) and *Top Hat* (1935); and

'Listen, sister, when are you going to get wise to yourself?'

Miriam in *The Women*

'Fasten your seat belts, it's going to be a bumpy night.'

Margo (Bette Davis) in *All About Eve*

character actors like Edward Everett Horton and Eric Blore began to make a name for themselves through playing pansies whose humour was all based around effeminacy.

In the mid-1930s, however, Hollywood decided to begin censoring its own films. The result was the infamous Hays Code, led by Postmaster General Will Hays, and while the Code didn't manage to completely eliminate the presence of gay characters in films, it ensured that filmmakers had to make them less obvious. So around this time writers and directors ditched the in-your-face camp sissy for another type of homosexual character: the unhappy, suicidal, desperate figure whose inevitable end was to be destroyed. In *Tea and Symphony* (1956) even the *false* accusation of 'Sissy Boy' was enough to nearly destroy the character. For decades, anyone of questionable sexuality would meet with a bad end by the close of the last reel. Gay characters found their natural comeuppance via bullets, fire or suicide.

Another image of the homosexual was as victimiser rather than victim, the shadowy psychopath, cold-hearted villain or perverted killer. This is a cliché resonating through such films as *Dracula's Daughter* (1936) and Alfred Hitchcock's *Rope* (1948). Hitchcock, always fascinated by the darker byways of sexuality, was a master of sneaking gay-shaded content past the censors and *Rope* was a barefaced attempt to pull the wool over their eyes. The director knew exactly what he was doing and slyly cast gay actors John Dall and Farley Granger in the parts of gay child-killers Leopold and Loeb. Scripted by Arthur Laurents, his film both perpetuated and subverted homosexual stereotyping.

Alfred Hitchcock's *Rope* (1948)

So although the Production Code was aimed at curbing social change and banning all reference to sexual diversity, filmmakers like Hitchcock were still getting away with it. Interestingly, if Hitchcock had been a filmmaker in France or Italy, he wouldn't have had to worry about the censors. In Europe, writers and directors were free to make great gay-interest films: Luchino Visconti completed the brilliant, Italian-based production *Ossessione* (1942); and in France, Jean Cocteau made the magical *Orphée* (1950). One exception, though, was Jean Genet's French production, *Un Chant d'amour* (1950), which was simply too explicit and remained unseen for decades.

Back in Britain and the US, gay characters were visible only through subtext and innuendo. Reined in by the Code, the prudishness of studio executives, and the pressures of social conformity, moviemakers learned to write between the lines. And audiences learned to view the films that way.

As soon as filmmakers wrote on the lines rather than between them, they were caught out. The Hays Production Code Director, Joe Breen, was successful in making many producers play by the rules. When Lillian Hellman's play *The Children's Hour* was filmed in 1936 by director William Wyler, its lesbian theme was cut and the film re-titled *These Three*; the sexual confusion strand in *The Lost Weekend* (1945) was also cut, as was the gay-bashing subject matter in *Crossfire* (1947).

Therefore most of the pre-1960s homosexual content only found its way into movies that simply winked at the audience. If you got the joke, you were one step ahead of the morality taskmasters behind the scenes. Take, for instance, Peter Lorre in *The Maltese Falcon* (1941). Or the John Wayne western *Red River* (1948), where six-shooters are phallic playthings and John Ireland says to Montgomery Clift, 'There are only two things more beautiful than a good gun: a Swiss watch, or a woman from anywhere. You ever had a Swiss watch?'

Censors were even fooled by directors who made epics from the era of Hollywood's studio system. Stanley Kubrick's epic *Spartacus* (1960), for example, included an attempt by Roman general Laurence Olivier to seduce his slave Tony Curtis as they shared a bath, yet this 'snails and oysters' scene was cut and remained unseen until the film's 1991 restoration and re-issue. Then there's the gay subtext in *Ben Hur* (1959) that subsequently sent Charlton Heston's blood pressure soaring.

During the 1950s, with 'masculinity' on the up, the vitriol against being gay grew more pronounced. One of the biggest stars of the era, Rock Hudson, like many male stars of the silver screen, had to be very careful to keep his homosexual experiences and lifestyles firmly in the closet. He is now known to have had gay affairs and in the latter part of the 50s a scandal sheet threatened to out him. His studio hastily arranged a sham marriage that lasted just three years. There were always teasers though, sprinkled by scriptwriters, throughout Hudson's movies of the 50s and 60s. Scenes in *Pillow Talk* (1959) involve Hudson having to drag up and get into bed with Tony Randall because his character poses as gay in order to get a woman into bed. A gay man impersonating a straight man impersonating a gay man – all

> 'There are only two things more beautiful than a good gun: a Swiss watch, or a woman from anywhere. You ever had a Swiss watch?'
>
> **John Ireland to Montgomery Clift in *Red River***

very amusing to those in the know at the time. Similarly, in *Lover Come Back* (1962) Hudson feigns impotence and says, 'Now you know why I'm afraid to get married'.

At the time, Hudson's fans wouldn't have given a second thought to the notion that he was really gay. It wasn't until 1984, when the actor revealed he had AIDS, that his sexuality became public. He died a year later.

Slightly more nonchalant about his experiences in the 50s and early 60s was Marlon Brando who was rumoured to be carrying on an affair with the actor Wally Cox. Later, the Hollywood great admitted: 'I have had homosexual experiences and I'm not ashamed.'

James Dean, who worshipped the ground Brando walked on, was known to frequent various backroom gay bars in LA and also dated several influential Hollywood execs. In his 1994 autobiography *Songs My Mother Taught Me*, Brando said he thought that Dean based his acting on his and his lifestyle on what he thought Brando's was. On the night before his death, at a Malibu party, it was reported Dean had stormed off after an argument with either a lover or friend over the actor dating women for 'publicity purposes'.

Another real American teen rebel in the 50s was Sal Mineo, who co-starred opposite James Dean in *Rebel Without a Cause* (1955). He played a rich, lonely, gay teenager called Plato who's not only in love with Alan Ladd (whose picture is pinned to his school locker), but also with his only friend, Jim, played by Dean. For his tender, soulful performance as the abandoned Plato, he earned a Best Supporting Actor Academy Award nomination. Unlike many of his 'confused' contemporaries, Mineo was probably the first major actor in Hollywood to publicly admit his homosexual lifestyle, and was a pioneer in paving the way for future generations of gay actors. It was rumoured for years that Mineo's 1976 knifing death was a result of his homosexual lifestyle. But in 1979, the killer was caught and convicted and it turned out Mineo was actually the victim of a robbery.

Unlike Mineo, one of the most handsome actors of the 50s, Montgomery Clift, kept his homosexuality quiet from his adoring public. Clift managed to get police charges for picking up a hustler on 42nd Street dropped so as to protect his on-screen persona. But his gay lifestyle was well known in Hollywood, and on the set of *The Misfits* (1961) Clark Gable referred to his co-star as 'that faggot'. Like James Dean and Sal Mineo, Clift died young. But

Lover Come Back (1962)

'If I had one day when I didn't have to be all confused and I didn't have to feel that I was ashamed of everything. If I felt that I belonged someplace. You know?'

Jim (James Dean) in *Rebel Without a Cause*

> 'Yeah, it's sad, believe me missy; when you're born to be a sissy... I'm afraid there's no denying; I'm just a dandy lion.'
>
> The Cowardly Lion (Bert Lahr) in *The Wizard of Oz*

> 'But, you're not a girl! You're a guy, and, why would a guy wanna marry a guy?'
>
> Joe in *Some Like it Hot*

San Fransisco drag party, circa 1959, from *Before Stonewall: The Making of A Gay and Lesbian Community* (1984)

Clift's death seemed to be brought about by the sheer torment he put himself through over his gayness. Eventually, through a mixture of drink and drugs, he died of a heart attack in 1966, aged 46.

While Montgomery Clift had pretty-boy good looks, Clifton Webb, another popular Hollywood actor of the 50s, wasn't traditionally handsome but more the suave, sophisticated type. Webb's sexual preferences were no secret amongst Hollywood circles; several young, fit actors reportedly came to him for a helping hand, most notably James Dean.

Back in Britain, actors were also finding it difficult to be open and honest about their gay lifestyles. The *Carry On* stars Kenneth Williams and Charles Hawtrey played sissies on screen throughout the 50s, but in private both were finding it tough to come to terms with their sexuality. Hawtrey turned to drink while Williams preferred to socialise with friends, opting for a sexless life without lovers. Another British comedian, Frankie 'titter-ye-not' Howerd was gay but preferred to present an on-screen image of a man never happier than when surrounded by a bevy of buxom beauties.

Gay audiences, like many of the stars they paid money to see, were also having to deal with life in the closet. In the 30s, gay men had latched on to the gay code dialogue in films like *The Wizard of Oz* (1939) and worshipped divas such as Judy Garland, Joan Crawford and Bette Davis. But even by the 50s, they were struggling to find gay-interest material in the movies. However, the clues were certainly there.

In *Gentlemen Prefer Blondes* (1953), one scene shows a gym full of bodybuilders working out and they have no interest whatsoever in Jane Russell who strolls through – and the well-oiled men are singing 'Ain't There Anyone Here for Love?' Meanwhile, in the 1959 Hollywood gender-bending comedy *Some Like it Hot*, Tony Curtis and Jack Lemmon have the time of their lives dragging up. When Lemmon, disguised as Daphne, tries to persuade Osgood (Joe E Brown) that they can't get married because Lemmon is really a man, Osgood remains unfazed, declaring, 'Nobody's perfect!'

By the end of the 50s, after lengthy discussions, the Motion Picture Production Code Office finally granted a special dispensation permitting *Suddenly Last Summer* (1959) to include the first male homosexual in an American film. The Production Code board felt they could compromise on the theme of homosexuality as long as it was 'inferred but not shown'. So the

22   OUT AT THE MOVIES

'H' word was never uttered, the gay character never spoke, and his face was never shown on screen. Nevertheless, director Joseph L Mankiewicz's film was a huge milestone. As the 60s approached it looked like the Production Code Administration was beginning to lose interest in its traditional hostility towards gay material.

'Is that what love is? Using people? And maybe that's what hate is – not being able to use people.'

Catherine in *Suddenly Last Summer*

THE FILMS

PANDORA'S BOX
(1928)

Germany, 100 mins
Director: GW Pabst
Cast: Louise Brooks, Franz Lederer, Fritz Kortner
Genre: Silent lesbian-interest drama

Based on two Frank Wedekind plays, *Erdgeist* and *Die Büchse der Pandora*, *Pandora's Box* is widely considered the finest film of its director, GW Pabst – an extremely significant figure of silent and early 30s cinema.

A silent screen classic, it's about a girl with loose morals who drifts from promiscuity to whoredom – and she's only interested in one thing: pleasure. One night she makes the fatal mistake of catching the eye of Jack the Ripper.

The film's portrait of a shameless callgirl surrounded by exploitative characters met with anger and derision at the time of its original release. Perhaps the reaction was something to do with the film's open critique of bourgeois sexual hypocrisy, its inclusion of the source's lesbianism (watch for an eloquently erotic dance scene that reminds us of Bertolucci's *The Conformist*) and adherence to Wedekind's Lulu as a 'personification of primitive sexuality who inspires evil unawares'.

Upon its release, *Pandora's Box* largely failed in Germany and was barely reviewed in the United States. The style of the film's star, Louise Brooks, was so natural that critics complained she either couldn't or didn't act.

However, *Pandora's Box* is now celebrated by most critics around the world and considered a landmark of the silent cinema, distinguished by expert compositions and expressionist lighting, along with the director's typically fluid editing that subtly cuts on movement to promote a sense of inescapable momentum towards an ultimate tragic destiny.

And then, of course, there's the cult of Louise Brooks. Central to the movie's success is her legendary performance as Lulu, the most *fatale* of all *femmes*. With a heightened naturalistic style and dark, dark, noirish leanings, the remorseless and fascinating journey of the anti-heroine to her date with destiny, in the form of a man who may be Jack the Ripper, exudes an hypnotic fascination.

Brooks is a twentieth-century icon. Her hair is her trademark. Universally recognised for a distinctive bob, its influence extended to the 'do' sported by Uma Thurman's Mia Wallace in *Pulp Fiction*. Brooks was later rediscovered and deservedly so. She certainly lights up this expressionistic slice of fatalism with incandescent star power.

Louise Brooks (centre) in *Pandora's Box*

Pandora's Box was considered such strong stuff that it was banned in several countries. Although it now feels pretty safe, it's easy to see what caused the censors to wince. Lesbianism, stripping serial killers – with so much of modern movie life here, the picture, like Brooks's beauty, defies the ravages of time.

MAEDCHEN IN UNIFORM
(1931)

Germany, 110 mins
Director: Leontine Sagan
Cast: Hertha Thiele, Emilia Unda, Dorothea Wieck, Hedwig Schlichter
Genre: Lesbian drama

Based on the play *Yesterday and Today* by lesbian poet Christa Winsloe, *Maedchen in Uniform* is the stunning story of a girl called Manuela (Hertha Thiele) who is sent to a boarding school for daughters of Prussian military officers. There, she rejects the repressive atmosphere and finds comfort in a tender relationship with one of the teachers, Fraulein von Bernbourg (Dorothea Wieck). While the headmistress declares Manuela's affections to be scandalous, her classmates are supportive.

An enduring lesbian classic, avant-garde director Leontine Sagan's film was immensely popular around the world when it was released in 1931. It was voted best film of the year in Germany while in New York a critic for the *World Telegram* dubbed it 'the year's ten best programs all rolled into one'.

Powerful and mature treatment of lesbian themes, coupled with erotic images and condemnation of authority, puts this all-female feature into the ranks of important cinema, presaging as it does the rise of conformity and oppression through Nazism.

Sagan's film was the first in a long line of lesbian-themed films set in boarding schools. Later, a 1958 remake featured actresses of international status (Romy Schneider, Lili Palmer, Christine Kaufman) but, although it was much more lavish, it didn't match the power of the original.

THE WOMEN
(1939)

US, 132 mins
Director: George Cukor
Cast: Joan Crawford, Norma Shearer, Rosalind Russell, Mary Boland, Paulette Goddard, Joan Fontaine
Genre: Comedy

Having been fired by producer David O Selznick from the set of *Gone with the Wind* after just three weeks, director George Cukor was handed the opportunity to direct MGM's *The Women*. Adapted by Anita Loos and Jane Murfin from Claire Boothe's hit Broadway play, the story required an all-female cast of 135, giving Cukor a great excuse to exploit the professional rivalries between the studio's stable of stars.

Joan Crawford (left) in a scene from **The Women**

The result is a gloriously camp and memorably bitchy work, a scathing story of love, betrayal and revenge. Starring Norma Shearer and Joan Crawford (long-time rivals at MGM), The Women is a Hollywood comedy of the Golden Age.

The plot centres around Mary Haines (Shearer), a member of New York's high society who discovers that her husband is having an affair with gold-digger Crystal (Crawford). Mary's mother advises her to say nothing and wait for Stephen to get bored of his new catch, but so-called 'friends', including the vindictive Russell, relish gossiping about Mary's humiliating predicament. After a confrontation with her rival-in-love at a fashion show, she heads off to Reno to get a quickie divorce. The news that Stephen has married Crystal confirms her worst fears, yet, in time, Mary develops the ruthless instincts necessary to try and win back her spouse.

Aside from what little plot there is, the film is basically an excuse for lots of megastars to exchange witty insults with each other. Cukor entered Hollywood when the talkies started as a dialogue director; and this is about as talky as any film you'll see. But just pay attention because this movie starts with a frenzy of dialogue and never really slows down. Lots of laughs, some good performances, and endless bitching and cattiness. A sugar-rush of pre-post-feminist comedy, this was Sex and the City for the 30s.

As in the play, no man appears – so it's a field day for the gals to romp around in panties and gowns. The acid-tongued one-liners delivered by Crawford et al are very funny and most of the members of the cast deport themselves in a manner best described by her at the end: 'There's a name for you ladies, but it's not used in high society outside of kennels'.

The Women, however, is a mass of contradictions in the way it both endorses and critiques patriarchal values. In the bizarre opening credits each actress is represented by a different animal that conveys their character's essential nature (Shearer is a fawn, Crawford a leopard, Russell a panther), and throughout much stress is laid upon the notion that women are inevitable rivals in their competition to win, and maintain their hold on, men. 'Don't confide in your girlfriends', admonishes Mary's mother. 'If you let them advise you, they'll see to it in the name of the friendship that you lose your husband and your home.'

Despite the conservative conclusion, Cukor's film still has a subversive potency in the way it undermines traditional notions of romantic love and the 'naturalness' of marriage. In the bad old days of the Code, this bitch-fest was about as gay as it could get without actually mentioning the word. Extolling the joys of the single life, near the end of the movie co-star Lucile Watson enthuses: 'It's marvellous to be able to spread out in bed like a swastika!'

THE WIZARD OF OZ
(1939)

US, 102 mins
Director: Victor Fleming
Cast: Judy Garland, Frank Morgan, Ray Bolger, Bert Lahr, Margaret Hamilton, Billie Burke, Jack Haley
Genre: Musical

'Lions and tigers and bears, oh my!' From the book by L Frank Baum, and springing from MGM's golden era with a then-staggering production budget of $3 million, *The Wizard of Oz* is everybody's cherished-favourite, perennial-fantasy film musical and has been *the* 'family classic' for decades. Its images – the yellow brick road, the Kansas twister, the Land of Oz – and characters such as Auntie Em, Toto, Dorothy, the Tin Woodman and the Munchkins, as well as the film's final line – 'There's no place like home' – and great songs such as *Over the Rainbow*, have gone down in cultural history.

One of the most popular and beloved motion pictures of all time, it has probably been seen by more people than any other over the decades. Yet there's no denying the film is also a gay favourite with the appropriation of its rainbow iconography and much of its dialogue becoming camp cliché and gay code.

As farm girl Dorothy Gale, Judy Garland endeared herself to the hearts of filmgoers for generations. The musical fantasy begins in black and white but soon whisks her on a Technicolor trip to the incredible land of Oz. Dorothy dreams of somewhere far away from the drab hog farm, a rainbow world where she can express herself and follow her dreams. How many gay guys aren't going to identify with that?

For generations of gay men growing up in backward-thinking small towns, escape has always been priority number one, the desire to get out of Humdrum Village and seek out a whole new world, whether it be in London, Manchester, New York, San Fran… or perhaps Oz.

On screen we are captivated by an adventure story which sees young Dorothy and her cute little dog Toto caught in a twister and whisked away from their Kansas home into an eerie land. There, she encounters strange beings, good and evil fairies (Billie Burke and Margaret Hamilton) and prototypes of some of the adults who comprised her farm world. Along the way, she's helped by her companions, the Scarecrow (Ray Bolger), the Tin Woodman (Jack Haley) and the Cowardly Lion (Bert Lahr). She faces a long trek, following the Yellow Brick Road, to the castle for an encounter with the mighty but wonderful Wizard of Oz (Frank Morgan), where she and her new friends will seek fulfilment of desire.

The film consists mainly of an extended dream sequence, the dream of a young girl, although it could just as easily be that of an old queen. Indeed, Dorothy's journey into fantasyland has resonated throughout the gay community over the years. The expression 'a friend of Dorothy' is one many gay

Dorothy with friends

IN THE CLOSET – PRE-60s **27**

men use to describe themselves and other gay people; the Garland reference 'My Judy' is often used by gay men to describe their best friend; and many gay bars around the world are still named after references to the film.

So why do gay men love all things *Oz*?

Most fear 'coming out' and if they're out they'll certainly remember that fear. In *The Wizard of Oz* the underlying theme of conquest of fear is subtly thrust through the action, so it's not surprising that gay fans of the film get hooked into the quest of its earnest central character. Dorothy finds herself in a dangerous world of people who either don't understand or appreciate her, or who are simply out to get her. Donning a pair of glittering red shoes, she hooks up with a motley crew of eccentric characters who are also seeking some kind of new life. A new non-biological family is formed, and a series of fantastic adventures unfolds. Gay men coming out onto the scene are also experiencing this kind of radical transformation, from a black-and-white conventional closeted world to a colourful, exciting and sometimes-freakish place, filled with other loners trying to discover themselves. The Land of Oz holds a special allure for those who are different because it's a community of eccentrics, a place that's fiercely tolerant of the outlandish. In the end, we see that the Scarecrow really *is* smart, the Lion *is* brave and the Tinman *does* have a heart – all they lacked was self-esteem.

The involvement of gay icon Judy Garland must also add to the movie's appeal, certainly with the older generation. The actress led a life of emotional turmoil and MGM made her take vast amounts of pills to help her through relentless filming schedules. Garland's tragic later life (she died of an overdose in 1969) makes her naïve and utterly beguiling Dorothy seem all the more poignant in retrospect.

Whatever the reasons for its popularity, *Oz* is an indelible part of our consciousness and our earliest childhood memories. The movie endures despite modern advances in film make-up and special effects and has become a TV classic, always pulling in high ratings, especially at Christmas. Just to hear 'Over the Rainbow' once again is worth tuning in for alone.

But all great films deserve to be seen on the big screen and, with that in mind, one gay film festival, 'Outsiders', based in Liverpool, recently showcased *The Wizard of Oz* in very special circumstances. A new digital print of the film was created with the music track stripped out leaving the voices and sound effects intact, and it was shown with live accompaniment from the Liverpool Philharmonic Orchestra, conducted by John Wilson. Fans attending were also asked to break

out their ruby slippers and come dressed as their favourite *Oz* character.

In addition to such special screenings, *The Wizard of Oz* was also brought back onto the cultural scene in 2006 with the opening of *Wicked*, a smash-hit Broadway musical which told the 'back story' of the witches of Oz, Elphaba the Wicked Witch and Glinda the Good Witch. Based on a novel by the gay author Gregory Maguire, the show later transferred to London's West End where it has enjoyed similar success.

Although nominated for Best Picture back in 1939, the Victor Fleming movie didn't win. Some Oscars, however, were awarded to *Oz*: Special Award to Judy; Best Original Score (Herbert Stothart); and Best Song for 'Over the Rainbow'. More recently the song claimed the number one spot in The American Film Institute's list of 'The 100 Years of The Greatest Songs'. The AFI board said 'Over the Rainbow' had captured the nation's heart and echoed beyond the walls of a movie theatre.

OSSESSIONE
(1942)

Italy, 160 mins
Director: Luchino Visconti
Cast: Massimo Girotti, Clara Calamai, Elio Marcuzzo
Genre: Neorealist drama

The Postman Always Rings Twice has been filmed five times, and even staged as an opera, but Luchino Visconti's version, his powerful first film, is an unauthorised – and partly homoeroticised – adaptation of James M Cain's classic 1934 suspense novel. Not only is *Ossessione* one of the most engrossing suspense films ever made – and a land-

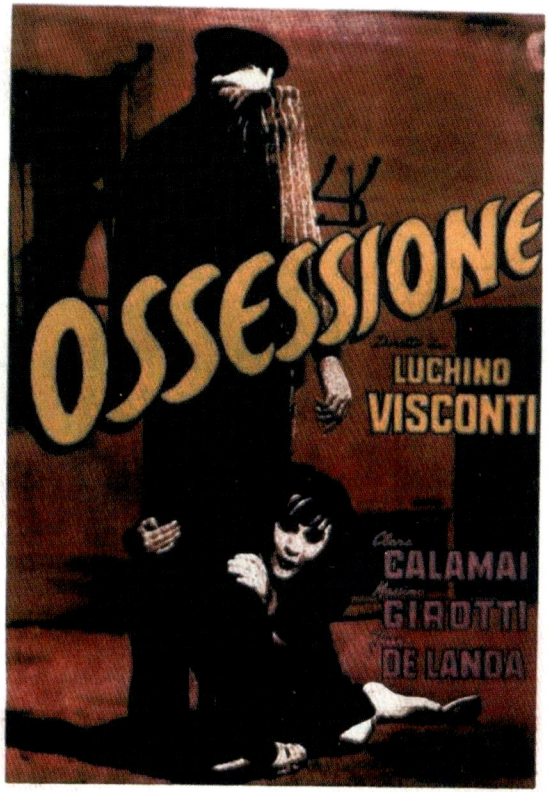

mark in the history of gay cinema – it also launched the extremely influential Neorealist movement in film, known for its rough, documentary-like technique, use of non-professional actors, and emphasis on working-class characters. Neorealism loosened up filmmaking styles around the world and it was, arguably, the most important development in cinema before the French New Wave.

In *Ossessione*, Visconti follows the main thrust of the original story, about a beautiful but frustrated wife Giovanna (Clara Calamai) who becomes obsessed with a strikingly handsome and virile drifter called Gino (Massimo Girotti) who's staying at her inn. Trapped in a loveless marriage with her obese and ill-tempered husband, Giovanna begs Gino to help her kill him so that they can collect his hefty insurance premium. However, after the murder, they find themselves caught up in a downward spiral of fear, deception and jealousy.

Visconti, who also co-write the screenplay, adds a fascinating new element to the story in the form of a beguiling gay vagabond Lo Spagnolo (Elio Marcuzzo), who offers Gino a chance at a better life, both before and after the murder. Gino and Lo Spagnolo's scenes, brimming with both sexual force and real tenderness, are astonishing for their period, and still deeply moving. Their relationship, as much as the illicit heterosexual pairing, may have caused the violent religious and political outrage which greeted the film. The Fascists went so far as to burn the negative; fortunately, Visconti was able to save a print. Because Visconti never secured the rights to Cain's novel, the film was long banned in the US, not appearing until 1975.

Visconti, the great, openly gay filmmaker, has been called the most Italian of internationalists, the most operatic of realists, and the most aristocratic of Marxists (of noble lineage, he was nicknamed 'the Red Count'). Although only a few of his twelve films contain important gay characters (*Ossessione* being one of them), they are essential to the evolution of gay cinema.

MILDRED PIERCE
(1945)

US, 109 mins
Director: Michael Curtiz
Cast: Joan Crawford, Zachary Scott, Jack Carson, Eve Arden, Ann Blyth, Bruce Bennett
Genre: Melodrama

More than a mere soap opera, this etched-in-acid film is a Joan Crawford classic, and was a triumph for her at a time when she'd been let go by studio MGM.

Ann Blyth (left) with Joan Crawford in *Mildred Pierce*

The film chronicles the flaws in the American dream as Mildred (Crawford) drives her husband away with financial nagging and then smothers her daughter with all the advantages she never had.

Mildred is a woman forced, after a failed marriage with Bert (Bennett), into waitressing. She succeeds in acquiring a chain of restaurants and enough money to satisfy spoiled, petulant daughter Veda (Blyth). 'My mother… a waitress!' she sneers. Next, enter the reptilian Monte (Scott), the owner of the property Mildred wishes to convert. Asked what he does, Monte replies, 'I loaf, in a decorative and highly decorative manner.' Monte, with his 'beautiful brown eyes' becomes Mildred's hubby number two. But what's a mom to do when she discovers that hubby is having an affair with his stepdaughter?

With its striking sets, bold cinematography and assured direction by Curtiz, *Mildred Pierce* is an undisputed classic. For sheer, unadulterated star power, Joan Crawford's return to fame, fortune and an Oscar is unrivalled. The amazing thing about this adaptation of James M Cain's bleak novel is that the entire cast and the surrounding talent also shine. There's not a single dud moment.

The film's appeal with gay film lovers lies with Crawford, a true diva and gay icon, and the fact it's as camp as they come. Before *Carry On* films, before *Absolutely Fabulous*, before Divine, there was *Mildred Pierce*, a tale with more drama than you can shake a stick at. The film snaps and crackles with sarcastic dialogue, memorable characterisations, and Crawford herself – an aura of glamour clings to her throughout.

The campiest scenes include Mildred slaving away in her fast-food-waitress uniform, the 'I wish you weren't my mother' tirade by her unruly daughter, and Mildred's visit to the dingy burlesque club to see her daughter dancing all over 50s taboos.

ROPE
(1948)

US, 80 mins
Director: Alfred Hitchcock
Cast: James Stewart, John Dall, Farley Granger, Cedric Hardwicke
Genre: Suspense thriller

Full of suspense and ingenious camerawork, *Rope* – Hitchcock's first film in colour – is all set on one stage and unfolds in unprecedented long takes. With a story relating to a real-life case, this truly frightening classic concerns two college boys who in 1924 murdered another student just for the fun of it, and to see if they could get away with a motiveless crime.

The screenplay, by gay writer Arthur Laurents in collaboration with Hume Cronyn and Ben Hecht, is based on the play *Rope's End* by Patrick Hamilton.

Hitchcock's take on the Leopold-Loeb case has the young men (Dall, Granger) murder a friend for the hell of it, then hold a cocktail party where the guests include the victim's father (Cedric Hardwicke), his fiancée (Joan Chandler) and the rest of his family. Plus the murderers' tutor (James Stewart), who returns to unmask their arrogant crime.

Jean Renoir, the great filmmaker and acerbic critic, dismissed the movie saying, 'It's a film about homosexuals, and they don't even show the boys kissing.'

However, watching *Rope* today is totally refreshing. Viewers should remember that, in the days of the Production Code, any mention of homosexuality was forbidden. Nevertheless, by casting gay actors John Dall and Farley Granger to play the parts of real-life gay child-killers Nathan Leopold and Richard Loeb, Hitchcock managed to pull the wool over the censors' eyes. Incredibly, the executives at Warner Bros were unaware of the gay implications until it was too late and the film was completed. They held their breath as it went to the censors' office and, amazingly, it slipped through the net.

Interestingly, Hitchcock wanted Montgomery Clift to play one of the murderers, with Cary Grant as the pair's mentor. But the homosexual subtext hit too close to home for Grant and Clift, and they dropped out.

Innovative filmmaking at its best, *Rope* is more like the theatre, with little editing, only when there's a change of time, a change of location or a change of point of view. Compared with the formulaic editing style of most of today's American or British films, Hitchcock's virtuoso long single takes and uninterrupted sequences are a welcome diversion. The experimental ten-minute takes serve to heighten the claustrophobia and tension of this disturbing thriller, allowing the action to unfold in the frame itself rather than movements created by editing. The audience can discover the heart of the material rather than allowing the camera to discover it for them.

The same story was filmed again ten years later as *Compulsion* (1959), directed by Richard Fleischer, with the homosexual aspect made more obvious. More recently, Tom Kalin's version of events, released as *Swoon* (1992), delved even further into the two men's self-destructive passion for each other.

ORPHÉE
(1950)

France, 95 mins
Director: Jean Cocteau
Cast: Jean Marais, Maria Casares, Francois Perier, Juliette Greco
Genre: Surreal Allegory

Jean Cocteau's fantastical updating of the Orpheus legend is cinematic poetry, a truly magical work. Unforgettable and profoundly influential, it defies comparison with anything else in cinema.

The French poet and filmmaker was prolific in the outpourings from his fertile imagination. Even today, 40 years after his death, we can say, 'Well, that's straight from Cocteau,' because he established such a distinctive style, a lyrical way of looking at the externalising of the inner world.

His fifth feature as director, *Orphée* is an hypnotically beautiful, allegorical retelling of the Greek myth set in post-war Paris, tantalisingly – and purposefully - open to a myriad of interpretation.

Cocteau believed that the cinema was a place of magic which enabled the artist to hypnotise an audience into dreaming the same dream. Here, Jean Marais is the object of desire and certainly many a gay man's dream. Marais was Cocteau's real-life boyfriend and one of the best-looking male stars of the era. In *Orphée*, he delivers an impressive performance as the eponymous poet, besieged by admirers, who hears voices from other worlds over the radio. He even meets Princess Death (Maria Casares), black gloved, when she comes through a mirror.

Cocteau makes brilliant use of a variety of cinematic effects, the most memorable of which is this mirror, representing the entrance to the hereafter: 'We watch ourselves grow old in mirrors. They bring us closer to death.'

As well as the beautiful Marais, like most of Cocteau's work, further queer iconography is there for all to admire: travelling between this world and the next via a chauffeur-driven Rolls Royce, Marais is escorted by a convoy of satanic, leather-clad motorcyclists, the errand boys of death.

In an article on *Orphée*, Cocteau affirmed that, 'There is nothing more vulgar than works that set out to prove something. Orphée naturally, avoids even the appearance of trying to prove anything.'

Orphée may well represent Jean Cocteau's most accomplished work as a director, remarkably consistent with the rest of his work and faithful to his own personal obsessions. It is a film which explores dreams and desire and the proximity of life and death, reality and illusion. It also shows Cocteau's total commitment to the world of his own artistry, which seems to have its own logic and its own laws. As the chauffeur in the film states: 'It is not necessary to understand, it is necessary only to believe.'

UN CHANT D'AMOUR
(1950)

France, 25 mins
Director: Jean Genet
Genre: Experimental

French novelist and playwright Jean Genet wrote and directed his only film, Un Chant d'amour, in 1950. A hymn to homosexual desire, it has been hailed as one of the most important films in gay cinema.

Set in a French prison, two inmates in solitary confinement communicate their desires to one another, principally through a small hole in the wall that separates their cells, exorcising their frustration and loneliness under the voyeuristic gaze of the prison guard. In Genet's silent, poetic and intensely physical vision of homosexual desire, the dynamic of warder and prisoner is explored as well as the possibility of personal freedom under repressive authority, and the effects of brutal institutionalisation. There is a remarkable range of emotions and motivations communicated through the visible machinations of desire – cruelty, domination, violence, defiance, as well as love and liberation.

Also revealed are the recurrent themes that unite Genet's work and the cinematic techniques – of collage, flashback and close-up – which he adopted in his novels, plays and poetry.

Shot on 35mm by an established cameraman and professional crew, the cast was chosen by Genet from his circle of Montmartre associates and lovers.

Originally intended for the eyes of only a few close friends, initially Genet and his circle were pleased with the film, but he later denounced it and refused the prize for 'Best New Film' of 1975 awarded by the Centre National de la Cinematographie.

Author Edmund White, in his preface to *Criminal Desires: Jean Genet and Cinema* by Jane Giles, comments: 'His rejection of *Un Chant d'amour* may have its roots in his fear that [unlike his first novel *Our Lady of the Flowers*] it was merely pornographic. Certainly by the time he denounced it definitively in the 1970s he had written several other film scripts, and his ideas about cinema as an art had evolved.'

Indeed, Genet was one of France's maverick artists, a man who exchanged a life of extreme deprivation and degradation for that of a novelist, playwright and poet and became something of an existentialist hero to the likes of Jean Cocteau and Jean-Paul Sartre. Although greatly influenced by the medium of cinema, and writing many scripts later on in his career, *Un Chant d'amour* is the only film he both wrote and directed. Long championed as one of the most emblematic films in gay cinema, it has unquestionably influenced generations of filmmakers, from the late Derek Jarman to Todd Haynes (his 1991 film *Poison* is directly inspired by Genet's work).

The subject of ceaseless controversy and international censorship, *Un Chant d'amour* was unseen for many years, becoming a cause célèbre of gay rights and freedom of expression, as well as being recognised as a masterpiece of underground cinema in its own right.

Heavily censored for many years and banned outright in the States until the late 70s on the grounds of obscenity, *Un Chant d'amour* is not for the faint-hearted. The British Film Institute later released an uncut version of the original, which features footage of masturbation, sexual climax and homosexual acts. The BFI DVD release added a vibrant new music score by Simon Fisher Turner who was composer on Derek Jarman's *Caravaggio*.

Looking at Genet's film over 50 years on, it is clearly both captivating and moving, giving us a glimpse of a great poet at work with film – although, unfortunately, it's the only glimpse there is.

ALL ABOUT EVE
(1950)

US, 138 mins
Director: Joseph L Mankiewicz
Cast: Bette Davis, Gary Merrill, Anne Baxter, George Sanders, Celeste Holm, Thelma Ritter, Marilyn Monroe, Hugh Marlowe, Gregory Ratoff
Genre: Camp comedy-drama

Joseph L Mankiewicz's jaundiced look at the show-biz battle zone better known as Broadway is probably the summit of Hollywood moviemaking.

Bette Davis gives the performance of her career portraying the just-turned-forty stage diva Margo Channing with a painful air of authenticity: the camp star, still awesome but aware of the ravages of time and the threat of younger actresses snapping at her heels. The actress is a living monument to enormous talent and volcanic temperament but what she needs is someone to follow her around, look after her and worship her, and that person seems to arrive in the form of Eve (Anne Baxter), an apparently innocent, adoring fan. But of course appearances can be deceptive. The younger woman is taken in as a kind of secretary and confidante to Margo but systematically sets about stealing her benefactor's man and career. Margo begins to realise what's happening but, through flattery and a series of double-crosses, Eve still manages to work her way to the top and cares little for Margo's misfortune.

Eve was originally written as a lesbian character but all overt references to her sexuality were dropped. Nevertheless, to those in the know, the gay subtext was fairly obvious: it's there in the voracious way in which Eve stalks Margo, through the subtle scene involving Eve's roommate, and in the giveaway line delivered by Margo to her boyfriend, Bill Sampson, 'Zanuck, Zanuck, Zanuck – what are you two, lovers?' Finally, in case we missed the point, Eve falls for the same trick she had herself relied upon: on finding a young female fan who's sneaked into her hotel room, she unwisely invites the girl to stay the night.

Mankiewicz triumphs as writer and director. What gives this cynical high comedy its emotional resonance and depth, however, is the poignance with which Davis plays Margo Channing. The piece, one of Hollywood's finest backstage dramas, fizzes with energy and the bitchy lines flow, largely from Davis's wickedly crooked mouth. The entire cast is on top form (Marilyn Monroe makes an early,

From left: Anne Baxter, Bette Davis, Marilyn Monroe, George Sanders

fleeting cameo appearance), although among the actors only Sanders won an Oscar for his superb turn as the camp theatre critic, Addison De Witt, who also serves as the film's narrator.

Alongside the lesbian subtext, the film's appeal amongst the gay community also lies in its star. Bette Davis, like Joan Crawford, was a true gay diva, a 'bitch' in every positive sense of the word. When Davis descended the stairs in *All About Eve*, regally gowned, her eyes burning with thoughts of vengeance, she was a portrait of strength. When she uttered that immortal line, 'Fasten your seat belts, it's going to be a bumpy night,' she put into words the thoughts of every gay man who struggled to come out, or get laid with a not-so-safe stranger.

REBEL WITHOUT A CAUSE
(1955)

US, 115 mins
Director: Nicholas Ray
Cast: James Dean, Natalie Wood, Sal Mineo, Dennis Hopper
Genre: Youth drama

One of the most influential films ever made, *Rebel Without a Cause* is a timeless masterpiece. Kids of today can still relate to its basic premise: of youth misunderstood, of wanting to belong. The clothes, hair and times may have changed, but the story of three teenagers, bonding as the world around them seems to cave in, is just as potent now as it was in 1955.

In his most famous film, James Dean delivers a knockout performance, playing Jim Stark, the nervous, volatile, soulful teenager lost in a world that doesn't understand him. It's his first day at a new

James Dean as Jim Stark

high school. The night before he is arrested for public intoxication. His dysfunctional parents don't know how to handle the situation: Mum is overbearing and self-centred while lily-livered Dad has good intentions, but is constantly overruled by his wife. Jim needs guidance and begs for it, in his rebellion.

The film's other teens in trouble include Judy (Natalie Wood) and John 'Plato', played to perfection by Sal Mineo (nominated for an Academy Award for Best Supporting Actor). When we first meet Plato, he is being questioned over why he shot a bunch of puppies, a horrifying way to introduce a character, but somehow Mineo makes us care about Plato, a rich kid with tons of problems: his dad's disappeared, and his mum's always away, leaving him in the care of the family maid. Plato is looking for somebody to be his friend, or family. And by the end of twenty-four hours, these three will make their own tightly knit little circle.

Rebel is all about the basic need to feel loved. In Jim, Judy has found her perfect soulmate. Plato loves Jim too, but it's a secret love and he's constantly having to come to terms with his latent homosexuality. Plato would love Jim to stay overnight with him: 'Hey, you wanna come home with me? ... If you wanna come, we could talk and then in the morning we could have breakfast...'

Made between his only other starring roles, in *East of Eden* and *Giant*, *Rebel* sums up the jangly, alienated image of Dean. He is heartbreaking, following the method-acting style of Marlon Brando but staking out a nakedly emotional honesty of his own. Dean is, of course, no longer an actor, but an icon, and *Rebel* is a lasting monument.

SOME LIKE IT HOT
(1959)

Tony Curtis (left) and Jack Lemmon drag up in *Some Like it Hot*

US, 122 mins
Director: Billy Wilder
Cast: Tony Curtis, Marilyn Monroe, Jack Lemmon, Joe E Brown, George Raft, Joan Shawlee, Mike Mazurki, Pat O'Brien
Genre: Comedy

Some Like It Hot is a cross-dressing comedy classic. Previously voted the best comedy film of all time by the American Film Institute, its campiness and kinkiness has also made it a real favourite of gay audiences around the world.

Tony Curtis and Jack Lemmon play two knockabout Chicago jazz musicians, Joe and Jerry, who happen to witness the Mob in bloodthirsty action during the infamous St Valentine's Day massacre. Needing a quick getaway, the pair disguise themselves as 'Josephine' and 'Daphne', and join an all-female choir.

Director Billy Wilder puts a flawless cast through some riotous capers, as the all-girl band heads for sunny Florida. Star attraction Marilyn Monroe is wonderful as Sugar Kane, the sexy Polish-American vocalist in search of a rich husband. Joe, ever the ladies' man, falls for the dazzling Sugar but is unable to reveal his true identity, so instead poses as a millionaire in an effort to woo the money-hungry singer. Jerry is also finding dilemmas of his own: lecherous millionaire Osgood Fielding (Joe E Brown) has his sights firmly set on Daphne/Jerry, which is okay so long as the gifts keep coming and the confused old horn dog is kept at a safe distance.

By the end of the movie Osgood has fallen so heavily for Lemmon's Daphne persona, he takes 'her' out in a boat and proposes marriage. After failing to dissuade him, in desperation she exclaims: 'Osgood you don't understand... I'm a man!' Unfazed, Osgood declares, 'Nobody's perfect!'

So if you thought that men-in-drag comedies had reached their pinnacle with *Priscilla* or *Too Wong Foo*, think again: this is a flawlessly scripted, superbly performed and endlessly witty comedy that deserves its place among the all-time greats.

SUDDENLY LAST SUMMER
(1959)

US, 114 mins
Director: Joseph L Mankiewicz
Cast: Elizabeth Taylor, Katharine Hepburn, Montgomery Clift
Genre: Psychological drama

Suddenly Last Summer is one of the big groundbreakers in gay cinema history. In 1959, the Motion Picture Production Code and the Catholic Church granted a special dispensation permitting the film to include the first male homosexual in American film. The word is never mentioned, the character did not speak and his face never appeared. His name was Sebastian Venable.

Gore Vidal's classy but stark screen adaptation of Tennessee Williams' powerful play not only landed Oscar nominations for stars Elizabeth Taylor and Katharine Hepburn (neither won), but also pulled off the trick of making Shepperton Studios near London look uncannily like New Orleans.

Set in 1937 New Orleans, Joseph L Manckiewicz's film explores the trauma of Catherine Holly (Taylor), whose homosexual cousin dies an unspeakable and gradually revealed death while travelling with her in Europe. Katharine Hepburn as the murdered man's wealthy mother, Violet Venable, can't bear to hear the details of her son's death, preferring instead to try and convince a doctor that he should have a lobotomy performed on her niece, insisting that the girl is mad. She thinks the lobotomy should remove the part of the brain which houses the memories of the day she witnessed Sebastian pursued and cannibalised by the hungry youths he had exploited. But Dr Cukrowicz (Montgomery Clift) is determined to explore the reasons behind the girl's inexplicable actions and words, and eventually the young neurosurgeon uncovers the secrets the mother wants to hide. By utilising injections of Sodium Pentothal, he discovers that

Catherine's delusions are in fact true. He then must confront Violet about her own involvement in her son's lurid death.

Williams' play explicitly stated why the murdered man's death so traumatised his cousin, but this adaptation written by Vidal, filled with wild, moody tension by director Joseph L Mankiewicz, allows viewers to read between the lines and form their own suspicions about Sebastian Venable's death. Taylor is on top form, radiating uncertainty and fear as the girl terrorised by her cousin's death and her fierce aunt's obsession to keep her quiet. Hepburn gives a similar tour-de-force performance, swaying with menace in one of her few, deliciously played roles as a villainess.

A classic in every sense of the word, *Suddenly Last Summer* touches on many subjects that were highly controversial at the time it was made, such as mental illness, homosexuality and cannibalism. Truth to be told, there's a lot of inference and not much shown. The cannibalistic murder, for instance, is left to the viewer's imagination, with the camera turning away as the street urchins destroy Sebastian. The inference only makes the film's themes stand out even more.

THE ACTORS AND DIRECTORS

JAMES BYRON DEAN
Actor
1931–1955

Undoubtedly one of the most admired and adored gay icons, James Byron Dean's impact on American youth culture is immense.

Born in Marion, Indiana, Dean began his career on the New York stage, and appeared in several episodes of such early-1950s episodic television progammes as *Kraft Television Theater*, *Danger* and *General Electric Theater*. After rave reviews in André Gide's *The Immoralist*, Hollywood and film stardom called.

Dean appeared in several uncredited bit roles in such forgettable films as *Sailor Beware*, but finally gained recognition and success in 1955 in his first starring role, that of Cal Trask in *East of Eden*, for which he received an Academy Award nomination for Best Actor in a Leading Role. In rapid succession, he starred in *Rebel Without a Cause*, also in 1955, and in the 1956 *Giant*, alongside Elizabeth Taylor and Rock Hudson, for which he was also nominated for an Academy Award. As Jett Rink, Dean once more played the brooding outsider, this time separated from his heart's desire by his lowly station in life. Cast in a villainous light, Dean remained the most fascinating presence in the film, especially in his brilliantly choreographed, climactic drunk scene. In fact, Dean played the cast-off loner in all three of his starring features, unable to draw attention to himself until forcing the issue.

Even before *Giant* was released, Dean was a major celebrity and he began enjoying his money by entering the world of automobile racing. He purchased a Porsche 550 Spyder and on September 30, 1955, after completing work on *Giant*, he zoomed off to a racing event in Salinas. Travelling at 115 miles an hour, he was killed in a head-on collison just outside Paso Robles, California.

One of only five people to be nominated for Best Actor for his first feature role, and the only person to be nominated twice after his death, Dean epitomised the rebellion of 1950s teens, especially in his role in *Rebel Without a Cause*. Many teenagers of the time modelled themselves after him, and his death cast a pall on many members of his generation. His very brief career, violent death and highly publicised funeral transformed James Dean into a cult object of timeless fascination. A life that's achieved mythic proportions, Dean's sexuality has also become a topic of endless fascination.

So was James Dean gay? Years after his death, in various biographies, writers and Hollywood insiders outed the original rebel actor. In Paul Alexander's biography, *Boulevard of Broken Dreams*, the author revealed publicly what many have acknowledged privately – that Dean's so-called 'sexual experimentation' was a convenient Hollywood euphemism for his lifelong attraction to men. In fact, later on, Dean became fascinated by sadomasochism, with studio make-up artists having to cover up the cigarette burns inflicted by his lovers.

When Dean moved to New York to pursue his acting career, many claim it was advanced when he became sexually involved with an ad man/director who introduced him to influential people in the city. Dean began dating a male producer who later cast him in *See the Jaguar* on Broadway.

The love of Dean's life, however, was allegedly his former flatmate William Blast and their relationship was documented in the 1976 TV movie *James Dean*, which dealt fairly explicitly with Dean's homosexuality.

Dean had also developed close relationships with actors such as Clifton Webb, Arthur Kennedy and Martin Landau and later was introduced to the young actor Nick Adams. While Dean was filming *East of Eden*, Adams was making *Mister Roberts* the same year. They became very close, with Adams making himself available for whatever services were required of him. In fact Adams was yet another actor who met an untimely death, dying of an overdose at 37 in 1968.

Despite his very short career in acting, James Dean has become a major figure in American culture. This most enigmatic of actors was a shy, deeply insecure man who never recovered from the early loss of his mother. Charismatic, ambitious and astoundingly gifted, he was also notoriously moody and difficult, his desperate need for affection and attention often manifesting itself in contradictory, ultimately self-destructive behaviour.

His deep and complex personality has intrigued all who have seen his performances, making everyone wonder how different the world would be if he had lived on to produce more great films.

JUDY GARLAND
Actress
1922–1969

Judy Garland remains the ultimate gay icon – the original diva who sparkled on screen long before Streisand, Cher and Madonna. Born Frances Gumm in 1922, she entered the public eye in 1939 as Dorothy in *The Wizard of Oz*, and sang her way through more than 30 films and dozens of stage appearances.

Her performance in *Oz* won her a special Juvenile Oscar, and it was this role, of course, that gave Garland her most famous song, 'Over the Rainbow'. It was also the film that resonated throughout the gay community. Dorothy was the misunderstood kid from a small town who has an amazing adventure in a Technicolor world. Despite intense fear, confusion and a series of trials, she finally makes it 'home' by realising that she possessed all of the heart, strength and courage needed to find the true happiness that lived within. That message resonated with gays of the era who yearned to come out into a colourful world and live what was inside them.

After *Oz*, Garland appeared in a string of classic MGM musicals, including *Meet Me in St Louis* (1944), *Easter Parade* (1948) and several with her friend, Mickey Rooney. Unfortunately, the same studio that made her a star unwittingly made her a drug addict, providing her with amphetamines to keep her energy levels high and her weight down. This kept her wide awake at night, so she was given barbiturates to help her sleep, and soon she couldn't live without these 'wonder drugs'. She also couldn't seem to live without a man, going through several affairs, often with older men, and by 1950 had been married twice, to bandleader David Rose and director Vincente Minnelli, with whom she had a daughter, Liza Minnelli. During this time her drug intake increased dramatically, and led to increasingly erratic behaviour. She often failed to show up on time at the studio and MGM eventually couldn't take it any more, terminating her contract in 1950.

Garland divorced Minnelli the following year and married producer Sidney Luft, father of her daughter Lorna and son Joey, who took it upon himself to orchestrate her comeback with a series of extremely successful concert tours. He also produced the film *A Star is Born* (1954), in which many feel she gave her greatest performance.

At her best, Garland gave everything to her audience. As 'the little girl with the grown-up voice', she often trembled, her strong vibrato sending shivers through her fragile frame. But her worst troubles – the drugs, the suicide attempts, failed marriages and breakdowns – seemed to draw the most die-hard fans. She was one of the first stars to show her bruised life to her public, and gay men felt her pain. Her songs of love, anguish and sacrifice touched a nerve with an invisible generation who identified with the dichotomy of her life; they too had to hide behind walls of perceived strength, all the time hoping that, somewhere over the rainbow, they would overcome their troubles.

Garland's true connection with gay men was rooted in her ability to overcome the inner conflict, instability and loneliness that defined her life even during stardom. She sang of intense loneliness and of delirious love, maintaining a 'stage presence' at all times despite her inner turmoil.

In the 1950s, Garland's concerts were major gay meeting places, and in her later years, she even made money singing at gay piano bars, performing to men who used the term 'friend of Dorothy' to refer to themselves in mixed company, in homage to Garland's character in *The Wizard of Oz*.

After her successful early-50s comeback, Garland concentrated on her career as a singer, winning legions of fans. She continued touring throughout the 1950s and 1960s, appearing in three more films and starring in her own television variety show in 1963. The show, however, had to be cancelled after one season because the competition, *Bonanza* (1959), was too strong. She divorced Luft and married actor Mark Herron, who she divorced when she found out he was gay, and married disco manager Mickey Deans. She continued to depend on prescription drugs, and finally the inevitable happened: on the night of 22 June 1969, she overdosed on barbiturates and died. Thousands mourned the world over. It was a sad way to end, but she left a great legacy: her many films and recordings, as well as her children, Liza and Lorna.

An emotional icon, the death of Miss Showbusiness in 1969 was considered by many to be a contributing factor that helped spark the Stonewall Riots, which took place over the same weekend in New York. This, in turn, launched the militant gay rights movement.

SAL MINEO
Actor
1939–1976

In the late 1950s, Sal Mineo was one of the hottest movie stars in the world. Twice nominated for an Academy Award, Mineo's career spans three decades, although he will always be fondly remembered for his role opposite James Dean in *Rebel Without a Cause* (1955).

Mineo earned his acting stripes on Broadway, appearing first in *The Rose Tattoo* (1951) and then in *The King and I* (1952), taking over the role of Yul Brynner's son. He effortlessly made the transition to the screen, appearing in *Six Bridges to Cross* and *The Private War of Major Benson* (both 1955) before earning celluloid immortality in the teen-angst classic *Rebel Without a Cause* as Plato, a tender portrayal which earned a Best Supporting Actor Academy Award nomination.

Mineo went on to play variations of the juvenile delinquent role in such films as *Crime in the Streets* (1956), *Dino* (1957), and *The Young Don't Cry* (1957). He was also nominated for Best Supporting Actor for his role in this movie and again for the role of Dov Landau in *Exodus* (1960). But in the 60s, after he started becoming more open about his sexuality, he found that fewer good parts were offered to him; he commented: 'Suddenly it dawned on me I was on the industry's weirdo list.'

He subsequently left Hollywood and began working all over Europe, where he was offered more interesting roles. He also found success on stage back in the States, as director of *Fortune and*

Men's Eyes and co-star of *P.S. Your Cat is Dead*, playing a bisexual cat burglar.

Discussing his sexuality, Mineo said, 'I like them all – men, I mean. And a few chicks now and then.' Unlike James Dean, Montgomery Clift, Rock Hudson et al, he seemed quite happy being out of the Hollywood closet. He once said: 'One time, when my Ma wondered how come I turned out gay, I asked her, "Ma, how come my brothers DIDN'T?"'

Preparing to open the play *P.S. Your Cat is Dead* in Los Angeles in 1976 with Keir Dullea, he returned home from rehearsal the evening of February 12th where he was attacked and stabbed to death by a stranger. In 1979, Lionel Ray Williams was convicted and sentenced to life in prison for the murder.

It's sad that his life had to end at the early age of 37, but the memory of Sal Mineo continues to live on through the large body of TV and film work that he left behind.

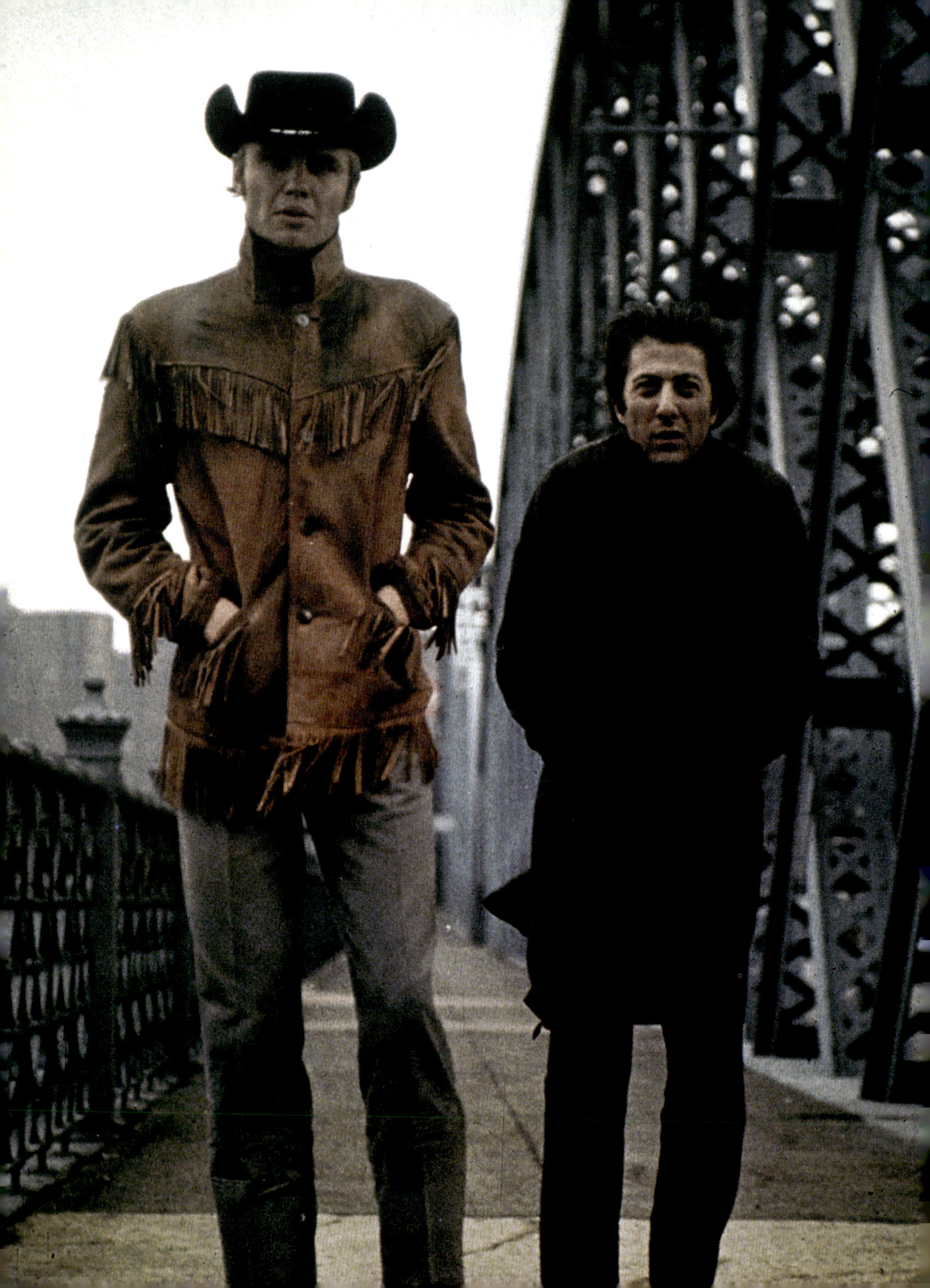

VICTIMS, VILLAINS AND SISSIES – THE 60s

'If you're old enough to vote, you're old enough to choose your own way of life.'

Galloway in *Victim*

Before the rise of independent cinema, it seemed that up to and throughout the 60s, gay and lesbian characters were portrayed as either villains to be feared, or tortured, suicidal individuals to be pitied.

For most of the decade, few of these characters of 'questionable sexuality' survived the final reel.

They were presumably paying rent and taxes, earning a wage and buying their groceries just like everyone else, but what the films told us was that homosexuality often led to Misery, Death, and The Destruction of Society As We Know It!

In 1961, Tony Richardson's acclaimed film *A Taste of Honey* had Rita Tushingham setting up house with an optimistic young gay guy she picks up at a carnival. Geoff, played by Murray Melvin, was one of cinema's first gay anti-heroes. Tushingham treats her effeminate homosexual friend as a sister, but Geoff, because of his sexuality, is seen as marginal to mainstream society. Significantly, on its initial release, *A Taste of Honey* was supplemented by a study guide, reprinted in *Life* magazine, on the 'causes and cures' of homosexuality.

In Brian Forbes' *The L-Shaped Room* (1962), based on the novel by Lynn Reid Banks, Leslie Caron starred as a pregnant, unmarried French girl who moves into a seedy London lodging house that's home to a variety of sympathetically observed but ultimately marginal inhabitants, including a homosexual black trumpeter called Johnny (Brock Peters) and an elderly lesbian music-hall artist (Cicely Courtneidge). Like the sexless Geoff in *A Taste of Honey*, Johnny in *The L-Shaped Room* is peripheral, although his understated

Jon Voight (left) and Dustin Hoffman in John Schlesinger's *Midnight Cowboy* (1969), the only x-rated movie ever to win an Oscar © Photofest affection for another male lodger is sympathetic and handled well, and he is in no way threatening.

The Leather Boys (1963), directed by Sidney J Furie, was another example of how filmmakers handled the gay lifestyle. Implied homoerotic tensions between two pals, Reggie (Colin Campbell) and Pete (Dudley Sutton), come to the surface when Reggie marries Dot (Rita Tushingham) but soon loses his sexual urge and opts to move in with his 'buddy' Pete. Despite Pete's insistent affection, his reluctance to associate with girls and his housekeeping ability, Reggie fails to wise up to the fact he's a homosexual. The plot is punctured somewhat by the fact that most viewers get the drift early on, and when Reggie realises that Pete really is 'queer' and rejects him, it becomes yet another example of a director who balks at a happy gay ending.

Throughout the 60s, more gay characters appeared, but despite the liberation of young men, cinema was not yet ready to liberate gays.

The 'pathology' of homosexuality, largely the result of the medical establishment's negative attitude, became rife in cinema with crazy queers appearing in such films as *Reflections in a Golden Eye* (1967) and *The Sergeant* (1968). It's interesting that both these films are set in a military environment, the implication being that such all-male environments are in danger of breeding homosexuality, which in turn creates murderous tendencies.

If they weren't villainous, they were suicidal. In Sidney Lumet's *A View From The Bridge* (1962), Raf Vallone implicates his own sexuality by accusing another man of being gay; eventually he too kills himself. Meanwhile, *Advise and Consent* (1962), produced and directed by Otto Preminger, features a scene set in a gay bar; also a suicide, which occurs when politician Don Murray is blackmailed for a past gay fling. In *The Children's Hour* (1962), the accusation of lesbianism (not entirely unfounded) ends with a rope suicide; and in *The Sergeant*, the title character kills himself after kissing a private.

Interestingly, while their gay characters paid the obligatory price by committing suicide, the stars of *The Children's Hour* (Shirley MacLaine), *The Sergeant* (Rod Steiger) and *Reflections in a Golden Eye* (Marlon Brando) all managed to survive the career threat of a gay role, as did two of Hollywood's most notorious heterosexuals, Richard Burton and Rex Harrison, who starred as a long-time gay couple in *Staircase* (1969).

> 'I'm not a lifebelt for you to cling to. I'm a woman and I want to be loved for myself.'
>
> Laura in **Victim**

> 'I wanted him! I wanted him, as a man wants a girl!'
>
> Melville Farr in **Victim**

As well as victims and villains, 1960s gay cinema was also full of sissies, characters who made their presence felt in a kind of leering, sniggering way. In the Rock Hudson vehicles *Lover Come Back* (1961) and *A Very Special Favor* (1965), the actor pretends to be a sissy in order to win over a girl, the irony of which isn't lost now that we know of Hudson's sexuality.

In British movies, Kenneth Williams and Charles Hawtrey's *Carry On* characters were two of the most popular of the series' gang. But they weren't gay, of course – they were sissies. Their limp hand gestures and airy-fairy 'ooh-I-say' tones put the representation of gay characters right back to the era of silent movies; and even by the late 60s, in the era of sexual freedom, many films still featured pitiable homosexuals who do everything for others but neither expect nor get happiness for themselves. It's an all too familiar notion that gays seem most loveable (or non-threatening) when rendered essentially sexless. And that's what these characters were – funny quirky, sexless people. Kenneth Williams' own highly personal diaries, published after his death, revealed his growing hatred of the stereotypical fairy types he was lumbered with, which not only typecast him but added to his own real-life personal insecurities.

But in one British movie, a character uttered the word 'homosexual' for the first time – and it wasn't a laughing matter. It was *Victim* (1961) that put down a marker for the serious consideration of homosexuality at a time when being outed could lead to a prison sentence. The film featured Dirk Bogarde, who broke free from his matinee idol image to play a gay barrister who's blackmailed by a young man who then commits suicide. When he tracks down a range of men who have been similarly compromised, he is faced with the choice of coming out or keeping silent. He opts for the latter.

Victim was extraordinary for two scenes. In one, the barrister explains to his wife the ins and outs of gay desire ('...and I wanted him! I wanted him, as a man wants a girl!'); and in the other a gentlemen's club is full of posh homosexuals who drink sherry and speak in very English clipped tones about 'our sort'. In insisting that there were a lot of them around, however, the film did a service to the gay community – despite the fact that the director, Basil Dearden, referred to gays as 'sexual inverts'.

Still, it's impossible to underestimate the importance of Dearden's film, however polite and quaint it feels today. It proved to be a major factor in the decriminalisation of homosexuality.

DETECTIVE INSPECTOR HARRIS: 'Someone once called this law against homosexuality the blackmailer's charter.'

MELVILLE FARR: 'Is that how you feel about it?'

DETECTIVE INSPECTOR HARRIS: 'I'm a policeman, sir. I don't have feelings.'

from *Victim*

> 'I've been telling myself that since the night I heard the child say it. I lie in bed night after night praying that it isn't true. But I know about it now. It's there.'
>
> Martha in
> **The Children's Hour**

In September 1961, the Motion Picture Producers and Distributors of America announced a revision of its Production Code: 'In keeping with the culture, the mores and the values of our time,' the revision advised, 'homosexuality and other sexual aberrations may now be treated with care, discretion and restraint.' Changes in the acceptable images of Hollywood films reflected mainstream Americans' limited willingness to view homosexuality in the mass media. Homosexuality could be portrayed and discussed as long as the images and discussions were 'safe' and 'discrete'.

The new Production Code revisions paved the way for the release of films like *The Children's Hour* (1963), an adaptation of Lillian Hellman's 1934 play that made it to the screen with its lesbian content intact as an example of a 'tasteful' treatment of homosexuality. The film had Shirley MacLaine committing suicide after she realises that lesbian rumours about herself are true – another example of a homosexual character not making it to the end without dying – but it did represent the first major release in the United States to deal clearly with lesbianism.

The Children's Hour also cleared a path for lesbian subplots in the mid-60s. Shelley Winters was a madam with a yen for Lee Grant in *The Balcony* (1963), Joseph Strick's film of the Jean Genet play. Jean Seberg's mental patient is openly bisexual in Robert Rossen's *Lilith* (1964) and Candice Bergen is the nice college girl who's also 'sapphic' in Lumet's *The Group* (1966).

The premiere of *The Group* marked the first time the word 'lesbian' was actually used in a Hollywood movie: when the film's central character, Lakey (Candice Bergen), returns from Europe with a butch baroness as her lover, Larry Hagman turns to her and says, 'I never pegged you as a Sapphie – to put it crudely, a lesbo.'

Another 'shocking' lesbian-themed film of this period came from Germany. *Therese and Isabelle* (1968) was a kind of lavish soft-core fantasy film about women who were in love with each other, notable more for its lush, lyrical photography and fabulous design than for its acts of passion. It is still well known, however, and appears on special edition DVD formats around the world, released for fans of films produced during the dreamy era of porno chic.

By the mid-60s, a vibrant underground film scene was burgeoning in New York's East Village with a large network of artists, writers, filmmakers and hangers-on. In 1963 alone, three of the most notoriously 'queer' avant-

Radley Metzger's
Therese and Isabelle (1968)

garde films of this period were produced: Kenneth Anger's *Scorpio Rising*, Jack Smith's *Flaming Creatures* and Barbara Rubin's *Christmas on Earth*.

And, as the 60s sexual revolution took hold, the avant-garde artist Andy Warhol was turning out a dizzying number and variety of films involving a host of different collaborators. Working in close collaboration with his protégé Paul Morrissey, the films were made in an East 47th Street studio dubbed 'The Factory', where Warhol developed his own start system. His performers included drag queens Holly Woodlawn and Candy Darling, women such as Bridget Polk and Edie Sedgwick, and hustlers Paul America and Joe Dallesandro. Films like *Blow Job* (1963), *My Hustler* (1965) and *Lonesome Cowboys* (1968) drew from the gay underground culture and openly explored the complexity of sexuality and desire. Indeed, *Blow Job* was basically a 35-minute close-up of a young man's face as he receives oral sex. Not surprisingly, many of Warhol's films premiered in gay porn theatres.

Lonesome Cowboys (1968)

Warhol described *My Hustler* in simple terms: 'It was shot by me, and Charles Wein directed the actors while we were shooting. It's about an ageing queen trying to hold on to a young hustler and his two rivals, another hustler and a girl; the actors were doing what they did in real life; they followed their own professions on the screen.'

Some critics hold his films in high esteem and many cite *My Hustler* as a classic of gay cinema. Others dismiss it as pointless and boring. But what is so frustrating is that it's impossible to assess most claims made about these films: controlled by his estate, they have not been made available for video or DVD release.

Warhol's contribution to gay cinema was immense, and it's a tragedy that his works are so little known today. In fact, many of his earlier short films have been lost or destroyed. Warhol, Smith and Anger's titles are now widely regarded as some of the most important and influential films of post-war underground cinema. Only recently, however, have critics begun to take seriously the fact that they were gay filmmakers whose films developed a distinctly queer aesthetic.

As Warhol was completing his most famous film, *The Chelsea Girls*, at the end of 1966, after 37 years of self-imposed censorship, the Production Code finally came down forever, giving new licence to Hollywood films.

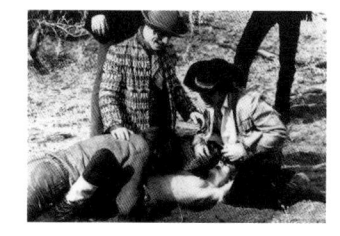

Pier Paolo Pasolini's *Teorema* (1968)

In 1968, Sandy Dennis and Anne Heywood were cast as lesbian lovers in *The Fox*, a sensitive dramatisation of DH Lawrence's novella; and in *The Detective*, also released in 1968, Frank Sinatra was playing a tolerant New York City cop investigating a messy murder of a young homosexual.

In Italy, Pier Paolo Pasolini's *Teorema* (1968) was causing controversy. Long before he was dragging up for *Priscilla, Queen of the Desert*, Terence Stamp played a divine stranger who insinuates himself into the sumptuous residence of an upper-class industrialist. One after another, he seduces the mother, the father, son, daughter and maid. Soon a telegraph arrives at the dinner table, and the stranger tells the family he must leave immediately. Their safe middle-class world having been screwed over, the family members now experience epiphanies of self-awareness, admitting to the stranger that he has awakened them to the shallowness of their lives. After he leaves, each of the family members immediately deviates from the status quo.

With its frequent homosexuality, Pasolini's film was designed to disturb its audience. Despite winning the Grand Prix at the Venice Film Festival in 1968, *Teorema* was publicly denounced by Pope Paul VI and banned as obscene in Italy. Pasolini was even arrested, but, in a much-publicised trial, acquitted of all charges. While it has certainly lost some of its subversive power over the last 40 years, it remains Pasolini's finest Marxist slap in the face to his hated bourgeoisie.

Back in Britain, one film that dealt intelligently and sympathetically with homosexuality was *The Killing of Sister George* (1968), a great breakthrough movie of the 60s, which marked a change of attitude from the public. The story of an ageing lesbian who loses her TV job and young lover was funny and entertaining from beginning to end but also dealt with homosexuality not as a problem or stigma but as part of the natural order.

Despite the demise of the Production Code, Hollywood didn't immediately put a stop to gay stereotypes. Producers continued to have gay and transgendered characters as the butt of all the jokes in comedies such as *The Producers* (1968) and *Candy* (1968). Meanwhile, Richard Burton and Rex Harrison were paired up to play two ageing homosexual hairdressers in *Staircase* (1969), but their characters seethed with guilt, shame, regret and self-loathing. To top it all, both wish they were straight!

ALICE:
'Not all women are raving bloody lesbians, you know.'

GEORGE:
'That is a misfortune I am perfectly well aware of!'

from *The Killing of Sister George*

In the same year, *The Gay Deceivers* was released, complete with the most flagrant gay stereotypes this side of Fairyland. A story of two young men (Lawrence Casey and Kevin Coughlin) who avoid the Vietnam draft by posing as gay lovers, the pair move into a gay apartment complex, with a bright pink bedroom, and a mincing, limp-wristed landlord (Michael Greer).

Variety reported that disgruntled gay cinema-goers were picketing *The Gay Deceivers* in San Francisco and quoted one protestor as saying: 'The producers of such rot [should] take note that this film is not only an insult to the proud and "manly" gay persons of this community but to the millions of homosexuals who conceal their identity to fight bravely and die proudly for their country which rejects them.' Many critics agreed, denouncing *Deceivers* as 'witless' and a 'travesty'.

The end of the Production Code did, however, result in one of the most impressive films of the decade – *Midnight Cowboy* – which won the Academy Award for Best Picture in 1969, the only X-rated movie to ever do so.

Directed by John Schlesinger, it was the first gay-themed Best Picture-winner in Oscar history, 35 years before Ang Lee's gay cowboys graced the silver screen. Of course, *Midnight Cowboy* could never have been as explicit, or as tolerant, as *Brokeback Mountain* (2005), but it caused quite a stir on its release.

Waldo Salt's screenplay – about a male hustler (Jon Voight) and his buddy (Dustin Hoffman) – did everything it could to avoid acknowledging the true heart of its narrative: that of two deeply lonely men who find a measure of grace in one another. Ultimately, their relationship was left as an 'are-they-or-aren't-they?' affair.

Schlesinger's film premiered in New York one month before the 1969 Stonewall riots that would mark the beginning of the gay-rights movement.

> 'Uh, well, sir, I ain't a f'real cowboy. But I am one helluva stud!'
>
> Joe Buck in *Midnight Cowboy*

> 'John Wayne! Are you tryin' to tell me he's a fag?'
>
> Joe Buck in *Midnight Cowboy*

THE FILMS

VICTIM
(1961)

UK, 90 mins
Director: Basil Dearden
Writers: Janet Green, John McCormick.
Cast: Dirk Bogarde, Sylvia Syms, Dennis Price, Anthony Nicolls, Peter McEnery, Derren Nesbitt
Genre: Thriller

'While we were filming, we were treated as though we were attacking the Bible... yet it was the first film in which a man said "I love you" to another man. I wrote that scene in. I said to them, "Either we make a film about queers or we don't."'

– Dirk Bogarde on *Victim*

Victim is the groundbreaking thriller that paved the way for the legalisation of homosexuality in Britain.

Writers Janet Green and John McCormick, producer Michael Relph and director Basil Dearden were the team that produced *Sapphire*, involving racial prejudice, and they adopted a similar technique with *Victim*. They provided a suspenseful thriller that followed a group of blackmailers targeting London's gay community, and at the same time argued a convincing case for gay rights and dignity, without resorting to unbalanced and contrived characterisations.

During a time when homosexual acts in private were illegal in the United Kingdom (as they still are in thirteen US states), Britain's most revered matinee idol, Dirk Bogarde, risked his career to portray Melville Farr, a closeted gay lawyer. The film was released in Britain in 1961, halfway between the Wolfenden Commission's recommendation of law reform in 1957 and the actual 1967 law reform.

In the opening scene of Dearden's film, a handsome, edgy-looking young man called Barrett is at a construction site. He looks down from a steel girder high above the ground to see a police car arriving. He flees in desperation. But he is not being chased by police who want to arrest him because he is gay; as we later find out, Barrett is actually embezzling money from the construction company to pay blackmailers. Barrett (lovingly called 'Boy Barrett' in the queer underground), however, is protecting a much bigger target, wealthy barrister Melville Farr (Bogarde), with whom he is in love. Farr is married and a non-practising homosexual, who is about to 'take the silk' (become a Queen's Counsel). He interprets Barrett's desperate phone calls as blackmail attempts, inadvertently triggering the young man's suicide in a jail cell.

Dirk Bogarde as blackmailed lawyer Melville Farr with Sylvia Syms as his wife Laura in Basil Dearden's ground breaker

As the blackmailers turn their attention to Farr himself, he must decide whether to expose them and ruin his career (and possibly his marriage) in the process, or continue to pay extortion 'for a kind of security' that he knows will keep the whole rotten system going.

Bogarde's portrayal of the increasingly beleaguered barrister is not only a knockout performance in itself but represented a major shift for the actor, who took the role after it was turned down by most of Britain's major stars because it was too controversial. Sylvia Syms, meanwhile, provides solid support as Laura, his equally stressed wife. She shines in her portrayal of a woman torn between her love for her husband and the realisation of the social implications of his homosexuality being made public.

In his memoirs, Bogarde said that *Victim* was 'the wisest decision I ever made in my cinematic life. The fanatics who had been sending me four thousand letters a week stopped overnight'. It was certainly a courageous move for the actor, then enormously popular for playing war heroes and heartthrobs, notably in the *Doctor in the House* comedies. After *Victim*, Bogarde's main fan base withered but he was taken far more seriously as a dramatic actor, and more extraordinary work followed – *The Servant*, *Accident*, *Darling*, *Death in Venice* and *The Night Porter*.

Victim was reviled in its day, and many crew members apparently worked throughout on set with obvious contempt. The film could not get a MPAA seal for American distribution, mainly because of the mention of the then-forbidden word 'homosexual' (though, as Vito Russo pointed out in *The Celluloid Closet*, the MPAA had just allowed the word 'faggotty' from the mouth of Sidney Poitier in *Raisin in the Sun*), and because 'sexual aberration could be suggested but not spelled out'.

In the week of release, *TIME*'s film critic was horrified: 'What seems at first an attack on extortion seems at last a coyly sensational exploitation of homosexuality as a theme – and, what's more offensive, an implicit approval of homosexuality as a practice.'

It is now clear that *Victim* was pioneering in its treatment of a long-repressed 'crime' and admirable for its sympathetic and non-stereotypical depictions of gay men. In Dearden's film, homosexuals are not caricatures but multi-layered human beings. Homosexuality is normalised (rather than glamorised), shown at every level of contemporary society – in every side street, factory, Rolls Royce and club in town.

On the British DVD, recently released, one of the extras – a half-hour interview with Bogarde shot soon after *Victim* – amusingly shows a journalist trying to taunt the actor with questions and comments: 'You must feel very strongly on this subject to risk losing possibly a large part of your following by appearing in such a bitterly controversial part.' But then, perhaps the interviewer knew what most people at the time did not, that Bogarde was in fact gay himself, a fact which surely contributed to his perfect performance as Melville Farr, complete with its nuances of guilt and terror. Ironically, unlike his character, he was never completely open about his private life (he lived with his longtime companion Tony Forwood). Yet, during the interview Bogarde is completely relaxed.

Today this black-and-white movie is still an entertaining drama, bolstered by strong performances and great attention to detail. But the real importance of *Victim* will always lie in its role in the eventual decriminalisation (in part) of homosexual acts between men of 21 years or over in England and Wales, through the Sexual Offences Act of 1967.

THE CHILDREN'S HOUR
(1963)

US, 109 mins
Director: William Wyler
Writer: John Michael Hayes
Cast: Audrey Hepburn, Shirley MacLaine, James Garner, Miriam Hopkins, Fay Bainter, Karen Balkin

The Children's Hour was the first major film released in the United States to deal clearly with lesbianism. Lillian Hellman's study of the devastating effect of malicious slander and implied guilt had already been brought to the screen once before in a film called *These Three* back in 1936 but had veered away from the touchier, more sensational aspects of Hellman's Broadway play. This time, however, director William Wyler chose to remain faithful to the original source.

The nature of the depiction of lesbianism in this film reflects the type of images that were considered tasteful to American audiences in the early 1960s. Hollywood was ready to release a film with lesbian content as long as lesbianism was treated as an unhealthy condition with no opportunity for happiness.

Shirley MacLaine and Audrey Hepburn co-star as headmistresses of a boarding school for young girls from wealthy families. After an irresponsible, neurotic child whispers to her grandmother a lie about a sexual relationship between the two women, the accusation spreads and the school is destroyed as parents remove their children.

The film is meant to illustrate how lies have the power to destroy the lives of innocent people; however, the movie takes an interesting turn as MacLaine's character, Martha Dobie, realises there may be some basis for the child's lie. Martha is forced to confront her own feelings for her friend Karen (Hepburn) and in an emotional scene she reveals her true feelings. In a speech filled with torment and self-hatred, she cries, 'I'm guilty! I've ruined your life and I've ruined my own. I feel so damn sick and dirty, I just can't stand it anymore.' The words 'lesbian' and 'homosexuality' are never used in the film but the implications are clear. Martha explains to Karen, 'There's something in you, and you don't know anything about it because you don't know it's there. I couldn't call it by name

French-born director William Wyler with Audrey Hepburn on the set of ***The Children's Hour*** (1963)

54 OUT AT THE MOVIES

before, but I know now. It's there. It's always been there ever since I first knew you.'

Around the time of making his film, director William Wyler stated: 'It's going to be a clean picture with a highly moral story.' And so Martha's self-realisation leads to her suicide. The little girl's lie revealed a truth that was so unacceptable to her that she chose death as the solution to her struggle with her lesbian feelings.

Admittedly, the stars of *The Children's Hour* made risky, admirable choices in their career by taking these roles on, rescuing the picture from box-office failure, but although the issue of invisibility was overcome, the increasing visibility of lesbians was now accompanied by portrayals of violent, predatory, overt or lonely homosexuals. *The Children's Hour* represents a typical characterisation in which lesbianism has to be seen as a hopeless lifestyle, which inevitably leads to destruction. Filmmakers could not have characters accepting or embracing their homosexual feelings and desires because the film industry would then be seen to be glamorising or encouraging homosexuality. The repressed, tortured homosexual character, therefore, has no choice but to commit suicide because, as films such as *The Children's Hour* suggest, it is the only viable option to dealing with such unacceptable sexual desires.

REFLECTIONS IN A GOLDEN EYE
(1967)

US, 109 mins
Director: John Huston
Writers: Chapman Mortimer, Gladys Hill
Cast: Elizabeth Taylor, Marlon Brando, Brian Keith, Julie Harris, Robert Forster, Zorro David
Genre: Military drama

John Huston turned Carson McCullers' novel about a latent homosexual US army officer into quite an interesting melodrama. Set in the pre-Second World War period, Huston's film features a veritable hothouse of repressed desires and fantasies, and six disparate characters: moody Marlon Brando's brooding latent homo; his wife Elizabeth Taylor, who's playing away with another officer; Brian Keith, whose own wife, Julie Harris, is having an affair with her houseboy, Zorro David; and finally Robert Forster, a young exhibitionist who Brando falls for.

Stuck in the married quarters of a Deep South army base, Taylor and Brando's marriage has seriously hit the rocks and they spend most of their time shouting and screaming at each other. One fight ends with Taylor completely disrobing and threatening Brando with being 'dragged out in the street and thrashed by a naked woman', causing Brando to yell out 'I hate you!', as the handsome young private (Forster) lurks outside watching.

Next door, unhappily married couple number two are just as frustrated. Julie Harris is still traumatised from the death of their infant daughter, whereupon she mutilated herself. As Taylor helpfully explains, 'I can't imagine. Cuttin' off your own nipples!', to which Harris's hubby Brian Keith replies, 'Well, the doctors said she was neurotic.' Harris ends up playing around with her Filipino houseboy Anacleto (Zorro David), and eventually Keith decides Harris needs to be committed and promptly drops her off at the local sanatorium.

While Taylor carries on her affair with Keith, Brando hopefully dogs the virginal young Forster, who's got a penchant for riding naked in the woods. At various junctures, in an attempt to fill the empty hours, he takes to his study so he can look at various mementos, which include photographs of gladiators and a tiny, antique-silver

John Huston directs Marlon Brando in *Reflections in a Golden Eye* (1967)

teaspoon. Later he obtains Forster's discarded Baby Ruth candy-wrapper, which he folds into a phallic shape and strokes. But however much he wants Forster, being the military man he is, he is forced to repress everything.

The soldier meanwhile takes to sneaking into Taylor's room to watch her sleep, and the film predictably ends in murder. As Forster breaks in, Brando barges into Taylor's bedroom to find him sniffing a nightgown, and shoots him dead.

It's not as muddled or pretentious as it sounds, and Huston's quirkish sense of humour is way ahead of other directors of the time. The script manages to lend genuine depth and credibility to the characters, far better than the other military-themed gay-interest movie of that time, *The Sergeant* (1968), a badly written tale of self-loathing.

Reflections in a Golden Eye captures the sheer frustration of it all – the boring lectures on military history, being stuck in classrooms during a hot summer, and the late-night drinks and card games which are more an effort to ease loneliness. All in all, it's a superbly controlled exercise in the malevolent torments of despair.

Interestingly, Brando developed his status as a gay icon not just through his early, stunning good looks and fantastic physique. His private life was dogged with rumours of gay affairs, most of which he didn't bother to deny, which only helped to secure an army of adoring gay fans. He lived in New York with his lifelong pal, actor Wally Cox, and did not contradict rumours that they were lovers. He even admitted: 'Like many men I have had homosexual experiences and I'm not ashamed.'

THE KILLING OF SISTER GEORGE (1968)

US, 138 mins
Director: Robert Aldrich
Writer: Lukas Heller
Cast: Beryl Reid, Susannah York, Coral Browne, Ronald Fraser, Patricia Medina, Hugh Paddick, Cyril Delevanti
Genre: Lesbian-interest black comedy

One of the great and infamous lesbian 'breakthrough' films of the 60s, Robert Aldrich's film concerns an ageing lesbian actress called June Buckeridge (Beryl Reid) who's the star of the hugely popular television soap opera *Applehurst*. Buckeridge has become so identified with her character – a sweet-natured district nurse called Sister George, who putters around her pretty little village on a motor scooter – that she's even known as George away from the set.

Outside the studio, however, she's an aggressive, hard-drinking, hot-tempered, cigar-chomping, foul-mouthed lesbian living with an immature young lover she's nicknamed 'Childie' (Susannah York).

George's domineering personality and self-destructive tendencies have placed her starring role in jeopardy, and she feels certain that 'Sister George' will soon be killed off. She vents her frustration on her lover and at one point even demands that Childie eats one of her cigars until she chokes and vomits from revulsion. Tired of being punished for breaking George's rules, she loses interest in the relationship and the soap star's world starts to fall apart.

On one of her drunken sprees, George goes too far and is accused of molesting two young nuns in a taxicab with behaviour so outrageous that one of them 'went into shock believing she was the victim of satanic intervention'. BBC executive Mercy Croft (Coral Browne) drops in on George at home and demands that she write a sincere letter of apology to the Director of Religious Broadcasting. Mercy also makes several subtle passes at Childie, which don't go unnoticed by George.

Tension builds as Mercy takes control of George's television career and her love life. Soon George is told by Mercy that she *will* be written out of the show: 'She'll be hit by a truck while riding her scooter – and the episode will nicely coincide with advertisements for Automobile Safety Week!'

Adding insult to injury, Mercy also advises George that she can still have a job: 'We do have an opening on one of our children's shows. You can play Clarabelle the Cow. All you have to do is wear a mask and say, "Moo!" – That's *if* you choose to accept the role.'

In the heartbreaking final moments, George returns to the empty set of her beloved TV show. On the dimly lit set, she finds the coffin destined for her character and begins to smash it – and the set – to pieces. As the camera tracks back to a long shot from above, George lets out a long, heart-wrenching 'moo', bringing down the curtain on a genuinely moving scene.

Susannah York (right) with Beryl Reid in *The Killing of Sister George* (1968)

The performances in *The Killing of Sister George* are exceptional and Beryl Reid's magnetic performance really should have earned her an Oscar nomination. Producers took a chance on Reid – known mainly for her comedy roles – by casting her in the original Broadway play, and she rewarded their gamble, winning the Tony Award for Best Actress. Despite reservations by Hollywood moneymen, Aldrich took another gamble and allowed Reid to recreate her role for the screen. The gamble paid off. Touching on many emotions, Reid creates a real human being who's easy to empathise with.

Because of its lesbian love scene, *Sister George* received an X rating, which limited its exposure in theatres. Aldrich filed a lawsuit with the aim of overturning the rating, but this was ultimately dismissed, and the film died at the box office.

Some critics point to what now seem caricatured portrayals of lesbian life, but, despite a few stereotypes, *Sister George* still remains an important work in early gay cinema. What is great about the film – and what made it way ahead of its time – was the fact that it treated homosexuality not as a problem or stigma but as part of the natural order.

STAIRCASE
(1969)

US, 101 mins
Director: Stanley Donen
Writer: Charles Dyer
Cast: Richard Burton, Rex Harrison, Cathleen Nesbitt, Beatrix Lehmann, Gordon Heath, Stephen Lewis

Staircase, investigating the lonely, desperate lives of two ageing male homosexual hairdressers in a drab London suburb, starred two icons of heterosexuality – Richard Burton and Rex Harrison.

Harrison is Charlie, the flighty, dagger-tongued roommate of fellow stylist Harry (Burton). Burton is excellent as the quieter of the two – he is very sympathetic, taking care of his bedridden mother as well as his long-time mate. He keeps his bald head wrapped in a towel turban to protect his business and is also self-conscious about his weight, tugging at his clothes throughout the film. It's one of the actor's overlooked roles but by no means his best work.

Admittedly, these two acting superstars took on risky roles, but Harrison seems far more concerned that the audience might think he is 'that way' and minces about in a parody of homosexual mannerisms. At the time, he was known as a bit of a homophobe, standing out among the usually tolerant actors of his day. Burton, however, told *People* magazine, 'Perhaps most actors are latent homosexuals and we cover it with drink. I was once a homosexual, but it didn't work.'

Together, the pair come across as a sideshow attraction. We never believe that any relationship, homosexual or otherwise, exists between them as they carp self-consciously at one another, coasting through roles they obviously don't take seriously in a film they don't respect. It's not so much a movie about homosexuals, but a movie about Harrison and Burton playing homosexuals.

MIDNIGHT COWBOY
(1969)

US, 113 mins
Director: John Schlesinger
Writer: Waldo Salt
Cast: Dustin Hoffman, Jon Voight, Sylvia Miles
Genre: Hustler movie

Nearly 40 years before *Brokeback Mountain* (2005), John Schlesinger made the original 'gay cowboy' movie.

But nobody called *Midnight Cowboy* a gay cowboy movie when it first screened. Everybody was too busy being shocked by its portrayal of street hustling and homeless life in New York City.

Midnight Cowboy takes place mostly in the cold, dark, dirty confines of the New York City streets, a

Jon Voight is hustler Joe Buck

58   OUT AT THE MOVIES

world away from the open-air, big-sky country of *Brokeback Mountain*. But the two movies share a central core: a love story involving two men.

Based on James Leo Herlihy's novel, *Midnight Cowboy* dramatises the small hopes, dashed dreams and unlikely friendship of two late-60s lost souls. Cheerful young Texas stud-for-hire Joe Buck (Jon Voight) travels to New York to make his fortune as a gigolo to older women, but he quickly discovers that hustling isn't what he thought it would be after he winds up paying his first trick (Sylvia Miles). He soon gets together with the tubercular Rico 'Ratso' Rizzo (Dustin Hoffman) who expands his services to the male population. The pair become companions as a result of their hard times and reside together in a one-bedroom apartment inside a condemned building.

Buck's incoherent flashbacks throughout the film throw some light on how he's ended up as a midnight cowboy. These brief sequences reveal he was raised by two women (his mother and grandmother) in a home without men, perhaps contributing to his homosexual leanings.

Joe and Ratso's lives continue to plummet, and after a strange run-in with the 'Warhol crowd', Ratso becomes deathly ill. The two friends have no means of financial support and a mean New York winter is upon them; thus Buck is forced to earn money for his friend and again finds himself on 42nd Street where the characters of the night reside, and much to his dismay – or pleasure (the audience is left in ambiguity) – must delve into various sexual encounters.

Midnight Cowboy's gay subtext wasn't really discussed at the time, although in an article entitled 'Midnight Revolution' by Peter Biskind (published in *Vanity Fair* in March 2005) Dustin Hoffman recalls that while making the film both he and Voight understood the gay themes. '"It hit us," observed Hoffman, "Hey these guys are queer. I think it came out of the fact that we were in the abandoned tenement. We were looking around the set and I said, 'So? Where do I sleep? Why do I sleep here and he sleeps there? Why does he have the really nice bed? Why aren't I – yeah, why aren't we sleeping together? *C'mon*.'"'

THE ACTORS AND DIRECTORS

DIRK BOGARDE
Actor
1921–1999

A celebrated actor of Belgian and Scottish descent, Dirk Bogarde was one of Britain's most popular leading men of the 1950s and early 60s, making his name in mostly routine light comedies (as Simon Sparrow in the popular Rank *Doctor* series) and melodramas before attracting serious attention for his role as a blackmailed homosexual lawyer in Basil Dearden's *Victim* (1961).

The response to his corrupt valet who comes to dominate his 'master' in Joseph Losey's *The Servant* (1963) seemed to convince Bogarde that he was not just handsome but intelligent and talented, and he took greater care in selecting his roles thereafter.

Bogarde subsequently favoured European cinema and he left Britain in the mid-60s to live in Provence with his friend and manager Tony Forwood. In the 1970s, Bogarde worked with some of the great European directors: he played Gustav von Aschenbach in *Death in Venice* (1971) for Luchino Visconti and in *Despair* directed by Werner Fassbinder in 1978.

Bogarde considered *Death in Venice* to be the peak of his career and felt he could never hope to give a better performance.

In his fifties Dirk Bogarde began a new career as a writer, producing eight autobiographies as well as a number of novels. When Forwood became seriously ill in 1983 they returned to London. In his book *A Short Walk From Harrods* in 1994, Bogarde describes how he nursed Tony Forwood for the last few months of his life until he died of cancer in 1988.

Dirk Bogarde was made a Chevalier de l'Ordre des lettres in 1982 and was awarded an honorary Doctor of Letters at St Andrews University. He was knighted on 13 February 1992.

In 1996 he was partly paralysed by a stroke and from 1998 required 24-hour nursing. This, and Forwood's long illness, made him an outspoken advocate of euthanasia, and he became vice-president of the Voluntary Euthanasia Society. He died of a heart attack at his Chelsea flat on 8 May 1999, aged 78.

ROCK HUDSON
Actor
1925–1985

'Rock Hudson's death gave AIDS a face.'
— Morgan Fairchild

With extreme good looks but no acting experience, Rock Hudson was very much a studio creation, borrowing his screen name from the Rock of Gibraltar and the Hudson River and taking singing, dancing and acting lessons before he made his debut in *Fighter Squadron* (1948). The tall, strapping young actor went on to become one of the leading male screen idols of the 1950s and 60s, reaching stardom and displaying his first signs of real ability in *Magnificent Obsession* (1954) and *Giant* (1956). Hudson later displayed a flair for comedy in a series of sex comedies, often opposite Doris Day, including *Pillow Talk* (1959), *Lover Come Back* (1961) and *Come September* (1964).

Despite such films as the fine science-fiction thriller *Seconds* (1966) and the sturdy actioner *Ice Station Zebra* (1968), Hudson's film career slowly petered out towards the end of the 60s, but his luck turned, however, with his role on the popular 70s police drama *Macmillan and Wife* opposite Susan Saint James. His death in 1985 was caused by complications resulting from AIDS, news of which revealed the homosexuality Hudson had long kept secret.

His last quote, read at an AIDS fundraiser, stated: 'I am not happy I have AIDS, but if that is helping others, I can, at least, know that my own misfortune has had some positive worth.' Indeed, his death did have an effect, bringing national attention to the disease and even forcing the then US president Ronald Reagan to actually acknowledge its existence, something he had failed to do throughout the early 80s.

JOHN SCHLESINGER
Director
1926–2003

One of the four major British film directors of the early 1960s, openly gay director John Schlesinger's debut feature *A Kind of Loving* (1962) fitted perfectly – if perhaps fortuitously – into the regional realism of British cinema of the time.

Schlesinger, though not particularly allied to them in any formal sense, found himself set alongside Tony Richardson, Lindsay Anderson and Karel Reisz as part of a wave of urban filmmaking dealing with hard-edged stories of working-class life.

Whatever else Schlesinger had in mind, he was keen on the frankness of the story about a young man who finds himself trapped by marriage to his pregnant girlfriend. This frankness brought him up against the censor. Referring to a scene in which characters attempt to buy condoms, Schlesinger was told, 'You could be opening the floodgates. Soon everybody will be doing it.'

Billy Liar (1963) and *Darling* (1965) showed Schlesinger moving away from the harsh realism that had typified early 1960s British filmmaking. In its place his films were becoming part of a highly fashionable 'Swinging London' scene.

Schlesinger's move to colour came with the big-budget *Far From the Madding Crowd*, shot by Nicolas Roeg. It marked perhaps the apotheosis of the fashionable 1960s British film, starring as it did both Julie Christie and Terence Stamp, the 'dream couple' for British casting directors of the time. *Far From the Madding Crowd* did not do well at the box office, but it marked his international acceptance as a director of stature, and paved the way for his move to Hollywood.

In America, he made his best-known work, *Midnight Cowboy* (1969), probably his greatest success commercially and critically, which won Oscars for Best Picture and Best Director and launched a long but rather turbulent Hollywood career for the director. Films such as *Sunday, Bloody Sunday* (1971), *The Day of the Locust* (1975) and *Marathon Man* (1976) all bear witness to Schlesinger's remarkable ability to weave meticulously observed, realistic backgrounds into his complex studies of human relationships.

Schlesinger's later films included *The Believers* (1987), a gripping contemporary horror story starring Martin Sheen and Helen Shaver, *Madame Sousatzka* (1988), about a London piano teacher (Shirley MacLaine) and her gifted young student, *Pacific Heights* (1990), possibly the first thriller to weave its plot around the problems faced by landlords in their attempt to evict a bad tenant, and *The Innocent* (1993), an adaptation of Ian McEwan's Cold War psychological thriller.

His final directorial outing was at the helm of the mild comedy *The Next Best Thing* (2000), which starred Madonna as a middle-aged woman whose biological clock has ticked so loudly she conceives a baby with her gay pal (Rupert Everett) and then struggles to raise the child with him. Although a fairly minor work in his otherwise bold canon, it was appropriate that in his last film effort before his death in 2003, Schlesinger, who was gay, again tackled the issues of homosexual life and love that had characterised his keenest work.

Many of Schlesinger's films all share a similar outlook. They are tales of lonely people, outsiders in some way, dependent on their illusions, adrift in a world that is bitter but not without sympathy; and to some extent this must have drawn from Schlesinger's own Jewish, gay background.

The strengths and weaknesses of that view are summed up by Schlesinger's comment in 1970 that 'I'm only interested in one thing – that is tolerance. I'm terribly concerned about people and the limitation of freedom. It's important to get people to care a little for someone else. That's why I'm more interested in the failures of this world than the successes.'

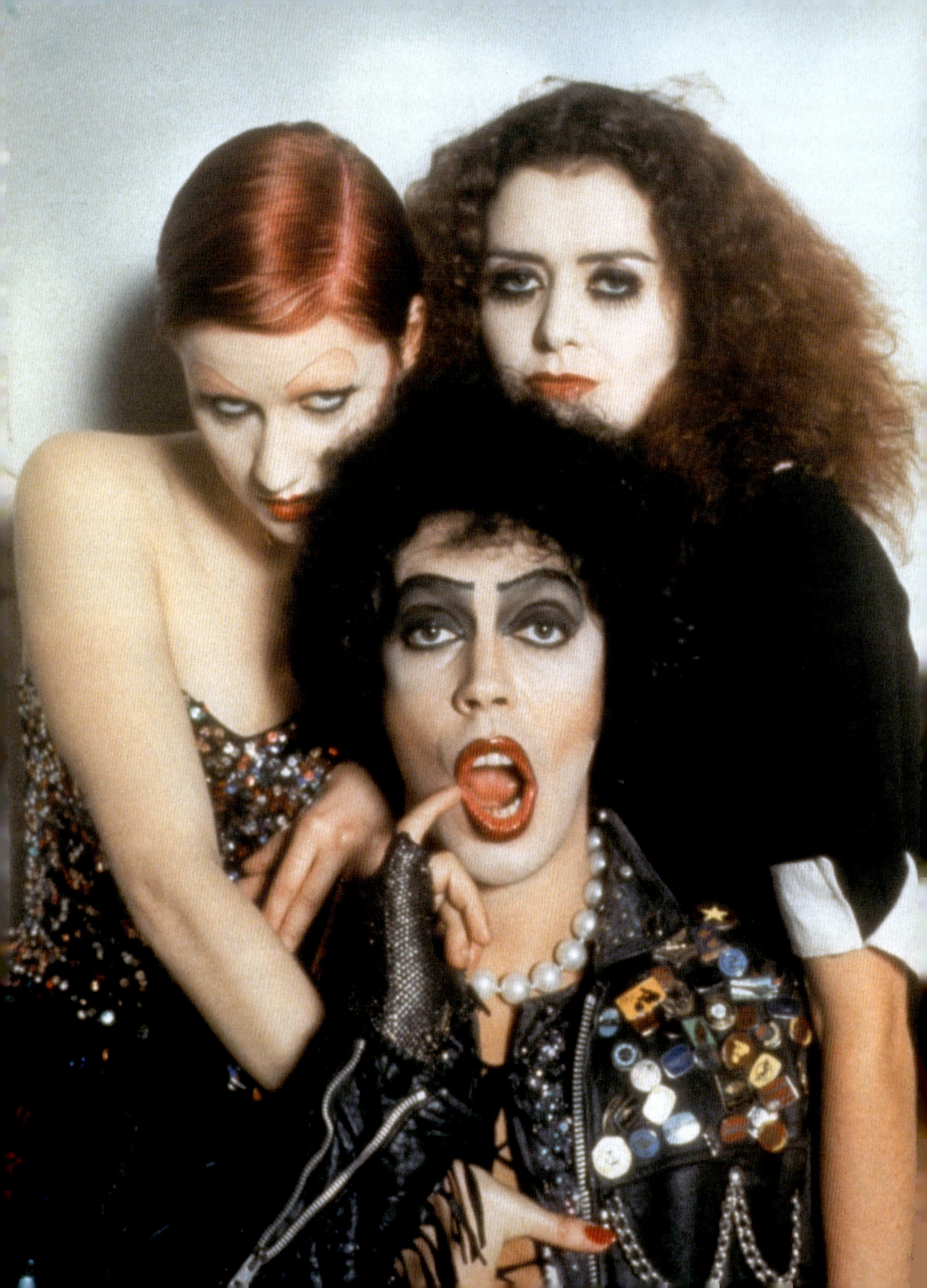

POST-STONEWALL CINEMA – THE 70s

'I'm just a sweet transvestite, from Transsexual, Transylvania.'

Frank in *The Rocky Horror Picture Show*

Already prominent in the mid to late 1960s were the women's, civil rights, black power and anti-war movements; developments which inspired younger gay and lesbian activists to radical action and social revolution. All it would take was one incident – any incident – for the Gay Pride movement to progress their cause to entirely new heights.

On Friday, 27 June 1969, the world mourned the death of Judy Garland. But the night would not simply be remembered for the Manhattan funeral of a gay icon. It was also to be a sensational turning point in the struggle for gay, lesbian and transgender equality.

On the night of Garland's funeral, New York City police officers chose to raid the Stonewall Inn, a small bar located on Christopher Street in Greenwich Village. Although mafia-run, the Stonewall, like other predominantly gay bars in the city, was raided periodically.

Typically, the more 'deviant' customers (drag queens, butch lesbians and 'coloured' gays) would be arrested and taken away while white, male customers looked on or quietly disappeared. On the night in question, the owners of the Stonewall were charged with the illegal sale of alcohol, although it was obvious to most that it had been busted simply because it was a gay bar. The raid began as they all did, with plainclothes and uniformed police officers entering the premises, arresting the staff, and throwing out the customers one by one onto the street.

As the police trashed the bar and smashed the cash register, the ousted gays gathered outside, frustrated that Stonewall was the third gay bar in the

Patricia Quinn and Little Nell getting friendly with Tim Curry in *The Rocky Horror Picture Show* (1975) © Photofest

> 'Truth? Justice? Human dignity? What good are they?'
>
> **Alfred in *Death in Venice***

> 'In just seven days, I can make you a man. Dig it if you can.'
>
> **Dr Frank-N-Furter in *The Rocky Horror Picture Show***

Village to be raided and closed in recent weeks. They started to get loud and rowdy; and then no one is really sure what happened next. Could the crowd have been incited by the butch lesbian who resisted arrest, yelling and screaming? Was it the defiant drag queen standing in high heels chanting 'gay power'? Perhaps emotions were still running high because of Judy Garland's death, or maybe it was simply the summer heat. But whatever the cause, the crowd, which had grown to several hundred people, totally erupted.

Police called for reinforcements while being hit with coins, bottles, bricks and even a parking meter. They tried to make arrests but hadn't expected queens to fight back. Surprised and in shock, officers were eventually forced to take refuge and lock themselves inside the Stonewall. To the delight of hundreds of gay onlookers, a group of drag queens taunted the police by singing at the top of their lungs, 'We are the Stonewall girls/We wear our hair in curls/We wear no underwear/We show our pubic hair/We wear our dungarees/Above our nelly knees!'

With the police holed up in the bar as the crowds chanted 'Gay Power!' it was clear the gay movement was underway. Similar riots occurred on succeeding nights, followed by protest rallies. The event marked the awakening of gay-rights organisations throughout the US and it's commemorated annually in Gay and Lesbian Pride Week.

As a result of the 1969 Stonewall riots and the subsequent shift in attitudes about homosexuality, the media was forced to acknowledge the existence of a gay community and the issues it faced. Although the events in Greenwich Village received little coverage initially, they served as a rallying force and soon many major newspapers and magazines featured in-depth stories concerning the new emergence of homosexual visibility. A *Newsweek* article commented of the Stonewall riots, 'In summers past, such an incident would have stirred little more than resigned shrugs from the Village's homophile population – but in 1969 the militant mood touches every minority.'

By October of 1969, a report issued by the American government's National Institute of Mental Health urged states to abolish laws against private homosexual intercourse between consenting adults. This report was interpreted by the author of an October *Time* article as a sign that some tolerance and even support for the gay activists was emerging in the 'straight' community.

Cinema also reflected these changing perceptions towards the gay community, and the events at Stonewall seemed to help make positive portrayals of gay characters possible. The release of Mart Crowley's *The Boys in the Band* in 1970 coincided with the new activist gay movement and provided Americans with personalised examples of male homosexuals and their struggles. The film centres around a group of unhappy but witty gay men who lacerate each other and themselves, characters like Larry and Hank, who are average guys who just happen to be gay. Friedkin's film was a major step forward in characterisation, although by no means perfect. It's often criticised for delving a bit too much into self-hating angst and demoralising confessions: not exactly supportive images for a minority struggling to become visible.

Although not quite as many gay villains, victims and sissies appeared in the 70s as the 60s, the revelation of homosexuality still caused suicides in *Ode to Billie Joe* (1976) and *The Betsy* (1978) and was regularly used to typify sleaziness and evil, from the animated features of Ralph Bakshi (*Heavy Traffic*, 1973; *Coonskin*, 1975) and blaxploitation films (*Cleopatra Jones*, 1973; *Cleopatra Jones and the Casino of Gold*, 1975), to espionage dramas (*The Kremlin Letter*, 1970; *The Tamarind Seed*, 1974; *The Eiger Sanction*, 1975), cop thrillers (*Magnum Force*, 1973; *Freebie and the Bean*, 1974; *Busting*, 1974), and prison films (*Fortune and Men's Eyes*, 1971; *Caged Heat*, 1972; *Scarecrow*, 1973). Homosexual rape also marred the backwoods trip of *Deliverance* (1972), and promiscuous hetero Diane Keaton got murdered by a gay man in *Looking For Mr Goodbar* (1977).

Nevertheless, throughout the 70s, there was a definite change for the better in gay cinema. Where, in the 60s, sympathetic though unhappy homosexual characters featured in major films like *A Taste of Honey*, *The Leather Boys* and *The L-Shaped Room*, it wasn't until a decade later that mainstream directors such as John Schlesinger and Bob Fosse would present homosexuality as a valid alternative lifestyle. Fosse's *Cabaret* (1972) and Schlesinger's *Sunday Bloody Sunday* (1971) proved that gay issues could be treated in a serious adult manner. While *Cabaret* was a bawdy but inspired musical exploration of 1930s Berlin seen through the eyes of a bohemian club singer (Liza Minnelli) and a pretty-boy bisexual (Michael York), *Sunday Bloody Sunday* was more low key – an understated, triangular love story in which Glenda Jackson and Peter Finch share the affections of bisexual Murray Head.

The Boys in the Band (1970)

'Do you know what lies at the bottom of the mainstream? Mediocrity.'

Alfred in *Death in Venice*

> 'You must never smile like that. You must never smile like that at anyone.'
>
> Aschenbach in ***Death in Venice***

Another powerful and poignant movie from the early part of the decade was Christopher Larkin's *A Very Natural Thing* (1973), about a young man who leaves the priesthood to settle down in New York, hoping to meet a man to love and share his life with. Honest and well acted, it tackled the subject matter without prurience. Larkin commented at the time: 'The idea of a film about gay relationships and gay liberation themes comes out of my own personal reaction to the mindless, sex-obsessed image of the homosexual prevalent in gay porno films.'

Meanwhile, director Sidney Lumet and writer Frank Pierson delivered a breakthrough box-office hit with *Dog Day Afternoon* (1975), a fact-based comedy/drama starring Al Pacino as a gay Brooklyn bank-robber trying to finance his male lover's sex-change operation. Filmmaking at its best, Pierson was rewarded with a much-deserved Oscar for Best Original Screenplay. Pacino later went on to play a sexually muddled cop in William Friedkin's *Cruising* (1980), also set in New York, this time centring around the S&M bars of the city.

Other celebrated gay-themed films of the 70s include various underground movies such as *Tricia's Wedding* (1971), which featured the drag troupe the Cockettes; Jim Bidgood's sensual fantasy *Pink Narcissus* (1971); the films of Jan Oxenberg, such as *A Comedy In Six Unnatural Acts* (1975); and the films of the late Curt McDowell, including *Thundercrack!* (1975) and *Loads* (1980).

From Italy, in 1971, came Luchino Visconti's interpretation of Thomas Mann's classic novella, *Death in Venice*. Dirk Bogarde starred as an ageing world-famous composer who reassesses his life when his eyes alight on a beautiful teenage boy. Quiet, thoughtful and beautifully composed, Visconti took a difficult story and treated it with restraint and sensitivity. Bogarde was quoted as saying that he'd never better his work in this film.

Meanwhile, in Britain, director Derek Jarman released some of his finest work, including the highly homoerotic *Sebastiane* (1976), a sincere, respectful story of the martyr. Jarman's film, infamous for its plentiful, non-exploitative male nudity and all-Latin dialogue, offered an honest detailing of the spirit of Christianity which led to Sebastiane's refusal of Roman orders to kill a young page.

Also from Britain came the made-for-TV movie *The Naked Civil Servant* (1975), a biographical film, based on the real life of Quentin Crisp, an

Björn Andresen as Tadzio in
Death in Venice (1971)

OUT AT THE MOVIES

Englishman who lived in London. Crisp was an effeminate homosexual, a flamboyant and witty exhibitionist whose conversation was as glittering as the lipstick and mascara he used for effect. The film, full of Crisp's dry and ironic humour, stars John Hurt in one of the highlights of his career, and explores the story of the extraordinary and courageous life of Crisp, who decided not to disguise his homosexuality, and use it as a weapon instead of a weakness. Although a TV movie, *The Naked Civil Servant* quickly became regarded as an invaluable document in the history of gay visibility in twentieth-century England.

A large batch of American television movies dealing with gay issues also seemed to surface in the 70s: *That Certain Summer* (1972) with Hal Holbrook as a gay father coming out to his son; *A Question of Love* (1978) starred Gena Rowlands as a lesbian mother fighting for custody of her child; and *Sergeant Matlovich Vs The US Air Force* (1978), which dramatised a real-life challenge to the military's ban on homosexuality.

The lighter side of the decade's gay cinema offerings came in the form of a bisexual named Frank-N-Furter (Richard O'Brien) in *The Rocky Horror Picture Show* (1975). Based on the British rock musical, it's primarily a spoof of old monster movies with scenes of bisexual flirtation and seduction thrown in. One of the most enduring examples of homosexuality in film, *Rocky Horror* bombed on its initial release. However, the marketing people at Fox decided to programme midnight showings and soon people started shouting at the screen, throwing objects across the cinema, and dressing up as their favourite characters. The midnight screenings encouraged even the most down-to-earth guys to dress up in high heels and fishnet stockings and, considering that a large portion of its audience was straight, *Rocky Horror* allowed heterosexuals to accept homosexuals, and even enjoy aspects of the lifestyle. Quite quickly, the movie became one of the most successful cult films of all time.

Meanwhile, the late, great drag queen Divine provided audiences with even more outrageous camp thrills, mainly courtesy of director John Waters. *Multiple Maniacs* (1970), *Pink Flamingos* (1972) and *Female Trouble* (1974) were sometimes-obscene black comedies extolling crime and exalting the 300-lb female impersonator. Waters' Divine-less *Desperate Living* (1977), a lesbian fairy tale, was one of the wildest of all his films.

> 'You cannot touch me now. I am one of the stately homos of England.'
> **Quentin Crisp in *The Naked Civil Servant***

> 'Let's do the time warp again!'
> **All in *The Rocky Horror Picture Show***

> 'I would like if I may to take you on a strange journey.'
> **The Criminologist in *The Rocky Horror Picture Show***

> 'Filth is my life!'
> **Babs Johnson in *Pink Flamingos***

> 'Oh my God Almighty! Someone has sent me a bowel movement!'
>
> Babs Johnson in *Pink Flamingos*

> 'There are two kinds of people, my kind and assholes.'
>
> Connie in *Pink Flamingos*

> 'It stinks of high heaven, and God, dressed as Marlene Dietrich, holds his nose.'
>
> Hedwig in *Fox and His Friends*

Yet these campier films tended to play better with audiences who felt more at ease laughing at gay lifestyles than understanding them. In fact, lesbians and gay men provided cheap laughs throughout the decade in films such as *There Was a Crooked Man* (1970), *MASH* (1970), *Little Big Man* (1970), *For Pete's Sake* (1974), *Sheila Levine Is Dead and Living in New York City* (1975) and *The Goodbye Girl* (1977). Some of the condescending farces that focused purely on homosexuality were simply horrendous: *Norman, Is That You?* (1976), *The Ritz* (1976) and *A Different Story* (1978) are just a few of the exploitative, politically incorrect 'comedies' that poked fun at faggots.

There were also gay supporting characters, however, who were actually funny, such as Antonio Fargas in *Next Stop, Greenwich Village* (1976) and *Car Wash* (1976), and Michael Caine in *California Suite* (1978). And *Foul Play* (1978), one of the funniest films of the 70s, had everything a gay man could ask for – San Francisco, camp disco music and saunas – but no gay characters! Like so much else at the time, you had to be in the know to see it as a gay film. Most didn't and it became an enormous popular success, restoring Goldie Hawn's box office and launching Chevy Chase and Dudley Moore into starring careers. Now it's far easier for people to pick up on its gay sensibility and many see Colin Higgins' film as a gay homage to Hitchcock.

Interestingly, Colin Higgins had previously scripted an earlier 70s gay favourite which also had no gay characters. *Harold and Maude* (1971) starred Bud Cort as a young man with a great flair for inspired sight gags, all relating to death, and a wacky 79-year-old woman (Ruth Gordon) as his companion in love and adventures. Higgins later revealed the film was a gay love story in disguise. He stated: 'I'd have written a wonderful gay love story. But who would have filmed it? So I did the next best thing – I wrote something very quirky and interesting and which hopefully challenged convention.'

By the end of the decade, one of the most successful foreign films ever shown in the US came out. *La Cage aux Folles* (1979) was a wildly hilarious French farce centring around a happy gay couple who are forced to pass as straight when one partner's son, from a previous moment of heterosexual abandon, brings home his prospective in-laws. The film was so successful it spawned a sequel three years later, followed by a third instalment in 1986. However, although *La Cage* featured out gay characters in a healthy committed relationship (and loving parents to boot), it was a very light-hearted affair and yet another example of how, over the course of the decade, gay-related films had shifted from serious post-Stonewall dramas (*Sunday Bloody Sunday*, *The Boys in the Band*, *Death in Venice*) to clownish camp antics and drag movies. Though in the decade that would follow, with the impact of AIDS, gay-themed movies were about to get a lot more serious...

THE FILMS

BOYS IN THE BAND
(1970)

US, 118 mins
Director: William Friedkin
Writer: Mart Crowley
Cast: Cliff Gorman, Laurence Luckinbill, Kenneth Nelson, Leonard Frey, Peter White, Frederick Combs, Robert La Tourneaux, Reuben Greene
Genre: Black comedy

Mart Crowley adapted his own acclaimed, award-winning 1968 play for the screen, the first Hollywood film in which all of the principal characters were gay. Unlike director William Friedkin's subsequent effort, *Cruising* (1980), this picture was well received on its release.

Set in New York, one rainy evening, the story centres around a bunch of gay men who get together to celebrate a friend's birthday party at a Manhattan apartment, the film's only setting. The party, for pot-smoking Harold (Leonard Frey), gradually turns into more of an ensemble character assassination as the drink flows and one of the guests, Alan (Peter White), reveals his heterosexuality to the group. The host, Michael (Kenneth Nelson), is the most dominant character but the least happy being gay. In fact, he's a Catholic riddled with guilt and ends up fleeing to Midnight Mass. Other characters include Michael's calmer pal Donald (Frederick Combs), a hustler called Cowboy (Robert La Tourneaux) and a bickering couple (Keith Prentice and Laurence Luckinbill).

The characters come out with some wonderful lines such as Michael's, 'Show me a happy homosexual and I'll show you a gay corpse,' and Emory's plea, 'Who do you have to fuck to get a drink around here?' As the evening wears on though, the quips become more and more waspish, and the bickering sinks into vengeful attacks.

The film has often been criticised for its stereotypical treatment of gay men, showing simply campy, bitchy behaviour. Certainly, the boys display varying degrees of queenish antics, with references to *The Wizard of Oz* ('He's about as straight as the yellow brick road') and *Sunset Boulevard* ('I'm *not* ready for my close-up, Mr DeMille, nor will I be for the next two weeks') and at one point, a guest is even seen perusing *The Films of Joan Crawford*. However, this film that so riled Gay Lib activists in the 70s has developed into an important historical document. Most now recognise its revolutionary qualities; that it was immensely valuable to have some acknowledgement of gay existence rather than silence. Although the film focused on the sadness and loneliness of being a homosexual, it gave a sense of various gay identities – the flamboyant queen, the clone, the straight-acting Ivy League Jock, the suited businessman, and so on. And none of them died at the end.

A breakthrough work on a taboo subject, *Boys in the Band* is certainly reflective of its times. 'I knew a lot of people like those people,' Crowley said of his characters. 'The self-deprecating humour was born out of low self-esteem, from a sense of what the times told you about yourself.'

Indeed, Crowley's entertaining yet quietly thoughtful script is full of pathos, bitchiness, loneliness and jealousy, and under William Friedkin's generally sensitive, guiding hand, the film builds to a powerful climax.

Written on the eve of Gay Liberation and released in 1970, less than a year after the infamous Stonewall riots, *Boys in the Band* finally put to rest the Production Code's repressive stance on gay subject matter and became a catalyst for future positive portrayals. The picture really was ahead of its time and, although it looks a little dated now, there is still much to enjoy.

DEATH IN VENICE
aka Mort à Venise (France)
Morte a Venezia (Italy)
(1971)

Italy/France, 130 mins
Director: Luchino Visconti
Writers: Luchino Visconti, Nicola Badalucco.
Cast: Dirk Bogarde, Romolo Valli, Mark Burns, Nora Ricci, Marisa Berenson, Carole Andre, Björn Andresen.
Genre: Period drama

'The theme is not only homosexuality, but there is homosexuality. Although no sex at all. Still, Hollywood wanted me to change the boy to a girl. They do not even know of Thomas Mann!'

– **Luchino Visconti**

Dirk Bogarde gave the finest performance of his career, in fact one of the very best ever on screen, in Visconti's superb 1971 version of the Thomas Mann 1912 novella.

Bogarde is the avant-garde composer Gustav von Aschenbach (loosely based on Gustav Mahler), taking a convalescent holiday at the Venice Lido after the death of his child, the disastrous reception of his new compositions and various complications in his personal life back in Germany.

Trying to escape this stressful period, relaxing in the inspirational but decadent city, he develops an attraction to a beautiful boy sporting on the beach. Having only intended to stay for just a short period, he soon becomes so entranced by the beauty of this young boy, Tadzio (Björn Andresen), that he finds excuses to stay there longer. Dismissing hotel staff and porters with a flick of his wrist and gazing longingly at the young boy's figure, Bogarde's Aschenbach is perfectly suited to the crumbling decadence of the Venetian locations. He lingers, despite possessing privileged knowledge about a cholera epidemic sweeping the city. Ultimately, he is thrown into epiphanic agony as he falls utterly in love with this adolescent who embodies his ideal of beauty, that which he has been striving to achieve in his work.

The composer continues to watch Tadzio, despite what he's heard about the onset of cholera. Convinced of a mad and passionate truth in this infatuation and pleased by the efforts of a barber to make him look younger, Aschenbach obviously cherishes his obsession with Tadzio. But when news of the epidemic spreads, the hotel guests begin to leave, and one morning Aschenbach goes down to the beach to find only Tadzio there. Sitting in his beach chair, he is mesmerised by the young boy who, posing like a Greek statue, raises his arm toward the horizon. As he watches the boy pointing, he thinks it's an invitation, so he reaches up too. But it's too much of a struggle and Aschenbach quickly collapses back into his chair and dies. His dying desire lives on.

The composer's demise is inevitable and evident from early in the film. From the thick black smoke of the steam train bringing him to Venice to the final hint in the barber's shop that he is being embalmed as a simulacrum of the way he might once have appeared, Aschenbach is on a path from which he cannot diverge. In a sense, he is dead from the start.

A surprisingly subtle and intriguing tale of an obsessive quest, this wonderfully slow-paced film is also about the spiritual history of a man who knows he is dying. Aschenbach knows he will meet his own doom, all in his quest to understand the meaning of perfection, as embodied in the form of Tadzio.

A film of undeniable but unconventional beauty, don't expect special effects, car chases or fights. But sometimes simple is best. Nor are there any perverted sex scenes; the interaction between man and boy is limited to stolen glances from afar and the occasional smile.

Death In Venice is indeed about Aschenbach's death but another death that we witness is a more abstract one; that of the composer's notions about the nature of art. Flashbacks reveal Aschenbach's colleague Alfred (Mark Burns) arguing about Art with him. Alfred's argument – 'Art is ambiguity, always' – wins through the person of Tadzio, a living embodiment of the ambiguity of physical perfection. Aschenbach thinks he is appreciating Tadzio on a spiritual level but he soon realises that this has become hopelessly confused with true feelings of love. This conflict can never be reconciled.

Mahler's Third and Fifth Symphonies are woven throughout the film. Particular emphasis is placed on the Adagietta of the Fifth, which first plays over the opening credits, then keeps reappearing. The music haunts the film, as do the quiet whispers of sound that help create the film's almost surreal environment. The delicacy of the soundtrack evokes the mood of Aschenbach's last days and his obsession with the face of Tadzio.

Pasquale De Santis's cinematography is also exquisite, while the beauty of Visconti's shots, particularly at the end, are sublime but also comforting, bathed in hazy Venice sunshine.

Visconti described the Thomas Mann novella from which the film was adapted as 'a mighty subject for a motion picture'. He fought hard to make *Death in Venice*. Arguments over casting and cuts in the original budget plagued the production. Originally the producers were horrified by the film's lyrical homoeroticism. However, the Warner Bros executives allowed Visconti to complete his film following large box-office returns from his previous feature *The Damned*.

Renowned for his uncompromising demands and need for perfection, a 20-minute featurette on the British DVD release of *Death in Venice* provides an interesting insight into life on set of this film – the endless takes and lengthy days waiting around for the correct conditions. The short documentary was made over a very long day of filming in which just one sequence of less than two minutes was shot. During the day, Bogarde described how Visconti concentrated on absolute craftsmanship: 'Everything has to be absolutely perfect for him,' he explained. 'The reflection of a glass dish on a child's face, in a scene where I am having a row with somebody else, is *equally* important to him as the row!'

Many critics were taken aback by the film's controversial subject matter, and *Death in Venice* was met with almost universal disapproval and misunderstanding when it was first released.

Nevertheless, Visconti's masterpiece won awards all round the world. Dirk Bogarde was deeply grateful to his director, saying, 'Visconti was the greatest teacher and professor I've ever had in my life. I've learned so much from him.' To top it all, in 1971, Visconti won the special Grand Prize at the 25th anniversary of the Cannes Film Festival, honouring the film and the career of its director.

PINK NARCISSUS
(1971)

US, 65 mins
Director: James Bidgood
Cast: Bobby Kendall, Charles Ludlum, Don Brooks
Genre: Erotic fantasy

James Bidgood's *Pink Narcissus* is an unwavering celebration of the male body within a fantasy world of epic indulgence. Complex, beautiful and very sexy, it's a film unlike any other. There is no dialogue but every scene is chockfull of symbolism.

An outrageous but breathtaking erotic poem, the film focuses on the daydreams of a beautiful young boy prostitute who, from the seclusion of his ultra-kitsch apartment, dreams a series of interlinked narcissistic fantasies. The self-obsessed boy imagines himself as a Roman slave chosen by the emperor, as a triumphant sparkle-suited matador vanquishing the bull, an innocent wood nymph romping in the woods, a harem boy in the tent of a sheik. But reality constantly intrudes through the depraved lives of the other street people, leather-clad bikers and slaves and visits from the johns.

Bobby Kendall in *Pink Narcissus*

His narcissism is marred by one great fear – growing old and losing his looks.

Filmed in richly saturated colours, brilliantly styled and created by Bidgood, *Pink Narcissus* was made in his own tiny apartment using homemade and improvised sets and props. It was shot over seven years in a haphazard fashion between 1964 and 1970 on 8mm. With its highly charged hallucinogenic quality, its atmosphere of lush decadence, and its explicit erotic power, *Pink Narcissus* is a true landmark of gay cinema. As filmmaker Richard Kwietniowski once wrote: 'Should the film be aligned with the work of Anger and Jarman in experimental cinema? Or in the art world, with photographers like Pierre et Gilles, who attempt similar levels of artifice? Is it just erotica from the beefcake era, or the most utopian home movie ever made?'

Pink Narcissus was shrouded in mystery following its initial release in 1971. The production company, Sherpix Productions, had edited the film without the creator's consent and so, as a result, Bidgood was credited as 'Anonymous', which led to critics surmising who had actually directed the film. Wrongly, it was attributed to filmmakers such as Kenneth Anger and Andy Warhol, until the truth emerged that it was in fact Bidgood.

The clues were there, however, with Bidgood having already achieved success as an artist and photographer, many of his photographs featuring the film's star Bobby Kendall. Throughout most of the 1960s, Bidgood had contributed photographs to physique magazines such as *The Young Physique* under the pseudonym 'Les Folies des Hommes'.

Considered lost for many years, film historians worked at restoring Bidgood's fantasy and, eventually, it was rescued from obscurity at the 1984 New York Gay Film Festival where screenings were packed out. More recently, in the summer of 2007, the film was released complete and uncut on DVD through the respected British Film Institute label. Accompanied by a world-exclusive filmed interview with the director, in it Bidgood stated: 'Most gay men are narcissists. We love men. We love ourselves, and that was what the film was about – someone who was in love with himself and had fantasies in which *he* was always the object of love or whatever.'

Thanks to the restoration of the film, *Pink Narcissus* will now always have a certain cult status as new generations of gay viewers become mesmerised by the film's stunning star – the gorgeous and enigmatic Bobby Kendall.

CABARET
(1972)

US, 124 mins
Director: Bob Fosse
Cast: Liza Minnelli, Joel Grey, Michael York, Helmut Griem, Marisa Berenson, Fritz Wepper
Genre: Musical

One of the most brilliant musicals ever made, Bob Fosse's *Cabaret* is a truly inspired version of Christopher Isherwood's 1939 memoirs and bisexual tales of pre-WWII Berlin.

In this dazzlingly choreographed story of love, decadence and Nazi storm troopers, Liza Minnelli stars as fame-hungry cabaret singer Sally Bowles, who becomes embroiled in a love triangle with an impossibly pretty bisexual English teacher Brian Roberts (Michael York) and wealthy German toff, Maximilian van Heune (Helmut Griem), in the rotting decadence of 1930s Berlin.

As the film opens, outside on the street, the Nazi party is growing into a brutal political force; but away from this, we are welcomed inside the Kit Kat Club, where the girls, the boys and even the orchestra are beautiful. Brian enters this strange café society and straight into starry-eyed Sally's decadent life – all fun, booze and sex. Straight sex, that is. Brian, having thought he was gay, is a little confused. Sally taunts him: 'Maybe you just don't sleep with girls.' He doesn't deny it. When Baron Maximilian arrives on the scene, he invites the pair to his mansion with the sole intention of corrupting them both. It's clear that the two men become more than just buddies. Although we don't see them in bed together, when Brian later shamefacedly rejects Max's gift of a gold cigarette lighter, the implication is that something has gone on.

Later, during a row about Max, Brian snaps at Sally, 'Screw Max!' 'I *do*!' she replies, and he retorts, 'So do I!' Sally soon winds up pregnant but has an abortion without telling him; she explains cryptically: 'How long would it be before you…'

Fosse makes such candid points about Brian's bisexuality with tasteful emphasis. The director also stokes *Cabaret* with an edgy desperation as the characters sweat blood to stay carefree in a world overshadowed by the Third Reich's leather-clad menace. Fosse handles the political material during the time of Hitler's rise to power with style and integrity and the film's energy, musical set pieces and performances still enthral to this day. Minnelli shines and sparkles throughout and York is excellent as the young bisexual Englishman, while Joel Grey's depiction of a grotesque cabaret MC is yet another highlight of this knockout musical. With patent-leather hair, rosy cheeks and thick drag-queen eyelashes, he relishes the creepy character's sleaziness and 'Money', his duet with Minnelli, is a showstopper.

This extraordinary adaptation of the Kander-Ebb musical won eight Academy Awards, including those for Best Director (Fosse), Best Actress (Minnelli) and Best Supporting Actor (Grey).

PINK FLAMINGOS
(1972)

US, 95 mins
Director/Writer: John Waters
Cast: Divine, David Lochary, Mink Stole, Mary Vivian Pearce, Edith Massey, Danny Mills, Channing Wilroy, Cookie Mueller
Genre: Cult camp comedy

If *Clockwork Orange* was a deliberate exercise in ultra-violence, *Pink Flamingos* is a deliberate exercise in ultra-bad taste. With no budget, grotesque images and the striking drag queen Divine, this movie soon attracted an endearing legion of admirers. It's still shown at select theatres and often at gay and lesbian festivals around the world with fans queuing to cheer for Babs and Cotton, hiss Connie and Raymond, quote endless lines, and have a great time.

The plot of this seminal camp flick follows the adventures of Sleaze Queen Babs Johnson (Divine), a fat, style-obsessed criminal who lives in a trailer with her mentally-ill, 250-pound mother Edie (Edith Massey), her hippie son Crackers (Danny Mills) and her travelling companion Cotton (Mary Vivian Pearce). They're trying to rest quietly on their laurels as 'the filthiest people alive'. But competition is brewing in the form of Connie and Raymond Marble (David Lochary and Mink Stole), 'two jealous perverts', according to the script, who sell heroin to schoolchildren. Finally, they challenge Divine directly, and battle commences.

Raymond and Connie try to seize Bab's title of 'filthiest person alive' by sending her a turd in the mail and burning down her trailer. The Marbles kidnap hitchhiking women, have them impregnated by their servant Channing (Channing Wilroy), and then sell the babies to lesbian couples. As Raymond explains, they use the dykes' money to finance their porno shops and 'a network of dealers selling heroin in the inner-city elementary schools'.

Pink Flamingos has cult qualities in the same way *The Rocky Horror Picture Show* does; everyone in the film has something odd about them and both movies joyfully celebrate their uniqueness. Waters' film has endless memorable moments (who could forget?) – the shrimping scene with David's blue and Mink's orange pubic hair, Divine's infamous faeces-snacking, brown teeth and all, sex with a chicken, eating people alive, incestuous fellatio with her son, and hard-core pornography. This commercial feature surely must be the first and only to end with the star eating dogshit.

Pink Flamingos is now 30 years old. Waters recently had the film blown up from 16 to 35mm and 'restored' ready for forthcoming video and DVD releases which feature a few never-before-seen outtakes, self-critical commentary by Waters ('You can see the bad continuity in this scene'), a new stereo soundtrack and the hilarious original trailer, which is made up only of shocked reactions from people who have just seen the picture.

Many won't enjoy either Crackers and Cookie's chicken-shagging scene or Babs' turd eating, but these sequences are what put the film on the map, brought Waters all the publicity, negative and otherwise, and gave *Pink Flamingos* a permanent place in camp film history.

THE ROCKY HORROR PICTURE SHOW
(1975)

UK, 100 mins
Director/Writer: Jim Sharman
Cast: Tim Curry, Susan Sarandon, Barry Bostwick, Richard O'Brien, Jonathan Adams, Nell Campbell
Genre: Cult camp comedy

Richard O'Brien's wacky stage show was turned into the definitive cult movie thanks mainly to Tim Curry's camp Dr Frank-N-Furter, Meat Loaf in a deep freeze, a script full of kitsch appeal, and that all-singing-all-dancing, toe-tapping 'Time Warp' finale. It was the movie that inspired us all to take a few steps to the left and showed us there's a disco queen inside each of us!

The Rocky Horror Picture Show is an outrageous assemblage of the most stereotypical science-fiction movies, Marvel comics, Frankie Avalon/Annette Funicello outings and rock 'n' roll of every vintage. Running through the story is the sexual confusion of two middle-American, 'Ike Age' kids confronted by the complications of the decadent morality of the 70s, represented in the person of the mad 'doctor' Frank-N-Furter, a transvestite from the planet Transexual.

O'Brien, who wrote the book, music and lyrics calls it 'something any ten-year-old could enjoy'. The original play opened in London at the Royal Court's experimental Theatre Upstairs as a six-week workshop project in June 1973, and was named Best Musical of that year in the London Evening Standard's annual poll of drama critics. Lou Adler, who was in London, saw *The Rocky Horror Show* and promptly sewed up the American theatrical rights to the play within 36 hours.

Filming of *The Rocky Horror Picture Show* began a year later at Bray Studios, England's famous House of Horror, and at a nineteenth-century chateau, which served once as the wartime refuge of General Charles de Gaulle.

The film version retains many members of the original Theatre Upstairs company. Repeating the roles they originally created in the theatre are Richard O'Brien (Riff Raff), Patricia Quinn (Magenta), Little Nell (Columbia) and Jonathan Adams (who played the Narrator on stage and in the film appears as Dr Scott).

With O'Brien co-writing the film's screenplay, the result is a faithful adaptation of the original...

On the way to visit an old college professor, two clean-cut kids, Brad Majors (Barry Bostwick) and his fiancée Janet Weiss (Susan Sarandon), run into tyre trouble and seek help at the site of a light down the road. It's coming from the Frankenstein place, where Dr Frank-N-Furter (Tim Curry), a transvestite from the planet Transexual in the galaxy of Transylvania, is in the midst of one of his maniacal experiments – he's created the perfect man, a rippling piece of beefcake christened Rocky Horror (Peter Hinwood), and intends to put him to good use (his own) in his kinky household retinue, presided over by a hunchback henchman named Riff Raff (Richard O'Brien) and his incestuous sister Magenta (Patricia Quinn), assisted by a tap-dancing groupie-in-residence, Columbia (Little Nell).

Meanwhile, an oafish biker, unwed Eddie (Meatloaf), ploughs through the laboratory wall, wailing on a saxophone. Frank puts a permanent end to this musical interruption without thinking twice until the old professor Brad and Janet set out to visit, Dr Scott (Jonathan Adams), turns up at the castle in search of his missing nephew, the juvenile delinquent Eddie. He knows that Frank-N-Furter is an alien spy from another galaxy, and goes to turn him in, but Frank moves too fast, seducing first Janet, then Brad into his lascivious clutches. Overwhelmed by a new-found libido, Janet hotly attacks the stud Rocky Horror while Brad is under the covers with Frank.

Before Dr Scott can bring justice and morality into this topsy-turvy Transylvanian orgy, Frank-N-Furter has turned his captives to stone, in preparation for a new drag revue 'experiment', and Riff Raff and Magenta reappear in Transylvanian space togs to wrest control of the mission from Frank-N-Furter, whose lifestyle is too extreme even for his fellow space travellers. When his lavish histrionic claims of chauvinism fail to soften up Riff Raff and Magenta, Frank-N-Furter tries to escape, only to be gunned down by their power ray-guns. Rock rushes to save his creator, but he, too, is blasted to outer space by the militants.

Tim Curry camps it up as Dr Frank-N-Furter in Richard O'Brien's *The Rocky Horror Picture Show*

Brad, Janet and Dr Scott are left in a fog, incapable of readjusting to the normalcy of the life they've left behind in Denton, now that they've tasted the forbidden fruits of the Time Warp.

Richard O'Brien's cross-dressing sensation will forever be an acquired taste but elicits a fiery passion in devoted fans. Like many cult movies, it was rejected by most viewers on its initial release; but after late-night screenings took place in New York, the cult began to develop. Devoted fans started to arrive at theatres in costume ready to join in the musical madness. One of the few movies that consistently inspires dancing in the aisles, throughout the film audience members recite the dialogue simultaneously with the characters on screen, many even mocking the characters or coming up with improvised quips aimed at the actors involved. Water pistols are squirted, toilet rolls thrown and playing cards tossed at the screen. Such screenings become major advertised events.

This camp classic always deserves another look and was the perfect picture for DVD. The various discs include an amazing line-up of essential extras for *Rocky* fans. Of course, they're not all on one edition and fans will have to buy special editions to collect them all. However, extras that are around include commentaries by O'Brien and other cast members, the deleted musical sequence 'Superheroes', which has been edited back into the film, 'The Theatrical Experience' – a branching function that gives you an in-theatre experience viewing option to allow DVD owners to see the crowd's reaction or the performers on stage at certain points as they watch the film – the engrossing documentary *Rocky Horror Double Feature*, deleted scenes, outtakes including 11 alternate takes on key scenes in the film, excerpts from VH-1's 'Behind-the-Music' and 'Where Are They Now?', featuring interviews with Susan Sarandon, Barry Bostwick, Richard O'Brien, Patricia Quinn and Meatloaf, two lively sing-along songs, two theatrical trailers and loads of photo galleries. The film company only release all of these special editions because the cultural movement surrounding *The Rocky Horror Picture Show* continues to this day. And the fact that there's still such huge interest more than three decades after the film's original release, is surely a testament to its status as the ultimate piece of interactive performance art.

THE NAKED CIVIL SERVANT
(1975)

UK, 80 mins
Director: Jack Gold
Cast: John Hurt, Patricia Hodge, John Rhys-Davies

Genre: Biopic

Quentin Crisp has been described as one of England's works of art. In 1908, in Surrey, England, Mrs Pratt, nursery governess and solicitor's wife, gave birth to her last child, Dennis. In the late 1920s, Dennis gave birth to the character that he would become for the remainder of his life, Quentin Crisp.

> *'Even a monotonously undeviating path of self-examination does not necessarily lead to a mountain of self-knowledge. I stumble toward my grave confused and hurt and hungry...'*

Thus ends Crisp's unflinching autobiography, *The Naked Civil Servant*, published in 1968. Seven years later, Thames Television adapted the book, turning it into a remarkable and poignant film. Featuring an award-winning performance by John Hurt, the drama of Quentin's youth is recaptured in 1930s England.

Crisp himself introduced the piece, which gave us the opportunity to compare Hurt's performance against the real thing. And *what* a performance. Not only are the mannerisms and affectations delivered with precision and realism, but the examination of the character within is poignantly and simply revealed.

Crisp's world was one of brutality and comedy, of short-lived jobs and precarious relationships. It was a life he faced with courage, humour and intelligence. He publicly declared his homosexuality at a time when this alternate lifestyle was still an offence punishable by imprisonment in Great Britain.

Given to blatant exhibitionism, Crisp endured almost constant beatings from local yobs who were threatened by his flamboyant style. He engaged for a time in street prostitution, although, in his own retrospection, he felt this was to look for acceptance more than income. Slowly, he began to assemble a group of friends who were in their own ways equally flamboyant and outrageous, and found himself in the arty world of Soho bohemia.

The film details how, just before the Second World War, he found work, lodgings and refuge by way of an unnamed ballet teacher, played outrageously in the film by Patricia Hodge. Exempt from war service due to his 'sexual perversion', he was employed at a government art school on the recommendation of the ballet teacher, thus becoming the 'naked civil servant'. In his own words, 'The poverty from which I have suffered could be diagnosed as "Soho" poverty. It comes from having the airs and graces of a genius and no talent.'

The film portrays an individual who finds himself an alien to all that convention provides. It is produced with an element of sophistry and bitter wit that seems to reflect Crisp well. Its narration plays straight to the audience, emphasised by the use of caption boards, reminiscent of old silent movies.

Crisp's search for enduring love remained unrequited, with the closest candidate being 'Barndoor' (John Rhys-Davies), with whom he shared his one-room Chelsea flat for a number of tumultuous years.

Crisp drifts from circumstance to circumstance in an amazingly passive way. In fact, the only time we see any self-generated activity is when he chooses to defend himself against charges of perversion and solicitation levelled at him by two London constables. Ever mindful of his audience, he stands in the witness box and exposes the inaccuracies of their testimony.

Having survived the court case, and with the war behind him, our last view of Crisp is in a park in London in the early 1970s. He wryly observes that the clothing that had earned him regular beatings from the town toughs is now the uniform of the youth culture. As four younger versions of those earlier toughs try to extort a pound each from him on threat of alleging he'd sexually assaulted them, he aloofly informs them that he is immune to their threats now. 'I'm one of the stately homos of England', he sniffs, and minces away as the credits roll.

This excellent film was a Prix Italia and Emmy winner, whilst John Hurt's memorable performance earned him a BAFTA award for Best Actor.

Fans of the film will probably already know that Crisp later moved to a studio flat in New York in the 1980s. Happily ensconced in Manhattan life, he was immortalised in Sting's song 'An Englishman in New York'. What many may not know, however, is that Crisp actually died on English soil, on 21 November 1999, while preparing for a one-man show.

FOX AND HIS FRIENDS
aka Faustrecht der Freiheit
(1975)

Germany; 123 mins
Director: Rainer Werner Fassbinder
Writers: Rainer Werner Fassbinder, Christian Hohoff
Cast: Peter Chatel, Rainer Werner Fassbinder, Karlheinz Bohm, Adrian Hoven
Genre: German Drama

Fox and His Friends was Rainer Werner Fassbinder's first specifically male gay-themed film and on its release in 1975 was described by a reviewer for *The Times* in London as 'one of the best films ever made about the life of homosexuals, their passions, their quarrels…' Meanwhile, a *New York Times* writer remarked that it was 'the first serious, explicit but non-sensational movie about homosexuality to be shown in this country'.

Franz Biberkopf, known as 'Fox' and played by Fassbinder himself, is a carnival worker at a loose end when his lover is arrested and the police shutter their carnival booth. In need of cash for his weekly lottery purchase, Fox lets himself be picked up in a public lavatory by an elegant older man named Max, an antique furniture dealer. At Max's house, he meets two younger gay men who have expensive tastes and images to uphold. The next day, Fox wins 500,000 marks in the lottery, and Max's friends suddenly turn into his friends, especially Eugen, the heir to a bookbinding firm that's short of cash. Fox and Eugen become lovers.

Fox, who's brash, uncouth, warm-hearted and naïve, dominates at first, or seems to, but soon he is tamed and exploited by the effete and bourgeois Eugen. Fox's winning lottery ticket is used to rescue Eugen's collapsing family business, and he is eventually jilted, broke and without recourse. His dead body is found next to an empty pill bottle by two teenagers who pick through his pockets while two of his old friends flee to avoid involvement.

There's a level of dry humour played throughout the story, which is both comedy and satire. Numerous scenes play up the differences between Eugen and Fox, and especially Fox's attempts to copy the social graces of the wealthy. Yet the overall effect is that of tragedy, as Fox allows himself to be used and abused, and in the final sequences come constant blows to any chance of a happy ending.

SEBASTIANE
(1976)

UK, 91 mins
Directors: Derek Jarman, Paul Humfress
Cast: Leonardo Treviglio, Barney James, Richard James, Neil Kennedy,

Genre: Historical drama

Derek Jarman's debut feature film shocked audiences with its frank portrayal of homosexuality, violence, and the ultimate martyrdom of the Catholic saint Sebastiane in 303 AD.

A visually striking fantasy, *Sebastiane* begins at the court of Emperor Diocletian in an unforgettable sequence of Roman excess and Bacchanalian sexuality. Similar in tone to the opening sequence of Ken Russell's grotesque historical drama *The Devils*, which Jarman designed in 1971, the film is also reminiscent of the orgiastic fantasies of Federico Fellini's *Satyricon* and Cecil B DeMille's *The Sign of the Cross*. Jarman is conscious of these allusions though, and at one point a Roman soldier in the film, dreaming of the golden era of Rome, mentions 'Cecilli Mille' and 'Phillistini's Satyricon'.

Accused of standing up for a Christian, Sebastiane (Leonardo Treviglio), friend of the emperor and captain of his guard, is demoted to mere soldier and banished from Rome to an isolated Sicilian encampment. This remote coastal place proves to be both a barren wasteland and an oasis of freedom where the men are free to act out homosexual fantasies and explore their hidden desires. However, Sebastiane angers outpost captain Severus by ignoring his sexual advances and devoting himself to God, resulting in a violent battle that ends ultimately with a stunningly homoerotic execution.

So, in Jarman's vision of the saint who died on a cross, Sebastiane is killed not simply for his Christian beliefs but because he refuses the advances of the sadomasochistic Severus.

The film contains probably *the* most classic homoerotic play-fight, which is thrilling, arousing and to some degree disturbing. In fact, the whole film is filled with memorable cinematography and symbolic imagery. Co-directed with Paul Humfress, this profoundly personal work is visually stunning. Though verging on the pornographic with its vast array of handsome naked men who practise for battle and have sex together, the film is more than an arty gay cult porno. It is an intriguing play on the male psyche and juxtaposes multiple themes: unrequited love; social acceptance of sexual thought; the demands of society upon the individual; sexual desire in an exclusively male environment; and the requirements imposed by religious values.

The film does, however, suffer from one, not-uncommon failing – that the best-looking actor is given the largest role but delivers the weakest performance. Treviglio's Sebastiane is oh-so-handsome yet far less interesting than the rest of the troubled, bullying, awkward or horny soldiers in the platoon.

Nevertheless, with its fabulous photography, Latin dialogue (with English subtitles), and an evocative, ambient-style score by Brian Eno, *Sebastiane* is a dreamlike, avant-garde exploration of the soul that benefited from a deserving, yet surprisingly strong, commercial release in Britain and major US cities.

LA CAGE AUX FOLLES
(1978)

France/Italy, 99 mins
Director: Edouard Molinaro
Cast: Ugo Tognazzi, Michel Serrault, Benny Luke, Michel Galabru, Claire Maurier
Genre: Farce

La Cage aux Folles, one of the most successful foreign-language films ever shown in America, was a huge hit. An undeniably loveable and unpretentious movie, audiences raved over the two main characters in this camp classic – gay lovers Albin and Renato.

Ugo Tognazzi stars as Renato, the owner of a nightclub that features a transvestite revue, while Michel Serrault plays his lover, a neurotic drag queen.

It's all a bed of roses for the quirky couple until Renato's love-struck son Laurent (the offspring of a youthful indiscretion) returns to announce that he is engaged to the woman of his dreams, a girl whose father happens to be a strict upholder of public morals. The father of the bride-to-be is a homophobic politician and, although Laurent is comfortable with his gay parents, he needs the man's approval if the marriage is to go ahead.

With no way of avoiding a meet with the future in-laws, Renato and Albin do their best to conceal their lifestyle, radically altering the décor of their home, from frilly flamboyance to a more subtle, understated style. Even the couple's maid, a handsome wannabe who usually struts around the house in little more than a skimpy pair of hot pants, is ordered to clean up his image and dress in a proper butler's uniform. But attempts to consign all signs of gayness to the closet meet with disaster and the increasingly frantic situation provides ample opportunity for slapstick laughs.

As the big night approaches, when they will finally meet the ultra-conservative in-laws-to-be, it becomes clear that Albin will have to pull off the performance of his life. With the aid of a wig, a dowdy housedress and a newly perfected, falsetto voice, he is introduced to the guests as Renato's wife.

It's Serrault and Tognazzi's fine performances that really make Edouard Molinaro's intrinsically theatrical comedy sparkle. They sail through the whole affair with seemingly boundless, kitsch conviction, but while there are many moments that are excruciatingly funny, there are also one or two others that are genuinely heartbreaking.

La Cage was so successful it spawned two sequels, a Tony-award-winning musical and a Hollywood remake. In *La Cage aux Folles II* (1981), directed again by Molinaro, the inspired lunacy of the first outing is turned into a caper film with the couple getting involved with gangsters, spies and the police. Meanwhile, five years later, in *La Cage aux Folles III: The Wedding* (1986), the couple stand to inherit a fortune if Albin can marry and produce an heir to validate his claim. The third instalment was the weakest though, proving that even the French can do bad sequels just like their American counterparts.

American remakes can be awful too, although *The Birdcage* (1996), with Robin Williams and Nathan Lane taking on the roles of the gay lovers, was actually quite impressive. Mike Nichols' update of *La Cage* had Williams as the outlandish nightclub owner, this time in Miami Beach, with Lane as his partner Albert.

THE ACTORS AND DIRECTORS

DIVINE
Female Impersonator
1945–1988

Born Harris Glenn Milstead, the 'world's most famous transvestite' Divine grew up down the street from high-school pal John Waters and became a cult figure as Waters' long-time leading performer. It was Waters, along with make-up artist Van Smith, who transformed the flamboyant and brilliantly talented actor into the horror show Divine, forever associated with vile, repulsive acts and attitude to match.

The oversized female impersonator developed his persona in such early Waters efforts as *Roman Candles* (1986) and *Eat Your Makeup* (1968), as a Jackie Kennedy-obsessed fashion groupie, *The Diane Linkletter Story* (1970), as the suicidal heroine, and the silent *Mondo Trasho* (1970), as a blonde bombshell who accidentally runs over a foot fetishist-pedestrian.

In 1970, Divine and Waters released their first full-length talking film *Multiple Maniacs*, the dark, funny and violent story of Lady Divine, leader of a Manson-like crime family. They followed with the classic *Pink Flamingos* (1972), a gritty, obscene but somehow heart-warming comedy of ill manners that firmly established both director and star. Starring as Babs Johnson, 'The Filthiest Person Alive', Divine turned in a star-making performance. Even his famed devouring of dog turds at the film's close couldn't overshadow his genuine comic gifts.

Divine was even more brilliant in the tour de force *Female Trouble* (1974), in which he aged from a rebellious, high-school girl into a deranged, death-row inmate. He also played his first male role in this film and, through the magic of cut-rate special effects, even had sex with himself.

Next, 'the most beautiful woman in the world' took his persona to the stage, first performing in San Francisco with a troupe called The Cockettes in such fare as 'Journey to the Center of Uranus' and 'The Heartbreak of Psoriasis'. He made his New York debut in Tom Eyen's *Women Behind Bars* (1976) and after its success there also played it to London audiences. Eyen's second play for Divine, *The Neon Woman* (1978), ran Off-Broadway and then to packed houses in San Francisco, Toronto, Provincetown and Chicago.

Divine returned to the screen for Waters in the amusing *Polyester* (1981), which featured the infamous Odorama cards for audiences to scratch and sniff scents depicted on screen, before working with other film directors. Paul Bartel's *Lust in the Dust* (1985) was the first major film in which the queen of drag parted company with Waters. Bartel's amusing sagebrush satire was quite a funny, irreverent send-up of the western, which reteamed Divine with his *Polyester* co-star Tab Hunter. Meanwhile, Alan Rudolph's *Trouble in Mind*, made in the same year, took Divine out of drag for his role as Hilly Blue, a powerful gangster in the fictitious RainCity.

Not only did he act, but Divine also found worldwide fame as a disco-diva recording star and club attraction, especially in gay venues. Beginning in 1978, he cranked out eleven international hit dance singles, including 'Shoot Your Shot' (a Gold single in Holland) and 'You Think You're a Man' (which reached number 17 on the British charts and number 5 in Australia). He recorded primarily with producer Bobby Orlando (who oversaw the Pet Shop Boys' first tracks), before switching to the team of Stock, Aitken and Waterman (whose line-up included Kylie Minogue and Dead or Alive). Divine toured the world with his solo cabaret act of disco and outrageous humour, performing over 900 times in more than 19 countries.

Divine's biggest hit came with Waters' mainstream comedy *Hairspray* (1988), playing both proud Mom Edna Turnblad (his trademark wigs and outlandish make-up somewhat toned down) and TV station manager Arvin Hodgepile. He was about to guest star as Uncle Otto on the Fox programme *Married...With Children*, a Bundy relative Fox was projecting as a regular, when his personal manager and biographer Bernard Jay discovered him dead in his hotel suite, with heart failure the cause.

Bartel's *Out of the Dark* (1988) featured him in a last cameo role as a gravelly voiced male detective.

DEREK JARMAN
Director
1942–1994

Much of Derek Jarman's early career was in theatre set design, which was always praised as avant-garde, and as a natural extension of this work he moved into film as a set designer on Ken Russell's *The Devils* (1971) and *Savage Messiah* (1972). The themes of these films – personal sexuality set against a violent religious structure – were to recur throughout Jarman's own cinematic career, and it was during this period that he began to experiment with his own super 8 shorts.

Jarman's first feature as director was *Sebastiane* (1975). Beautifully shot in an almost surreal, sun-drenched setting and spoken entirely in Latin, it's the story of Sebastiane, a Roman exiled to a men-only outpost in 300 AD. The film establishes themes which characterise all of Jarman's work – homosexuality, religion and persecution. Slow-motion sequences of naked Roman soldiers cavorting in the sea shocked audiences when it was eventually broadcast on British television (in a late-night spot), and Jarman's debut feature was greeted with an unparalleled number of complaints about graphic content.

Sebastiane was the first of four films through which Jarman explored gay history. In 1986 he created *Caravaggio*, the life and death of the last great painter of the Italian Renaissance, openly homosexual, artistically revolutionary and ultimately doomed. This film was followed five years later by a violent reworking of Marlowe's *Edward II* (1991), a savage presentation of the treatment of the only openly gay British monarch, and the stark *Wittgenstein* (1992), a bold, offbeat biography, personalised in Jarman's unique style to address the politics and sexuality of the great but troubled philosopher. The result was no dry treatise, but a treat for eyes and mind alike.

The Last of England (1987) was the first film made after the director discovered that he was HIV positive earlier in the same year. A pessimistic look at the country he once loved and a personal commentary on England and London under the Thatcher government, there is no linear plot line as such and only one recognisable 'character'. It's a mixture of fact and fiction, with Jarman employing arresting images, rock & roll, gay erotica, and his own home movies to create a searing survey of 80s Britain, devastated by greed, violence and environmental disasters.

Jarman followed *The Last of England* a year later with *War Requiem* (1988), in which the poetry of Wilfred Owen is employed in a comparison of war with the ravages of AIDS.

In *The Garden* (1990) the setting moved to the director's beach house in the shadow of a nuclear power plant. Various images were intercut together – the director, now suffering from AIDS, his curiously beautiful garden, extreme sexuality, the persecution of a gay couple and Catholic iconography. In other words, the world through Jarman's persona, his own world of dreams.

As mentioned earlier, *Wittgenstein* (1992) was to be Jarman's penultimate film, and was infused with the sense of artistic adventure, intelligence and playfulness that characterised his life and work.

Perhaps the most personal of all Jarman's work came with his last film in 1993. *Blue* is an unchanging blue screen over which voiceover, music and sound effects give a portrait of Jarman's battle against AIDS. Composer Simon Fisher Turner wrote the hypnotic soundtrack; actors Nigel Terry, John Quentin and Tilda Swinton read the voiceover. *Blue* received a simultaneous broadcast on television and radio; at this time the director's sight was failing and he was shortly to die of an AIDS-complicated illness.

At the New York Film Festival in October 1993, Jarman appeared on stage to introduce his final film. The greeting he received was overwhelming. First he commented on the disease that was killing him: 'It has destroyed my sight, I couldn't make another film now because I cannot see enough.' But there was no room for bitterness. He told a *New York Times* reporter: 'You can sit there and feel sorry for yourself or you can get out and attempt to do something. I've tried to do the latter.' Like Andy Warhol, Jarman constantly used the same production base: Brian Eno worked on the scores of *Sebastiane* and *Jubilee*, Simon Fisher Turner on *Caravaggio*, *The Last of England*, *The Garden*, *Edward II* and *Blue*. Nigel Terry starred as Caravaggio and narrated *The Last of England* and parts of *Blue*. Tilda Swinton was Jarman's most frequent performer, appearing in *The Last of England*, *War Requiem*, *The Garden*, *Edward II*, *Wittgenstein* and *Blue*. Just like Warhol's body of work, there's a truly coherent vision running throughout.

Jarman's influence on contemporary gay culture in Britain cannot be underestimated. An opulent, sensual stylist whose stock-in-trade was the abandon with which he painted his visuals, Jarman's homosexuality was central to his films. They are gay and proud, and not surprisingly they received screenings on the fourth British television channel when it was trying to establish a contentious modern identity for itself in the 1980s. Channel 4 wanted to be radical and different, so they chose an authentic dissenting voice; and his films certainly offer a genuine alternative to the mainstream. Love him or loathe him, the man was a visionary.

LUCHINO VISCONTI
Director
1906–1976

Aristocrat and Marxist, master equally of harsh realism and sublime melodrama, Luchino Visconti was without question one of the greatest film directors of the mid-twentieth century. Immensely rich and a bit of a dilettante, he went to Paris in the 30s to escape the stifling culture of Fascist Italy. In Paris he met, and fell in love with, the fashion photographer Horst P Horst. But even more formative was his meeting with Jean Renoir in the heady political atmosphere of the Popular Front.

After a short stint in the military, Visconti became a designer. Soon he'd befriended Coco Chanel, and by 1937 he was working with the French filmmaker Jean Renoir on *Une partie de campagne* and was imbued with a lifelong love of cinema. Returning to Italy, he took part in the Resistance and became a convinced Marxist, which he remained until his death.

His first feature, *Ossessione* (1942), came under fire from Mussolini's government. An unauthorised – and partly homoeroticised – reworking of James M Cain's *The Postman Always Rings Twice*, about a woman who murders her husband, the film angered the authorities with its gritty representation of everyday life, and was severely censored.

Visconti's political leanings were expressed in his second film *La Terra Trema* (*The Earth Trembles*) (1947), which tells the story of class exploitation in a small, Sicilian fishing village. This theme continued with the 1960 film, *Rocco e i Suoi Fratelli* (*Rocco and his Brothers*).

As one of the 'Big Three' of post-war Italian cinema – along with Fellini and Antonioni – he enjoyed huge creative freedom and was often dubbed a 'genius' who made 'masterpieces'.

In his later work, Visconti seemed to move away from the neorealist style towards more historical and literary themes. The battle between progress and nostalgia is constantly fought in his work, but towards the end of his career Visconti seemed to favour the latter with a definite air of scepticism about the value of progress.

Many of Visconti's films feature few homosexual characters but many handsome young men. From the 1960s, his films became more personal, focusing on themes of sadness, ageing and death with somewhat of an autobiographical strain emerging, first in *The Leopard* (1963). Visconti's lush adaptation of *The Leopard*, Giuseppe di Lampedusa's 1958 novel, chronicles the decline of the Sicilian aristocracy during the Risorgimento, a subject close to his own family history.

Another film with an autobiographical strain was *Death in Venice* (1971). Having undergone various peaks and troughs of popularity, it's a great film of extraordinary scenes, an inspired soundtrack and a remarkable central performance. The celebrated story of homosexual desire, a man obsessed by ideal beauty, it's a ravishing piece of cinema. An adaptation of Thomas Mann's novella, it explores the world of moribund composer Gustav Aschenbach (Bogarde) who, abroad on a rest holiday, glimpses 14-year-old Björn Andresen, who inspires him to give way to a secret passion and question the validity of his entire life.

Earning its maker a Cannes Film Festival Special 25th-Anniversary Prize, *Death in Venice* – with a soundtrack feast of Gustav Mahler music and a haunting Bogarde performance – is Visconti at his best.

Like Aschenbach, Visconti is an artist obsessed: his films are awash in mood, period detail and emotions which seethe beneath placid surfaces.

Not the easiest of directors (leading lady Clara Calamai called him 'a medieval lord with a whip'), Visconti nonetheless commanded the greatest respect from his actors. Despite his famed ill treatment of Burt Lancaster on the set of *The Leopard*, the actor still felt that Visconti was 'the best director I've ever worked with... an actor's dream'.

Openly bisexual, as was his father, Visconti's films have few explicitly gay characters, although there is often an undercurrent of homoeroticism. He favoured attractive leading men, such as Alain Delon, and his final obsession was Austrian actor Helmut Berger, whom he directed in *The Damned* (1969), *Ludwig* (1972) and *Conversation Piece* (1974).

His smoking (up to 120 cigarettes a day) led to a stroke and subsequent ill health, but he rallied long enough to make *The Innocent* (1976) before dying in the same year, at the age of 69, in Rome. Luchino Visconti's funeral was attended by President Giovanni Leone and Burt Lancaster.

JOHN WATERS
Writer/Director
1946–

The openly gay, self-proclaimed 'Prince of Puke' certainly lives up to his reputation, having provided us with a body of work which encompasses drag queens, rock 'n' roll, capital punishment, sexual roles and gender bending. Waters once said: 'If I see someone vomiting after one of my films, I consider it a standing ovation.'

Growing up in Baltimore in the 50s, Waters was completely obsessed by violence and gore, both real and on the screen. With his weird, counterculture friends acting, he began making silent 8mm and 16mm films in the mid-60s, which he screened in rented Baltimore church halls to underground audiences drawn by word-of-mouth and street leafleting campaigns. He gathered together interested friends and neighbours to form his own stock company, the undisputed star of which was Harris Glenn Milstead, a former high-school chum and 300-pound cross-dresser who billed himself as Divine.

Success came when *Pink Flamingos* (1972) – a deliberate exercise in ultra-bad taste made for just $10,000 – took off in 1973; helped no doubt by lead actor Divine's infamous dog-shit eating scene. He continued to make low-budget shocking movies with his Dreamland repertory company, until he went into partnership with New Line Cinema in 1981 and made *Polyester*, which had Divine as the heroine Francine Fishpaw, who has a lot on her plate – a slutty daughter (Mary Garlington), a criminally insane son (Ken King) and a cheating porn-king husband (David Samson) who drives her to alcoholism. Although lacking in the harsh edges of his earlier work, *Polyester* gained Waters his first real mainstream success.

Hollywood crossover success also came with *Hairspray* in 1988, a surprisingly wholesome slice of early 60s nostalgia starring Ricki Lake as hefty Tracy Turnblad who longs to be on a lily-white local TV dance show. As a result, Universal Pictures noted the resounding success of *Hairspray* and duly obliged by handing over $8 million to Waters to direct a hipper, funnier variation of *Grease*. The result was *Cry-Baby* (1990), starring Johnny Depp alongside his regulars, Mink Stoole, Patty Hearst and ex-porno star Traci Lords.

Obviously, having 'gone Hollywood', some changes were made. Not that he actually went to Hollywood, shooting the Depp movie instead in his beloved Baltimore once again. Though the ditching of the grotesque elements associated with Waters' films was clearly designed to bring his sensibilities to mainstream audiences, his manic energy was still on show.

Waters' *Serial Mom* (1994), with Kathleen Turner, was even more glossy, and the Edward Furlong-Christina Ricci comedy *Pecker* (1998) fairly tame, although it was still set in Baltimore.

Into the new decade, a bit of the vintage Waters crept back in with *Cecil B Demented* (2000), which, though not as humorous as the films that built his shock legacy, seemed charged in a way that Waters' work had not been since the 70s. In the film, a reactionary band of filmmakers, led by a guerrilla director, force a Hollywood actress to star in their low-budget movie.

A Dirty Shame (2004) was another example of him documenting the awakenings of suburban repression, with Tracey Ullman playing a sex-addict housewife who ends up in a local sex cult. The film didn't skimp on trademark bodily excrement and fluids, proving that Waters hadn't lost his passion for the deviant flipside of mainstream culture.

In 2006, came *This Filthy World*, a celluloid representation of Waters' regular and ever-evolving, filthy-minded solo show, which he'd toured America with for three decades. In Jeff Garlin's film of the show, the man William S Burroughs called 'the Pope of Trash' addresses the crucial issues of the day – from the theory and practice of 'teabagging' and the home life of Michael Jackson, to why Charlize Theron didn't thank Aileen Wuornos in her Oscar acceptance speech, and what it's like to attend children's movies alone when you look like a child molester. The 86-minute concert film also includes reminiscences about working with Divine, poppers, swivel chairs and his country's unheeded cry for an all-voluntary lesbian army: 'They could find Bin Laden!' At one point, the great man admits, 'I was the only kid in the audience who didn't understand why Dorothy would ever want to go home to that awful black-and-white farm, when she could live with winged monkeys and magic shoes and gay lions…' Filmed at New York's hallowed Harry De Jur Playhouse, Garlin's film was an unforgettable and bizarrely endearing session in the company of one of the world's greatest and most gleefully original entertainers.

This Filthy World is just a small part of what seems to be a John Waters revival recently. In 2007, his 1988 movie *Hairspray* enjoyed a Hollywood remake, with John Travolta dragging up to take on Divine's role of Edna Turnblad, and the stage musical in London's West End followed soon after. Waters is also said to be planning a Broadway revival of his 1990 Johnny Depp movie *Cry-Baby* and has another interesting idea in mind too: '*Pink Flamingos* would make a great opera, 'cos the fat lady sings and eats dog shit at the end. That would work!'

On whether he intentionally makes gay-interest cinema, Waters stated recently: 'I think they're funny movies with gay appeal, hopefully, but I never just wanted to ghettoise and say I'm a gay filmmaker. I'm a filmmaker who's gay. I'm not trying to get out of being gay or anything but I make films for straight people as much as gay people.'

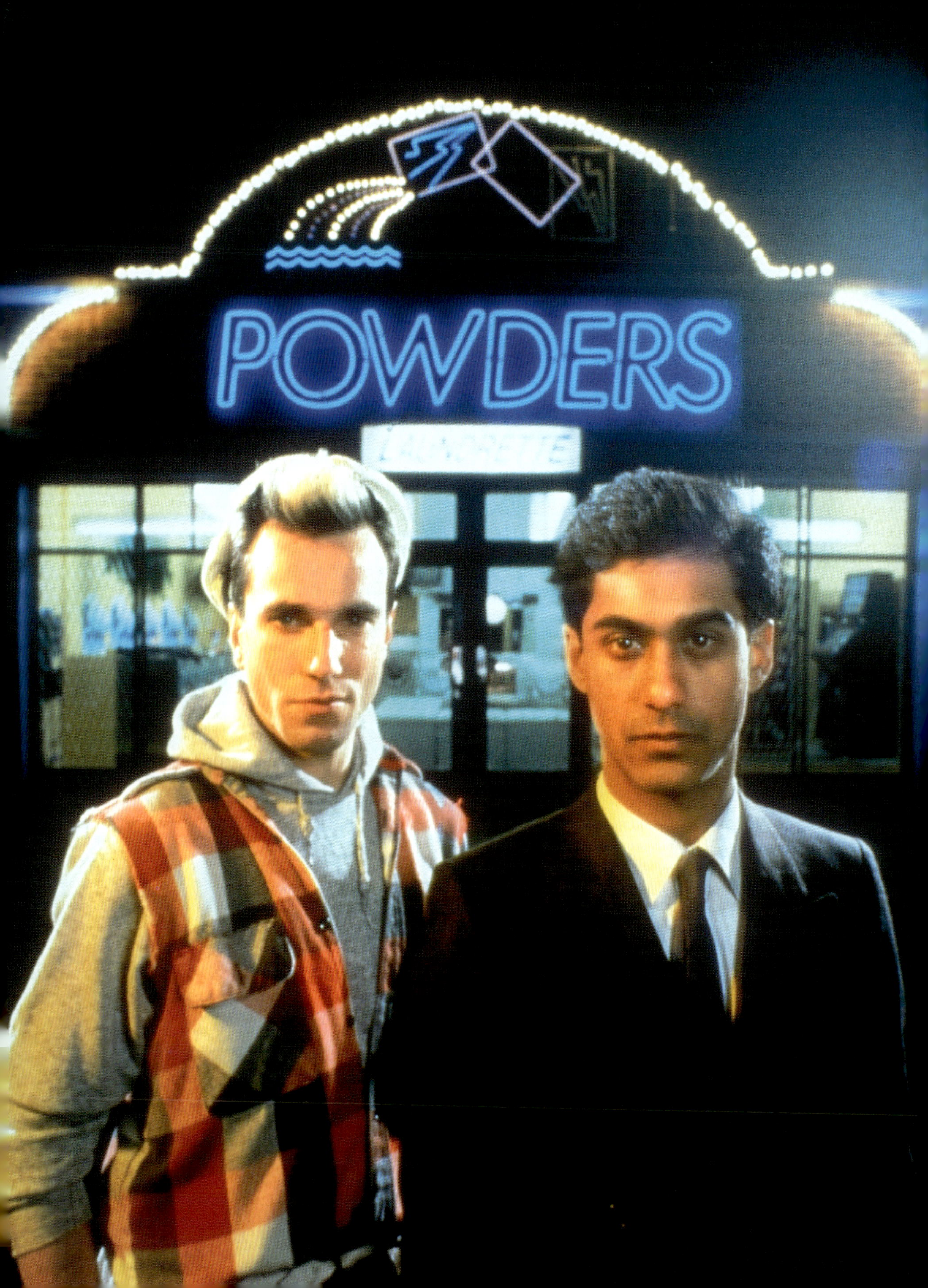
POWDERS
LAUNDRETTE

THE INDIE YEARS – THE 80s

'The 70s are dead and gone. The 80s are going to be something wonderfully new and different, and so am I.'

Samantha in *Can't Stop the Music*

It was the decade of dosh, and the 1980s were all about money, consumption, yuppies and greed, not to mention dirty dancing and designer drugs.

In 1980, to kick the decade off, American cinema dished out two very different gay-interest movies – the Village People disco extravaganza *Can't Stop the Music* and the Al Pacino police thriller *Cruising*. While *Can't Stop the Music* bombed at the box office, mainly down to the fact that people had ditched disco for punk or new wave rock, *Cruising*, on the other hand, attracted much attention. In fact, it caused more controversy than director William Friedkin could ever have imagined.

His film explored the S&M life of New York City with Pacino as an innocent young cop chosen to go underground in search of a killer. After a string of hot encounters with men in Greenwich Village's seedier gay bars, he starts to question his own sexuality.

'This isn't a film about gay life,' Friedkin stressed. 'It's a murder mystery with an aspect of the gay world as background.'

But despite the director trying to play down his film's lurid depiction of gay life, activists got together anyway for protests outside theatres, in a bid to bury the movie. They felt that *Cruising* did not show a 'positive representation' and was therefore deemed a homophobic distortion. But there is actually something quite distorted about this logic. The truth is that the gay scene, whether it be S&M bars or the commercialised dance-club culture, has always been decadent. Drugs, wild parties, seedy bars, anonymous sex. So *Cruising* wasn't all that inaccurate. Gay life isn't always pretty rainbows, Pride marches and Will & Grace re-runs. In fact, *Cruising*, when watched now, nearly 30 years later, is actually quite entertaining and a not-too-unrealistic

Daniel Day-Lewis as Johnny and Gordon Warnecke as Omar in the British gay classic *My Beautiful Laundrette* (1985) © Photofest

> 'It's your music that's bringing all of these talented boys together. They ought to get down on their knees!'
>
> Helen in *Can't Stop the Music*

> 'There's a lot you don't know about me'
>
> Steve Burns (Al Pacino) in *Cruising*

glimpse into gay life in the pre-AIDS days.

Admittedly, there are homophobic elements to Friedkin's film, especially in the dialogue uttered by the cops about 'fags', but there were far more homophobic movies around in the early 80s. That same year, Gordon Willis directed *Windows*, in which bad lesbian Elizabeth Ashley stalks good heterosexual Talia Shire. Meanwhile, evil gay men came to foul ends in *American Gigolo* (1980) and *Deathtrap* (1982).

One film that was certainly more homophobic than *Cruising* was James Burrows' 1982 one-joke 'comedy' *Partners*, about two cops – one homosexual (John Hurt), the other one straight (Ryan O'Neal) – posing as lovers in order to crack a murder case in Los Angeles' gay community. All the gay characters are raving queens, either prancing around with their limp wrists in the air or swooning as soon as O'Neal enters the room. Hurt, usually dressed in pink or lilac, tries his best to help solve the crime but is, naturally, more content to bake a soufflé or stare doe-eyed at O'Neal as he adoringly serves him breakfast in bed. The film is utterly horrendous and painful to watch, although, interestingly, didn't seem to attract the same furore as *Cruising*. Perhaps homophobic filmmaking is more acceptable in comedy than it is in drama.

Actually, the gay activists who targeted *Cruising* back in 1980 needn't have bothered. After all, this was the early 80s when people were already wary of such subject matter, and there were plenty of other activists complaining about the film; no shortage of 'normal' suburban types complaining that they didn't want these kinds of films being shown at their local family movie chains.

As if in answer to the controversy surrounding *Cruising*'s depiction of gay life, Arthur Hiller made the all-too-well-meaning and rather sickly gay love story *Making Love* (1982). The story of a married couple forced to confront the husband's homosexuality when he becomes attached to an openly gay writer, Hiller's film aimed to present a 'non-stereotypical' view of gay men dealing openly and honestly with their sexuality – as opposed to Pacino's character in *Cruising*, whose curiosities about muscular men and hard sex all took place in a darker, more promiscuous environment.

Later in 1982, a bigger stride forward seemed to come in the portrayal of lesbian characters. In fact in *Personal Best* (1982) they were visible in a Hollywood film that refreshingly did not end with self-hatred and suicide. The film depicted a lesbian relationship between two athletes who meet at the Olympic trials. Although the relationship doesn't last, the main characters, Tory and Chris, are not depicted as abnormal. They are young and attractive women involved in a relationship that lasts over three years. The two women are in no way ashamed of or embarrassed by the set up, and sex scenes develop without either character breaking down in tears or feeling 'sick' about themselves.

A year later, *Silkwood* (1983) depicted lesbianism as more than simply an adolescent phase. Cher starred as Dolly, Karen Silkwood's lesbian roommate and best friend. Although the lesbianism wasn't the central theme of the film, Dolly's character is highly visible and her relationships are given enough attention to be considered a significant strand of the film. In an early scene that foregrounds Dolly's lesbianism, her lover emerges from the bedroom one morning. Surprised for a split second, Karen's live-in lover Drew quickly turns to her and says, 'Well, personally, I really don't see anything wrong with it.' Karen agrees and replies, 'Nope, neither do I.'

Both *Personal Best* and *Silkwood* scored quite well at the box office (*Silkwood* grossed over $35 million in the United States) and garnered good reviews.

Despite these gains, however, another backlash against homosexuals would soon follow, resulting from one of the key milestones of the 80s – the AIDS epidemic.

Unknown at its beginning, by 1989 the terminology of the disease was familiar wherever English was spoken: *HIV*, *PWA*, *AZT* and so on. The official answer was 'safe sex': not an easy concept to popularise at a time when the media were obsessed by 'bonking'. It also didn't help that the 1980s were ruled by staunchly right-wing politicians. In Britain, the Conservative Thatcher government had come into office in 1979 and, in1980, Ronnie Reagan beat Jimmy Carter in a landslide US election.

Despite the discovery of the AIDS virus in 1981 and thousands of cases in the following few years, the Reagan administration remained silent on the issue until after the death of movie star and international icon Rock Hudson from the disease in 1985, by which time there were approximately 8,000 cases. In fact, Reagan did not publicly utter the word 'AIDS' during the first

> 'If it feels good, do it. You don't get any points for playing by the rules.'
>
> **Bart in *Making Love***

six years of his administration and his first public mention of the disease didn't come until a press conference in which he discussed the federal government's role in fighting it in May 1987.

The spread of AIDS across the United States brought about widespread public panic and fear back in the UK, much of which, thanks to British tabloid newspapers, was directed at gays as perceived carriers of the virus. Thatcher's government did little to allay fears or educate people about the reality of the disease, preferring instead to vote in the now-repealed Section 28, which prohibited local councils from promoting materials on homosexuality. This only served to inhibit the teaching of safer sex among young gay men, those with the highest death rate from AIDS infection.

Many believe that it took a movie star's death to legitimise the need for political action. They are probably right. So, in the early part of the decade, with politicians staying tight-lipped, it was left to filmmakers to get the issue onto the agenda.

Soon after AIDS appeared, an 'AIDS cinema' emerged, coinciding with the mid-80s American indie production boom. Films like *An Early Frost* (1985) and *As Is* (1986) were typical of this genre, which portrayed the plight of white middle-class gay folk in a somewhat maudlin way as they came to terms with the spread of the new terminal disease. Most AIDS movies made at the height of the epidemic tended to be high-minded dramas awash in mournful, teary-eyed scenes, promoting an image of martyr-like victims that much of the gay community really wanted to ditch.

Parting Glances (1986) enjoyed more success and is a better example of entertaining, perceptive independent filmmaking. Director Bill Sherwood's film concerns a young writer whose present lover is leaving him for a foreign-based job, while his ex-lover Nick (Steve Buscemi) is dying of AIDS. *Parting Glances* succeeds because the film indulges in no special pleading, merely regarding the disease as another fact of gay life.

The late writer/director Arthur J Bressan Jr made a poignant low-budget drama in *Buddies* (1985) about a young man who volunteers his spare time as a 'buddy' to help care for a dying person with AIDS. Less widely distributed than *Parting Glances*, *Buddies* is regarded as the first AIDS feature film. Skilful and moving, Bressan does not forget to include an erotic dimension in his depiction of a community coming together to mourn a loved one's fade-out.

Away from the United States, European cinema provided two of the best gay-themed films of the 80s. Unlike a rather nervous, twitchy Hollywood, filmmakers in Europe tended to embrace gay subjects and, in 1982, German director Rainer Werner Fassbinder gave us *Querelle*, a surreal, sweat-drenched adaptation of Jean Genet's novel about an enigmatic, drug-dealing sailor (Brad Davis) on leave in a seedy seaport. Amidst the sultry, highly charged atmosphere, he embarks on a journey of sexual self-discovery. With its striking iconic imagery, set against the orange glow of a permanent sunset, Fassbinder's last film was a dreamlike experience and a unique piece of gay cinema.

A few years later, from Spain, came *Law of Desire* (1987), a deliciously overwrought gay soap opera about a trendy film director yearning to be swept up in all-consuming passion. Part fantasy, part murder mystery, part erotic comedy, it wowed gay audiences with its steamy man-on-man sex scenes and also featured a pre-Hollywood Antonio Banderas. Pedro Almodovar's film became a hit at the Berlin Film Festival and led to the director being dubbed a 'Spanish John Waters'.

The British film industry delivered a few hit gay-themed movies in the 80s too. In 1983, adapted by Ronald Harwood from his hit 1980 play, came, arguably, one of the best films ever made about the theatre. *The Dresser* featured Tom Courtenay as the very camp gay dresser who is infatuated with the ageing, spoiled actor played by Albert Finney. Courtenay is the only person who can handle the crotchety old man whose love of theatre supersedes all other considerations. Both actors are outstanding and, in 1984, both were nominated for an Oscar for Best Actor. Courtenay also won the Best Actor Golden Globe.

Also from the UK, in 1985, came *My Beautiful Laundrette*. With its multifaceted depiction of a society turbulently struggling with issues of class, race, gender and sexual orientation, Stephen Frears' film seemed to announce a new departure for both British cinema and gay cinema. Set within the Asian community in London, Hanif Kureishi's unusual love story concerned itself with identity and entrepreneurial spirit during the Thatcher years and featured an inter-racial gay affair between a white, left-wing punk (Daniel Day-Lewis) and an Asian laundrette manager (Gordon Warnecke).

My Beautiful Laundrette was just one British gay-themed film from the 1980s which seemed to celebrate heroic homosexuals, a stance which would have been unthinkable before 1960 when the subject was almost never mentioned in films. The ultimate outsiders, gay men were shown in a variety of historical eras defying the system, social prejudice and middle-class morality in a string of UK productions: *Another Country* (1984), *An Englishman Abroad* (1985), *My Beautiful Laundrette* (1985), *Maurice* (1987) *Prick Up Your Ears* (1987) and *We Think the World of You* (1988).

British actor Gary Oldman excelled in both of these last two films, but although *We Think the World of You* was an interesting movie – it had a bisexual Oldman in jail while his lover Alan Bates transferred his affections to Oldman's dog – it was a peculiar tale, too indifferently made to have much impact. *Prick Up Your Ears*, on the other hand, was always destined for success, with Oldman playing Joe Orton in Stephen Frears' follow-up to *Laundrette*. A powerfully acted film, it traced Orton's stormy relationship with his lover Kenneth Halliwell, from their college days to the stressful time of Orton's first success.

Prick Up Your Years was released around the same time as the other hit British gay-themed movie of 1987, *Maurice*, a superior Merchant Ivory production about gay love across the class divide, starring Hugh Grant, Rupert Graves and Denholm Elliott.

It was quite a brave move for director James Ivory and producer Ismail Merchant to follow up their hit *A Room with a View* with this less commercially viable EM Forster adaptation, but its success pointed to the fact that gay cinema had, at least in Britain, moved quite a few steps forward.

Most of the internationally distributed British art cinema came about through the advent of Channel 4 funding in the mid-80s. A UK government policy came out in February 1980 stating that ten per cent of the new channel's budget should be used on regional film funding. These new initiatives, together with British Film Institute funding, helped acclaimed British *auteur* Derek Jarman finance his landmark *Caravaggio* (1986), a pastiche period biopic based on the life of Italian seventeenth-century painter Michelangelo da Caravaggio. Jarman, working on a minuscule budget, still managed to produce an avant-garde masterpiece.

> 'I'm an unspeakable of the Oscar Wilde sort.'
>
> **Maurice in *Maurice***

Another British auteur who achieved notable success in the 80s was the gay Liverpudlian director Terence Davies. Although he'd started work on a trilogy of films back in 1976, the three films were eventually released together in 1984. Taken together, the three films traced the biography of a man over seven decades. In the first part of the trilogy, *Child* (1976), a young Robert Tucker is victimised at school and deeply attached to his emotionally unstable mother. The second film, *Madonna and Child* (1980), found Tucker as a middle-aged man, torn by the conflict between his Catholic faith and his gay sexuality. The final film, *Death and Transfiguration*, depicted Tucker (now played by Wilfrid Brambell, famous from the classic TV comedy show *Steptoe and Son*) as an 80-year-old man dying in a hospital bed. The trilogy put Davies on the cinematic map as one of the most original British filmmakers of the late twentieth century and led to funding for *Distant Voices, Still Lives* (1988), which had similar, grim subject matter, and a focus on guilt and unfulfilled longing.

Back in the States, towards the end of the decade, it was also left to indie filmmakers, rather than Hollywood, to carry the torch for gay cinema. Although mainstream American filmmakers were still happy producing comedies with a gay slant, notably Blake Edwards' transgender farce *Victor/Victoria* (1982) and the Dustin Hoffman drag comedy *Tootsie* (1982), serious big-budget, studio-produced gay dramas were nowhere to be seen.

Instead, the smaller film company New Line released Paul Bogart's *Torch Song Trilogy* (1988), an adaptation of its star Harvey Fierstein's semi-autobiographical play. The touching story spanned nine years, detailing the life and loves of gay New Yorker Arnold Beckoff, a flamboyant drag queen.

The decade's best American indie film, however, came from the openly gay director Gus Van Sant. Shot in black and white on a shoestring budget, *Mala Noche* (1985) was his first feature, a classic tale of doomed love between a gay liquor-store clerk and a Mexican immigrant. The film, which was taken from Portland street-writer Walt Curtis's semi-autobiographical novella, featured some of the director's hallmarks, notably an unfulfilled romanticism and a dry sense of the absurd.

Six years later, Van Sant would stay with similar themes for his even more successful hustler movie *My Own Private Idaho* (1991).

THE INDIE YEARS – THE 80s

So thanks to the advent of American independent cinema in the 1980s, together with British and European hits, gay and lesbian characters finally became out and proud, and the success of many of these films proved that gay-themed movies could appeal to more than just a niche audience. There were certainly a handful of landmark 80s movies which demonstrated remarkable progress, but it was only in the next decade that the path to understanding and acceptance, at least in the cinema industry, would widen...

THE FILMS

CAN'T STOP THE MUSIC
(1980)

US, 123 mins
Director: Nancy Walker;
Writers: Bronte Woodard, Allan Carr
Cast: Village People, Valerie Perrine, Bruce Jenner, Steve Guttenberg and Paul Sand
Genre: Musical Comedy

'Be kind' – the words of Nancy Walker at an early preview screening of her sole directorial effort *Can't Stop the Music*. Perhaps she had realised that disco was all but over by the time this movie was ready for distribution.

After the huge success of *Grease*, flamboyant producer Allan Carr tried to hit box-office pay dirt again by using the then-popular disco group The Village People, whose worldwide hit 'YMCA' had sold more than 10 million records, and whose carefully crafted, macho-satirising image won them a large gay following.

However, by 1980, with the emergence of punk and new wave rock, disco really was on its last legs. Not surprisingly, coupled with the fact that Carr had insisted the film was 'not gay-themed', the gay press ended up shunning the movie, especially following one EMI exec's comment that, 'A million or two million gay men can make an album a hit, but we have to enlist the 'hets' to make a hit of a major picture.' Arthur Bell dubbed the film, 'a stupid gay movie for stupid straight people'.

In fact, looking back it is hard to see why the critics gave the film such savage reviews. Was the plot of *Can't Stop the Music* really ever important? A New York songwriter Jack Morell (Steve Guttenberg) needs just one big break to get his music heard and land a record deal. So with the help of his retired, supermodel roommate (Valerie Perrine) and an uptight tax attorney (Bruce Jenner – yes *that* Bruce Jenner), they bring together six singing macho men from the Greenwich Village scene for an outrageous adventure full of fun, fantasy and disco fever. Hardly Shakespeare but then who cares? It features unforgettable dialogue, unimaginable performances and unbelievable production numbers such as 'YMCA', 'Liberation', a song about milkshakes (draw your own conclusions) and the wonderful grand finale featuring the title song: 'You Can't Stop the Music!'

Unfortunately, at the time, critics chose to do just that. Despite its many detractors, however, af-

The Village People

ter two decades the film has begun to find a new audience. As people get nostalgic over 80s culture, the entire movie is being reappraised as pure camp delight, a telling display of how gay culture still managed to celebrate itself under the watchful eyes of 80s conservatives.

In fact the movie flows well and is full of charming gay camp, and while the acting isn't great, the 'let's put on a show' attitude behind it *is* very sincere. If you manage to find a copy of the latest DVD release, you'll find yourself laughing rather than cringing all the way until the final, jaw-dropping, gay-studded ending.

CRUISING
(1980)

US, 106 mins
Director/Writer: William Friedkin
Cast: Al Pacino, Paul Sorvino, Karen Allen, Richard Cox, Don Scardino, Joe Spinell, Jay Acovone, Keith Prentice
Genre: Serial killer thriller

Nearly three decades after its original release, William Friedkin's *Cruising* has transformed from a political issue to an intriguing cultural document.

The 1980 thriller, about a series of murders set against the background of New York's gay S&M club scene, can be seen as a glimpse of a pre-AIDS gay subculture. Or as an opportunity to see Al Pacino's naked butt on screen.

Back in late 1979, tempers flared over the White Night Riots, the gay community's response to the minimal sentence given to former San Francisco City Supervisor, Dan White, for killing George Moscone (then mayor of San Francisco) and Harvey Milk (an openly gay supervisor of San Francisco). So

Al Pacino as undercover cop Steve Burns

there was a lot of gay anger around and it seems strange that much of it was channelled at the release of Friedkin's film. Perhaps it was just the wrong film released at the wrong time, but it was seen by much of the gay community as anti-gay.

Now, though, *Cruising* can at last be viewed as a piece of filmmaking, one of the most original thrillers of the 1980s. It's a lurid, twisted film that draws you into its world and completely works you over. It never declares itself to be a movie about 'gay life', but rather a murder mystery with an aspect of one part of the gay world as its background.

On the surface, it's a slasher pic. A killer works his way through the S&M clubs, picking up guys, tying them up and hacking them to death. The killer (Richard Cox) is tall and thin, and wears the regulation sunglasses, chains, biker jacket and hat. Pacino is Steve Burns, a cop who goes undercover to catch the homophobic killer.

But Friedkin's film is beyond a run-of-the-mill slasher with a strange, one-of-a-kind setting and impassioned direction. The director knows how to make you care and knows how to get you scared. The first killing, presented from the likable victim's point of view, is agonising to watch. In fact, much of the film involves horrific killings, coupled with seedy thrills – male nudity, simulated fisting and lurid sweaty dancing.

Cruising is a unique thriller in that the main source of interest isn't in the cop-and-killer angle, but in the hero's psychological state. It is clear the Pacino character, Burns, is himself sexually frustrated, perhaps even more so than the killer he's chasing. He uses his wife Nancy as little more than relief. After a night undercover in the gay district he returns to her for a night of hard sex and angrily warns her, 'Don't let me lose you.'

The film concludes by shifting back to Pacino for an eerie ambiguous finish: a wonderfully chilling close-up of his reflection staring back at him with strange, cold satisfaction. Was Burns gay? Was he the killer?

MAKING LOVE
(1982)

US, 113 mins
Director: Arthur Hiller
Cast: Michael Ontkean, Kate Jackson, Harry Hamlin, Wendy Hiller, Arthur Hill, Nancy Olson, John Dukakis, Asher Brauner
Genre: Coming-Out Drama

One of the first Hollywood movies to take a positive look at homosexuality, this domestic drama of a man's 'coming out' presented a non-stereotypical view of same-sex desire.

Michael Ontkean plays Zack Elliot, an LA doctor, married happily (it seems) to fast-rising TV exec Claire (Kate Jackson). But when novelist Bart McGuire (Harry Hamlin) walks into his office, his long-repressed homosexuality comes to the fore. In a move which leaves him wracked with guilt, Zack cancels dinner with his wife in order to go out with Bart. He is inexplicably drawn to this man and embarks on a secret affair with him, although the writer seems intent on keeping him at arms' distance. Bart is used to having a good time, loves no-strings sex and hates the idea of commitment, so won't allow their relationship to grow. Exasperated, Zack asks Bart, 'Do you snore? Does anybody ever get a chance to find out?'

The character of Bart is not a negative portrayal. He's not a screwed-up gay, just footloose and fancy free, a well-off, self-reliant and confident gay guy who doesn't need anyone or anything, and likes playing the field. Zack, on the other hand, is used to commitment and wants a stable, romantic, monogamous relationship – a state he has become quite used to during his marriage to loyal, intelligent Claire.

As Zack's absences become more and more frequent, Claire's concern manifests itself in the suspicion that he is having an affair with another woman. Jilted by Bart and feeling alone for the first time in his married life, Zack resolves to tell Claire the truth about himself. He knows his marriage is over and so he tells her exactly what's going on.

Michael Ontkean (left) with Kate Jackson and Harry Hamlin

Predictably, Claire is shocked that she could have known so little about the man she has loved for so many years and accuses him of deceiving her from the very start. With emotional recriminations underway, it's not long before Claire is tearing her husband's clothes out of the closet and throwing them on the floor.

Making Love was certainly a breakthrough film, the first Hollywood-produced and marketed gay-themed film for a general audience and one of the first American mainstream movies to show two men kissing.

A Scott Berg conceived the story after six of his friends came out after marriage. 'What the black movement was in the 60s, and the feminist movement in the 70s, the gay movement will be in the 80s,' he said. Working from Berg's original concept, his partner, Barry Sandler, penned a fairly absorbing screenplay, utilising elements of classic melodrama to tell a modern love story. Sandler has explained that the script was the direct result of his decision to write from his personal identity and experience.

Director Arthur Hiller, on the whole, elicited strong performances from his actors – Jackson is suitably overwrought, Hamlin exudes sexuality – but Ontkean frequently looks as though he wishes he was elsewhere. Hiller also has the trio directly addressing the audience with their thoughts from time to time, a device which seems to pay off. That said, although *Making Love* was a brave movie at the time, these days it's got less power than the average soap opera.

Writing in *The Advocate* in 2002, recounting how his gay love story somehow got made by a Hollywood studio, Sandler stated: 'There were hurdles. Hollywood in the Reagan 80s was a conservative, closeted, chickenshit town. Showing gay characters in a positive light – were we crazy? Agents and talent shunned the project, deeming it too risky. But at 20th Century Fox, [producers] Sherry Lansing and Dan Melnick quickly committed, sensing a groundbreaker. A few brave actors stepped up, damn the sceptics, and the movie was made.'

Those few brave actors did *not* include Harrison Ford, Michael Douglas and Richard Gere – they all turned down the male lead, expressing reservations about the subject matter.

Publicity surrounding the film was exhaustive. Sandler decided to come out publicly as the movie opened, so the studio sent him on a cross-country tour, taking in appearances on huge mainstream US shows – *Today*, *20/20*, and so on. In 2002, he told *The Advocate* magazine: 'I was announcing that yes, I was gay, so what? But more important than promoting the film, my reason for these appearances was that I thought if, instead of seeing the sick gay stereotype they were used to, people saw this ordinary guy being open and unashamed about his sexuality, then maybe they'd see there was no shame in it. Neither my body nor my career was harmed, contrary to what I'd been warned.

'To the gay community this was more than a movie – it was a celluloid insignia that told the world we're as good as everyone else. When it failed to make a fortune, some declared it the death knell for positive gay-themed movies. Well, it wasn't; in fact, scores more followed. But we were the first. Someone had to be.'

QUERELLE
(1983)

France, 107 mins
Director/Writer: Rainer Werner Fassbinder

Cast: Brad Davis, Franco Nero, Jeanne Moreau, Laurent Malet, Hanno Poschl, Gunther Kaufmann, Burkhard Driest
Genre: Sadist drama

Fassbinder is the auteur who contributed more gay representations and instigated more debates on gay male cinematic representations than any other in the 70s. This, his final film, made in 1982, is set in a phallic dreamscape where romance is synonymous with cynicism and brutalism with love.

A sexy, moody hunk of a French sailor called Querelle arrives in Brest and soon starts frequenting a strange bordello. He discovers that his brother Robert is the lover of the lady owner, Lysiane, played by Jeanne Moreau. Here, you can play dice with Nono, Lysiane's husband: if you win, you are allowed to make love with Lysiane; if you lose, you have to make love with Nono... Querelle is soon mixed up in this strange world and loses on purpose...

No one is more enamoured of Querelle than his own commanding officer, Lieutenant Seblon (Franco Nero), who narrates his lust into a tape recorder and watches Querelle from afar. But Querelle has other plans: he wants to prove himself a criminal mastermind, capable of engineering two perfect murders – that of a fellow sailor and his own execution.

After murdering the sailor, he pins the blame on known homosexual Gil. But when Querelle finds himself in a sexual relationship with Gil, his dangerous circumstance becomes even more complicated.

Based on Jean Genet's novel, *Querelle* marked the end of the controversial directorial career of Rainer Werner Fassbinder. The director chose to bow out with a morally disjointed story where legal and sexual standards shift constantly. Fassbinder

Brad Davis and Franco Nero get close in *Querelle*

mocks morality, and himself, even blotting out a plaintive, romantic song by one of the characters with the sounds of a cheap video game. And he certainly doesn't want the film to be easy to watch – the film is meant as a challenge to its audience, a final act of defiance by a director who certainly had nothing left to lose. In the spirit of this resistance to convention, Fassbinder even shot *Querelle* in English, as opposed to his native German.

Critically savaged (and possibly misunderstood) upon its 1983 release, Fassbinder's swansong offers a uniquely surreal and dreamlike tone and a wealth of fascinating imagery to the adventurous viewer, including a hugely erotic scene of anal intercourse that's still very rare in film. The poster alone is unforgettable, and the movie needs to be seen to be believed.

MALA NOCHE
(1985)

US, 78 mins
Director/Writer: Gus Van Sant
Cast: Tim Streeter, Doug Cooeyate, Ray Monge, Nyla McCarthy, Sam Downey, Bob Pitchlynn
Genre: Youth Drama

The seeds of Gus Van Sant's later work *My Own Private Idaho* (1991) can be seen in *Mala Noche*, the director's 1985 debut feature, about a group of Mexican street kids in Portland and the gay bohemian who falls in love with them.

Walt (Tim Streeter) is the lovesick liquor-store worker who is openly gay and lives his life surrounded by the winos and illegal workers of Portland. He becomes infatuated with the manipulative Mexican youth Johnny (Doug Cooeyate) and although he knows he has no chance of developing anything serious with him, he clings on hopelessly. Sixteen-year-old Johnny exploits Walt's feelings and the pair live on the edge of ruin and have a blast doing it for as long as they can, taking thrill rides in the country and fighting like puppies. But, frustrated by Johnny's abusive and taunting behaviour, Walt eventually finds consolation with Johnny's friend, Roberto, another handsome Latino boy.

There are echoes in *Mala Noche* of Martin Bell's powerful documentary of the same year, *Streetwise*, about how homeless kids in Seattle survive by prostitution, panhandling and robbery. An early example of 'new queer' cinema, with a brilliant self-effacing script, Van Sant's film also shares the same bored-youth-punk feel as Alex Cox's brilliant 1984 genre-buster debut *Repo Man*. Both are very low-budget declarations of a new vision, inspired by punk rock, although Cox was more overtly referential.

Unlike most low-budget debuts (Van Sant shot it on grainy 16mm black-and-white stock with a tiny budget of $25,000), *Mala Noche* features some fine understated performances, an interesting script and a good sound mix. It also happens to feature one of the most likable and most realistic gay characters ever to grace the screen.

MY BEAUTIFUL LAUNDRETTE
(1985)

UK, 90 mins
Director: Stephen Frears
Writer: Hanif Kureishi
Cast: Daniel Day-Lewis, Gordon Warnecke, Saeed Jaffrey, Roshan Seth, Shirley Anne Field
Genre: Racially-mixed gay love story

My Beautiful Laundrette will remind you of those mid-80s days when Thatcherism ruled the earth (or so it seemed) and money was king. Set within the Asian community in London, Stephen Frears' low-budget adaptation of Hanif Kureishi's subversively critical play captures the contradictions of that time in a way that's as fresh today as when it was new.

Omar (Warnecke) is the aspiring capitalist given an opportunity by his uncle Nasser (Jaffrey) to grab a share of Britain's wealth by 'squeezing the tits of the system'. The wheeler-dealer Nasser sums it up when he says, 'In this damn country, which we hate and love, you can get anything you want.'

Nasser sets up Omar (Gordon Warnecke) with a rundown laundrette and the instruction to

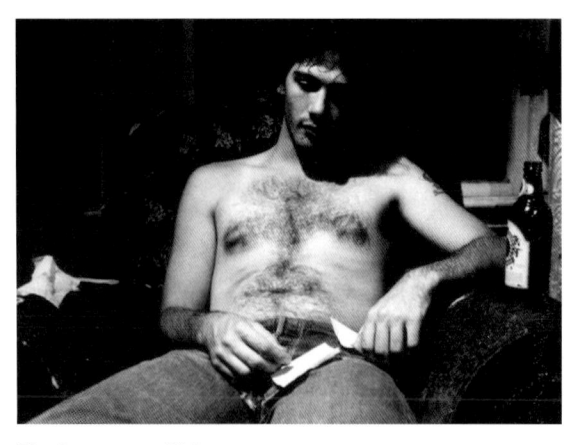

Tim Streeter as Walt

Gordon Warnecke (right) with Daniel Day-Lewis in *My Beautiful Laundrette*

make it a glittering palace of commercial success, which Omar temporarily does, with the help of his childhood friend (and ex-National Front member) Johnny (Daniel Day-Lewis). But Johnny is confused: his days as a Union Jack-loving thug have not improved his station in life and now he 'just wants to do some work for a change'.

Bringing together two such different characters as Omar (Asian, ambitious, for whom success is defined by wealth) and former childhood friend Johnny (white trash, ex-National Front) was utterly inspired. Watching their friendship develop into love, with the ensuing bitterness and misunderstanding that they suffer from friends and family, is very poignant.

My Beautiful Laundrette isn't, however, an exploration of alternative sexuality. Instead, Kureishi treats his gay couple as he would do any young lovers who have to struggle against insurmountable odds to be together. Each character is rounded and well defined, imbued with depth and complexity, and the central gay relationship is (for its time) remarkably free of guilt and not used as an incendiary plot device.

Omar and Johnny's romance successfully survives the racial battle between native Britons and Pakistani newcomers, the moral battle between liberalism and conservatism, the intellectual battle between idealism and pragmatic capitalism, and the political battle between Prime Minister Thatcher and the inner-city, working class.

Funny, touching and anger-inducing, Stephen Frears' movie wears its age lightly and its era proudly. This complex study of race, politics and sexuality has a consistently comic touch, is expertly acted throughout and remains a definitive snapshot of British life in the 1980s.

Interestingly, *My Beautiful Laundrette* was originally developed for television but given a cinematic release instead. It was the first movie from the Eric Fellner/Tim Bevan powerhouse partnership and their UK company, Working Title Films (*Four Weddings and a Funeral*/*Bridget Jones's Diary*).

PARTING GLANCES
(1986)

US, 105 mins
Director/Writer: Bill Sherwood
Cast: Richard Ganoung, John Bolger, Steve Buscemi, Adam Nathan, Patrick Tull
Genre: AIDS drama

Bill Sherwood's 1985 film *Parting Glances* was described by the *Seattle Times* as 'the best movie ever made about gays in the United States... you can't help wondering why most films can't move this well or look this good'.

Praise indeed, but deservedly so – this funny and unashamedly romantic feature is a triumph for anyone who has ever been in love, straight or gay.

Sherwood's only feature spends a day with yuppie Manhattan gay couple Robert (Bolger) and Michael (Ganoung) who have been lovers for years.

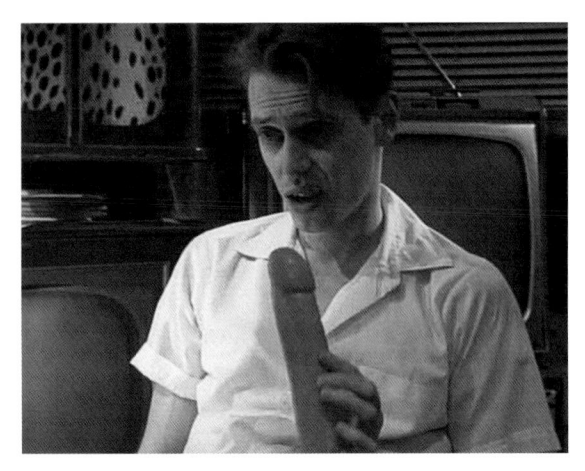

Steve Buscemi as Nick

We meet them, however, on the eve of Bolger's work-enforced departure to Africa. Choosing to bid farewell in the company of their best friends, the pair come to terms with the end of their six-year relationship, a termination skilfully mirrored in an early cinematic portrayal of an AIDS sufferer (their best friend Nick, played with oodles of caustic wit by Buscemi).

It just so happens that punk-rock star Nick is also Michael's former lover and it is Michael who must encourage him to attend Robert's going-away party (hosted by *The Drew Carey Show*'s Kathy Kinney), meanwhile trying to get Robert to stop avoiding Nick.

Sherwood basically follows Michael around town, as he visits a record store, gets pursued by a cute young cashier, has dinner with a married couple, criticises Robert for his callousness, and tries to nursemaid Nick, whose defiance against convention, pity and a couple of bathetic Don Giovanni-inspired nightmares makes him the firm moral centre of the film, rather than a victim.

Sherwood, who died aged 38, from an AIDS-related disease in 1990, refuses to handle the illness with kid gloves but, as in the rest of the film, informs the subject with humour, intelligence and warmth. He keeps issues unresolved and his characters very much alive, indulging in no special pleading, merely regarding the disease as another fact of gay life.

CARAVAGGIO
(1986)

UK, 93 mins
Director/Writer: Derek Jarman
Cast: Nigel Terry, Sean Bean, Garry Cooper, Spencer Leigh, Tilda Swinton, Michael Gough, Dexter Fletcher
Genre: Biopic

This excessive but imaginative portrait of the Renaissance painter overcomes its tiny budget with ravishing pictorial compositions that seek to convey the essence of Caravaggio's own striking artwork.

Michelangelo Merisi Caravaggio (1573–1610) was one of the greatest and most controversial painters of the Italian Renaissance. His erotic paintings of naked saints caused much scandal at the time. Derek Jarman struggled for seven years to bring his portrait of the seventeenth-century artist to the screen. The result was well worth the wait, and was greeted with critical acclaim: a freely dramatised portrait of the controversial man and a powerful meditation on sexuality, criminality and art – a new and refreshing take on the usual biopic.

Jarman's film centres on an imagined love triangle between Caravaggio, his friend and model Ranuccio, and Ranuccio's low-life partner, Lena. Conjuring some of the artist's most famous paintings through elaborate and beautifully photographed *tableaux vivants*, these works are woven into the fabric of the story, providing a starting point for its characters and narrative episodes.

Nigel Terry plays Caravaggio with intense passion, alongside Sean Bean as his rugged lover, Ranuccio, and Tilda Swinton as Lena, his beautiful mistress who comes between the pair. Swinton was to become Jarman's muse and long-time collaborator.

The film distinctively merges fact, fiction, legend and imagination in a bold and confident approach that will probably leave serious art enthusiasts and casual viewers outraged by the complete disregard for accurate, historical storytelling. Jarman deliberately dabbles in anachronisms – a car, typewriters, passing trains, tuxedoes and pocket calculators are all thrown into the film – making use of a similar revisionist theory to that which Caravaggio applied to his paintings.

Not surprisingly, the director caused a furore in the art world, and generated accusations of everything from irreverence to downright dishonesty regarding the artist's alleged homosexual and violent impulses. Certainly, Jarman imposes a homosexual interpretation on the proceedings, depicting the artist's murder of Ranuccio as the result of a lover's spat. In fact, the murder charge sent Caravaggio into exile, virtually all that is really known about the artist's life.

Beyond its homoerotic slant, the film can actually be viewed as something of a satire on the shallowness of the burgeoning 80s art scene, of which Jarman was very much a part. Although the film was seven years in preparation, it was only five weeks in production, shot at a disused East London warehouse. The result is something rather special.

Caravaggio is an inventive and unashamedly pretentious work of modern cinema that deserves a wider audience. With a cast of (now) very well-known faces, such as Sean Bean, Tilda Swinton, Michael Gough, Dexter Fletcher and Robbie Coltrane, not to mention some of the most beautiful photography ever committed to film, Jarman's work represents an impressive, and for the most part enjoyable, combination of art and cinema that is ripe for rediscovery.

Dexter Fletcher as the young Caravaggio

MAURICE
(1987)

UK, 134 mins
Director: James Ivory
Writers: Kit Kesketh-Harvey, James Ivory
Cast: Hugh Grant, James Wilby, Rupert Graves, Denholm Elliott, Simon Callow, Billie Whitelaw, Barry

Foster, Judy Parfitt, Phoebe Nicholls, Ben Kingsley
Genre: Period Drama

In his first major starring role, Hugh Grant gives a compelling performance (proof, if you needed it, that he can do more than just bashful) as a young, upper-class Edwardian student torn apart by a love affair with fellow Cambridge student James Wilby.

This adaptation of EM Forster's controversial novel offers everything we expect from a Merchant Ivory film – beautiful locations, a who's who of top British actors and an insight into the world of the repressed upper classes. We also get a delicately handled expression of homosexual love and an account of the difficulty of being gay at a time when it was illegal for men to have sex.

Maurice Hall (Wilby) and Clive Durham (Grant) are close friends whose attachment is actually something more. Clive expresses his love for Maurice, but is only looking for an idealised, platonic relationship, whereas the initially reluctant Maurice is after a more sexual communion. Both men, however, are frightened off when their gay friend is arrested and sentenced to six months hard labour. Clive takes refuge in a respectable marriage, while Maurice's psychiatrist advises fresh air, country walks and the shooting of small animals as a 'cure' for his homosexuality.

Fortunately Maurice finds the honesty and strength to face up to his true nature when a man from a completely different social world enters his life: the attractive, young gamekeeper Alec Scudder (Graves). Together the pair take on society's social and sexual prejudices, and face some pretty tough times. As Lasker-Jones (Kingsley) puts it: 'England has always been disinclined to accept human nature.'

The director makes much play of how posh Edwardian society struggles to decide which is worse – that Maurice is bedding a man or that he's bedding a commoner. Watching the film today reassures us that, as bad as things can be nowadays, we've come a long way.

It goes almost without saying that the period is evoked wonderfully well, with lots of floppy haired youths lying around Cambridge colleges and English stately homes, and the acting is universally good. Hugh Grant is worryingly convincing as the effete Clive, while Wilby and Graves conspire to make their slightly unbelievable relationship convincing.

Forster's 1914 novel *Maurice* hadn't been published until after his death in 1971 and was the first-ever novel involving a gay romance to have a happy ending. Turning this novel into a film had always been a pet project of producer/director team Ismail Merchant and James Ivory. It was only when they made the film of Forster's gay story did the media pick up on the fact that Merchant and Ivory weren't simply filmmaking partners. In 25 years as 'collaborators in art and in life', as *People* magazine commented, it was the first time the media revealed that the pair lived together.

PRICK UP YOUR EARS
(1988)

UK, 105 mins
Director: Stephen Frears
Writer: Alan Bennett
Cast: Gary Oldman, Alfred Molina, Vanessa Redgrave, Julie Walters, Richard Wilson, Frances Barber, Wallace Shawn
Genre: Biopic

Stephen Frears' film *Prick Up Your Ears* is a celebration of the outrageous playwright Joe Orton (Gary Oldman) and his stormy love affair with Kenneth Halliwell (Alfred Molina) from their college days to the stressful time of Orton's first success.

Orton was one of the 1960s golden boys, from working-class Leicester lad to national celebrity, from sexual innocent to grinning satyr, from penniless student to icon of Swinging London. He became a star by breaking the rules – sexual and theatrical. But while his plays, including *Loot, What the Butler Saw* and *Entertaining Mr Sloane*, were all hugely successful, his private life was sometimes sordid, often farcical, and also ended in tragedy.

Orton and Halliwell met at the Royal Academy of Dramatic Art. The inarticulate Orton fell for the seemingly sophisticated Halliwell, and for a while the film dwells on Orton's promiscuity, at a time when homosexuality was still illegal in the UK. Then, seemingly out of nowhere, Orton becomes an overnight success. He pens West End hits and even gets commissioned to write a script for the Beatles.

However, the conclusion is one of tragedy. Frears depicts the lovers' life in their apartment as totally claustrophobic and, while Orton enjoys his status as a popular playwright, Halliwell is simply his personal assistant, as he defines himself, trying to find a purpose in a life that he considers useless. He never attains success. Joe doesn't love him and doesn't have sex with him any more. He cannot share success with Joe. Inevitably, Halliwell gets terribly depressed... and then the tragedy. Halliwell spirals downwards, from Orton's lover to his bludgeon killer.

The modern-day framing device has Lahr (Wallace Shawn) researching his book through interviews with Orton's agent Peggy Ramsay (Vanessa Redgrave), and the diary he wrote, a clever device which ends up drawing a provocative parallel between Orton and Halliwell's relationship and that of Lahr and his wife (Lindsay Duncan).

With that in mind, at the time of its release, director Stephen Frears commented: 'Orton and Halliwell's life together was as natural to them as a more conventional heterosexual life is to others. This is the way it was – no excuses or explanations. But the fact that they were gay is secondary to their story. It's about marriage, with many of the same problems as any other marriage that goes wrong, except between two men.'

Frears, fresh off the back of the gay-themed *My Beautiful Laundrette*, manages to balance our

Gary Oldman (left) as Joe Orton with lover Kenneth Halliwell (Alfred Molina)

sympathies for both the protagonists, while the leads give what may in retrospect look like the standout performances of their careers: Gary Oldman is excellent as Orton, right down to the remarkable resemblance, while Alfred Molina is superb as an amusing and tormented Halliwell.

TORCH SONG TRILOGY
(1988)

US, 120 mins
Director: Paul Bogart
Writer: Harvey Fierstein
Cast: Harvey Fierstein, Anne Bancroft, Matthew Broderick, Brian Kerwin, Karen Young, Eddie Castrodad, Charles Pierce
Genre: Autobiographical drama

Gruff-voiced Tony Award-winning actor and playwright Harvey Fierstein recreates his role as the unsinkable, 40-ish, drag queen Arnold Beckoff in this film adaptation of the smash Broadway play *Torch Song Trilogy*.

Originated as separately staged one-acters, the play, when finally mounted as a unified work in 1982, proved bracing in its frank depiction of gay sex life, both promiscuous and committed.

Personal, funny and poignant, *Torch Song Trilogy* chronicles Arnold's search for love, respect and tradition – while looking good in a dress – in a world in which he doesn't easily fit. In the opening scene we see Arnold in drag as Virginia Hamm (working with Ken Page as Marcia Dimes and Charles Price as Bertha Venation). Away from the drag performances, Arnold is rather gun-shy of romance, though still allows himself to be picked up in a gay bar by Ed (Brian Kerwin), a handsome, straight-acting schoolteacher who openly announces his bisexuality. They become lovers but Ed can't really accept his own gayness and chooses to marry.

In what is effectively Act Two, Arnold meets Alan (Matthew Broderick), a stunning young model who used to be a hustler and is 15 years his junior. The two are perfectly matched. For Arnold it's love at first sight, while Alan is actively seeking out Arnold for his human, as opposed to superficial, qualities. They go beyond being partners: they are soulmates.

Act Three, the more conventional of the sections, is given over to Arnold and Alan adopting David, a disadvantaged gay teenager. Then one night Alan heroically attempts to rescue an elderly man who's been set upon by gay-bashers and ends up fatally beaten by the gang, leaving Arnold to raise David on his own. Arnold's greatest challenge remains his complicated relationship with his mother (Anne Bancroft), who comes to visit and refuses to see Arnold's relationship with Alan as being as valid as hers with her own late husband. Although she eventually comes to understand her son more, that he wasn't simply going through a phase, she leaves as soon as his back's turned, suggesting she hasn't yet fully come to terms with him.

Finally, the mixed-up schoolteacher Ed comes to terms with his sexuality, leaves his wife to be with Arnold and they both raise David together.

Torch Song Trilogy was the last major gay-themed film of the 80s and, although it occasionally sinks into bathos, it is nevertheless worthy viewing for the easy-to-love romantic tangles, the smart one-liners and strong performances, especially the hilarious Fierstein.

It certainly took guts to release this cosy gay film in the late 80s. After all, the box-office charts were dominated by macho men Arnold Schwarzenegger and Sylvester Stallone. However, at the time of release, back in 1988, Fierstein stated: 'This is the perfect time to do the film, because it's all too easy for people to think of gays as a high-risk group and nothing else. I mean, aren't you a little sick of every time seeing a gay person on-screen with an IV in his arm?'

Fierstein also pointed out: 'If every gay person in this country went to see it, it'd be the largest-grossing movie ever. We forget how many of us there are...'

THE ACTORS AND DIRECTORS

SIMON CALLOW
Actor/Writer/Director
1949–

Simon Callow is the ever-jovial British actor who's been lighting up the stage and screen for years, often in roles that highlight his versatility.

Born in London, Callow became infatuated with the great British actor Laurence Olivier who at the time was heavily involved with the Old Vic Theatre. Callow wrote to him and was amazed to get a response. Olivier wrote back, telling the young Callow that if he was interested in acting, he should consider taking a job at the Old Vic's box office. He did so and in no time at all was appearing in numerous productions over the years.

Callow made his film debut with a supporting role in 1984 in Milos Forman's *Amadeus* before Merchant Ivory gave him the substantial role of the Reverend Beebe in *A Room with a View* (1985) and a strong supporting role as Mr Ducie in their gay-interest drama *Maurice*, alongside Hugh Grant in 1987.

Callow turned in a mesmerising performance as the flamboyant Gareth in *Four Weddings and a Funeral* in 1994. His character's open, unapologetic relationship with another man (John Hannah) was among the hit film's highlights, and had few parallels in American movies at the time. It also drew attention to Callow's status as one of Britain's openly gay actors, which also had regrettably few parallels across the Atlantic.

Callow was hilarious as the convener of a men's therapy group in Rose Troche's gay-themed comedy *Bedrooms and Hallways* and as the dour Master of the Revels in John Madden's *Shakespeare in Love* (1998). He has also appeared in various American films (even *StreetFighter* and *Ace Ventura*), directed a film, *Ballad of the Sad Café*, written biographies of Charles Laughton, Orson Welles and agent Peggy Ramsay, an intriguing autobiography, *Being an Actor* (1984), and continued to work on stage, mainly in the UK.

Keeping busy into the new millennium, one of Callow's most notable appearances was among the ensemble cast of Mike Nichols' critically acclaimed HBO mini-series *Angels in America* (2003), a political epic about the AIDS crisis during the mid-80s.

TERENCE DAVIES
Writer/Director
1945–

One of the finest, most individual talents the British cinema has produced, Terence Davies has directed films both in the UK (*Trilogy*, 1984, *The Long Day Closes*, 1992) and in the States (*The House of Mirth*, 2000).

Davies's *Trilogy* is divided into *Children* (1976), *Madonna and Child* (1980), and *Death and Transfiguration* (1983), each segment telling the life of Robert Tucker – his birth and formative years in school, his father's death's impact on him, his closeted homosexuality, still living at home with his daunting mother, and finally his mother's death and his own impending doom.

In his first full-length feature, *Distant Voices, Still Lives* (1988), Davies conjured intimate family memories in free-form images, sometimes bleak and brutal, at others tender and nostalgic. His film was a strikingly intimate portrait of working-class life in 1940s and 1950s Liverpool and focused on the real-life experiences of his mother, sisters and brother, whose lives are thwarted by their brutal, sadistic father (a chilling performance by Pete Postlethwaite). Davies used the traditional family gatherings of births, marriages and deaths to paint a lyrical portrait of family life – of love, grief, and the highs and lows of being human.

Distant Voices, Still Lives was recently revived by the British Film Institute, touring the UK again at prestigious festivals. It was also released in a special edition DVD format.

Filmed mostly on location in a grey and rainy Liverpool, *The Long Day Closes* (1992) was another personal portrait, this time of 'Bud', a friendless, probably gay, 11-year-old boy growing up in an ordinary working class Catholic family in Kensington Street, L5 (a street that no longer exists). Set in the early 1950s, Bud, isolated from everyone but his loving sisters and mother, lives for the pictures – the cinema – and in particular for the colour and life of the Hollywood musicals. A truly beautiful film, *The Long Day Closes* is considered by many to be the director's masterpiece.

Davies has also proved he can move beyond personal material with two adaptations: of John Kennedy Toole's *The Neon Bible* (1995) and Edith Wharton's *The House of Mirth* (2000). Both had good reviews, but failed to establish his commercial credentials and he hasn't made a feature since.

Recently, Davies has been trying to obtain finance for a new script: *Mad About the Boy*, which he describes as 'a ménage à trois set in the fashion world in London and Paris: a contemporary romantic comedy, in colour and with a happy ending'.

But the fact that Davies, one of our finest directors, is struggling for funding and hasn't been given the money to make a string of planned projects is a tragedy, some would say a national disgrace.

Davies was once quoted as saying: 'I don't like being gay. It has ruined my life. I am celibate, although I think I would have been celibate even if I was straight because I'm not good-looking; why would anyone be interested in me? And nobody has been. Work was my substitute.'

BRAD DAVIS
Actor
1949–1991

Brad Davis was both ruggedly handsome and amazingly versatile, a male lead who made his compelling film debut as an American drug smuggler incarcerated in a Turkish prison in Alan Parker's *Midnight Express* (1978).

Davis's relatively sparse screen roles include off-beat classics such as American Olympic runner Jackson Scholz in *Chariots of Fire* (1981); the title character – a gay sailor – in Rainer Werner Fassbinder's *Querelle* (1982); and his only comedic role as the eccentric pilot in Percy Adlon's *Rosalie Goes Shopping* (1989).

A risk-taking stage actor, Davis won acclaim as Ned Weeks, alter ego of playwright and Gay Men's Health Crisis-founder Larry Kramer, in Kramer's harrowing AIDS drama *The Normal Heart* (1985). He also starred in Steven Berkoff's avant-garde adaptation of Kafka's *Metamorphosis* at the Mark Taper Forum.

Davis's reputation for bad behaviour both on and off set meant that good parts were rarely offered to him and his roles in *Midnight Express* and *Querelle* remain the only ones for which he is remembered. His friend, Larry Kramer, stated: 'He was one of the first straight actors with the guts to play gay roles.'

Davis contracted the AIDS virus in 1985 but hid the fact from Hollywood execs in order to keep working. In the last few years of his life the actor became a committed AIDS activist, speaking out about Ronald Reagan's policies and describing the American president as 'an unbelievably ignorant, arrogant, bigoted person'. Davis continued: 'How could he possibly think that his opinion on homosexuality had anything to do with a devastating disease that was ravaging people, reducing them to skeletons and killing them.'

The actor, who had been suffering with complications from AIDS, reportedly committed suicide at age 41, not before leaving a handwritten statement blasting Hollywood homophobia: 'I make my living in an industry which professes to care very much about the fight against AIDS, that gives umpteen benefits and charity affairs. But in actual fact, if an actor is even rumoured to be HIV-positive, he gets no support on an individual basis – he does not work.'

His widow, Susan Bluestein Davis, who continues with Davis's activist work, is the author of the only published biography of her husband. Worth reading, it gives a fascinating insight into a hugely complex character, although readers will be left feeling that she probably knew her husband rather less well than many of the others in his life.

RUPERT EVERETT
Actor
1959–

Dubbed the new Cary Grant in the 80s, British actor Rupert Everett was born in Norfolk, England. Educated by Benedictine monks at Ampleforth College, he dropped out of school and ran off to London to become an actor. In order to support himself, he worked as a rent boy, something he admitted to *US Magazine* in 1997.

His breakthrough was in the 1982 West End production of *Another Country*, playing a gay schoolboy opposite Kenneth Branagh, followed by a film version with Colin Firth two years later.

Everett came out as gay in 1989, which many agreed harmed his career for a few years; the movies he appeared in around this time, such as *The Comfort of Strangers* (1990), had little success.

His comeback came with *My Best Friend's Wedding* (1997) in which Everett almost single-handedly conquered Hollywood with his turn as Julia Roberts' gay friend. As the handsome, elegant and gay George, Everett ushered in a different kind of gay sensibility in Hollywood, one that, rather than begging audiences for acceptance, simply told them to get over it.

In the following year, in *Shakespeare in Love*, Everett had a supporting role as playwright Christopher Marlowe, and in *B. Monkey*, in which he played Jonathan Rhys Meyers' criminal lover. 1999 proved to be an even more fruitful year and he featured in leading roles in four mainstream films. He first played Oberon in Michael Hoffman's *A Midsummer Night's Dream*, with an all-star cast including Michelle Pfeiffer, Kevin Kline, Christian Bale and Calista Flockhart. Next came the role of Madonna's gay best friend in *The Next Best Thing*, followed by Oliver Parker's adaptation of Oscar Wilde's *An Ideal Husband*, for which Everett garnered positive reviews in his central role as the delightfully idle Lord Goring. Finally, he camped and vamped it up as the resident villain of *Inspector Gadget*, once again demonstrating to audiences why it could feel so good to be so bad.

While Everett will always be dubbed Hollywood's Gay Prince, he has certainly proved that his roles aren't simply limited to gay ones – in fact, in recent years, most of his work has been in high-profile movies, playing heterosexual leads.

RAINER WERNER FASSBINDER
Director/Writer
1945–1982

Fassbinder is probably the best-known director of the New German Cinema. He's also been called the most important filmmaker of the post-WWII generation. Exceptionally versatile and prolific, he directed over 40 films between 1969 and 1982; in addition, he wrote most of his scripts, produced and edited many of his films, and wrote plays and songs, as well as acting on stage, in his own films and in the films of others. Although he worked in a variety of genres – the gangster film, comedy, science fiction, literary adaptations – most of his stories employed elements of Hollywood melodrama from the 1950s, overlaid with social criticism and avant-garde techniques.

Fassbinder was always a rebel, even declaring his homosexuality to his shocked father at the early age of 15. In his early to late teens, when he wasn't watching Hollywood movies, he was frequenting gay bars.

He made various films of interest to a gay and lesbian audience, including *The Bitter Tears of Petra von Kant* (1971), adapted from his play. The title character is a dress designer whose heterosexual marriage fails as she falls for Karin (Hanna Schygulla), a beautiful working-class model. Meanwhile, in *Fox and His Friends* (1974), a queeny older gent destroys a sweet but unsophisticated working-class homosexual, fleecing his lottery winnings and trying to mould him into a more sophisticated type.

Fassbinder's best-known work *Querelle* (1982), about a sailor (Brad Davis) anchored in Brest, is a surreal look at a young man discovering his sexuality. Based on Jean Genet's novel *Querelle de Brest*, the film deals with various forms of sexuality and love. By the time he made this – his last film – heavy doses of drugs and alcohol had apparently become necessary to sustain his unrelenting work habits. When Fassbinder was found dead in a Munich apartment on 10 June 1982, the cause of death was reported as heart failure resulting from interaction between sleeping pills and cocaine.

The script for his next film, *Rosa Luxemburg*, was found next to him. He had wanted Romy Schneider to play the lead.

HARVEY FIERSTEIN
Actor/Writer
1954–

Actor/playwright Harvey Fierstein made his off-Broadway debut in Andy Warhol's *Pork* at the famed La Mama. He soon began writing about his early experiences (he came out at the age of 13) and, in 1982, Fierstein wrote and starred in the stage play *Torch Song Trilogy*, a bittersweet three-part comedy concerning the homosexual experience in the AIDS era. The play won two Tony Awards and became one of the longest-running Broadway productions in history, totting up 1,222 performances. Fierstein repeated his stage characterisation of Arnold Beckoff for the heavily rewritten and severely shortened 1988 movie version of *Torch Song Trilogy*, the essence of which was still autobiographical, since he began performing as a drag queen in Manhattan clubs as early as age 15.

The actor's crossover performances in mainstream roles have often been quite successful, notably his appearance as the likable cosmetician brother of Robin Williams in *Mrs Doubtfire* (1993).

Outspokenly homosexual, Fierstein has successfully smashed previous 'gay' stereotypes with his deep, ratchety voice and his engaging 'You got a problem with that?' belligerence.

However, since his successes of the late 80s and early 90s, Fierstein's career seems to have been put on permanent hold, due to a mixture of bad choices and bad luck. In 1994, he co-starred in the dreadful, short-lived Dudley Moore TV series *Daddies'*

Girls, unfortunately lapsing into some of the clichéd gay mannerisms he had managed to avoid in most of his previous work. More recently, Fierstein has stuck to TV projects or voiceover work.

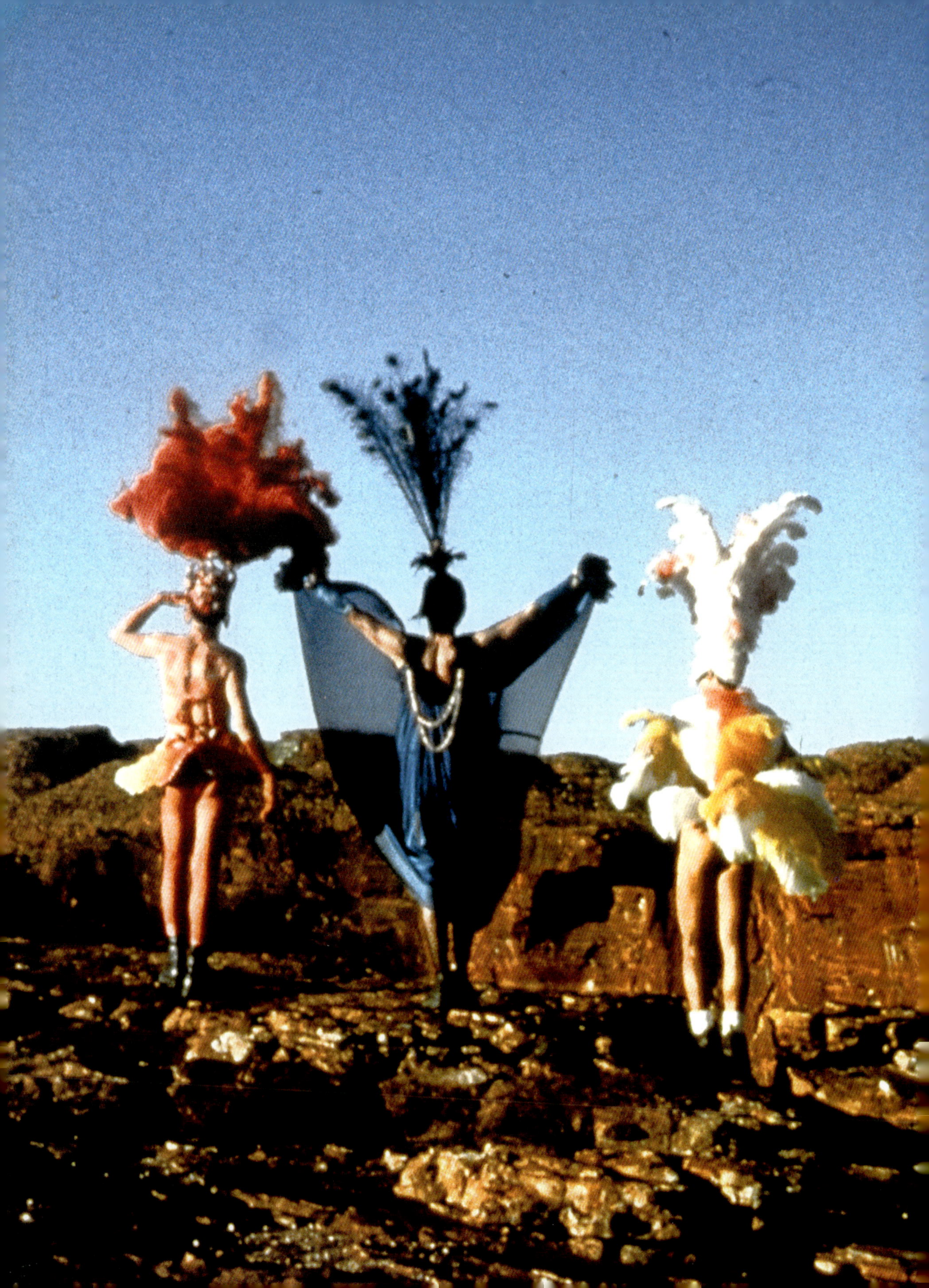

LIFE AFTER AIDS – THE 90s

> 'Just what this country needs: a cock in a frock on a rock.'
>
> Bernadette in *Adventures of Priscilla, Queen of the Desert*

Remember the 1990s? Dot-com booms, Desert Storm and presidential impeachment. It's an era that's oh-so-close, yet already so far away – the decade of *Forrest Gump*, grunge and Gay Pride.

But in the world of gay movies it was the decade of drag and quirky camp comedies, a response to all the AIDS-based dramas of the 80s. Certainly, the early 90s threw up the major work in the AIDS cinema genre, *Philadelphia* (1993), but the bulk of the decade was made up of outrageous queens and gorgeous leading men with gym-toned bodies in heart-on-the-sleeve films that reassured us there was life after AIDS...

Before gay filmmakers began playing it for laughs though, in the early part of the decade, independent cinema was electrified by a further bumper crop of 'serious' gay-themed films which emerged from the more politically minded gay filmmakers of the late 80s: Tom Kalin's *Swoon* (a 1991 retelling of the Leopold and Loeb murders), Christopher Munch's 1991 release *The Hours and Times*, a fictionalised account of John Lennon and Brian Epstein's 1963 Spanish holiday together; Richard Glatzer's *Grief* (1993), set in the world of trash TV, and Todd Verow's *Frisk* (1995), about the exploits of a gay serial killer set in an erotic world of sado-masochism.

Dubbed the 'new queer cinema' by renowned critic and feminist academic B Ruby Rich, the most successful example of these films was Todd Haynes' feature debut, *Poison* (1991), one of the most original American films in years.

None of the American 'new queer' films, however, made much of a dent at the box office, with the exception of Gus Van Sant's *My Own Private Idaho*, one indie release which really smelt like new queer spirit. A worldwide

> 'Why don't you light your tampon and blow your box apart, because it's the only bang you'll ever get, sweetheart!'
>
> Bernadette in *Adventures of Priscilla, Queen of the Desert*

> 'Oh, for goodness sake get down off that crucifix, someone needs the wood.'
>
> Felicia in *Adventures of Priscilla, Queen of the Desert*

Cocks in frocks on a rock: Guy Pearce, Terence Stamp and Hugo Weaving as we'd never seen them before © Photofest

> 'Why, you wouldn't even look at a clock unless hours were lines of coke, dials looked like the signs of gay bars, or time itself was a fair hustler in black leather.'
>
> Scott in
> *My Own Private Idaho*

> 'I'm a connoisseur of roads. I've been tasting roads my whole life. This road will never end. It probably goes all around the world.'
>
> Mike in
> *My Own Private Idaho*

hit, mainly due to the presence of the two lead actors, River Phoenix and Keanu Reeves, it is still remembered for producing some of the most iconic images in gay cinema.

Following on from its success, *My Own Private Idaho* seemed to become the parent of various indie, gay hustler films during the 1990s. Successfully strutting down the same celluloid street came Scott Silver's astonishing 1995 directorial and screenplay debut, *Johns*, set on a hot Christmas Eve in Los Angeles. In *Johns*, life on the game consisted of violence, theft and sick clients, and like *My Own Private Idaho*, the film examined friendship between prostitutes. Although writer/director Scott Silver had been working on *Johns* since 1992, Bruce La Bruce got in a few months earlier with the release of his film *Hustler White*, which owed just as much to *My Own Private Idaho*.

Even German gay cinema had a 90s entry in the hustler genre with *Lola and Billidikid* (E Kutlug Ataman 1998), set in Berlin's Turkish gay scene, and centring on an enclave of Turks living there as drag queens and hustlers.

Many of the new queer movies coming out of America during the 90s were concentrating on AIDS storylines, such as Richard Glatzer's *Grief* (1994). Other new queer efforts dealing with AIDS included Greg Araki's HIV-positive road movie *The Living End* (1992), John Greyson's outrageous and satiric AIDS musical *Zero Patience* (1993) and Norman Rene's *Longtime Companion* (1990), an absorbing account detailing the effects of the disease on the American gay community through the 1980s, as seen through the eyes of two friends who watch their social circle die around them.

Having ravaged millions of both sexes, including children, especially in Africa, AIDS was still seen in the West predominantly as a gay disease. What had begun as a health crisis quickly became a social crisis, with a steep rise in homophobia and discrimination. So it was a substantial, if calculated, risk for a major movie studio to finance the expensive 1993 mainstream film *Philadelphia*, Hollywood's attempt to deal with AIDS.

Immediately following *Philadelphia* came the much-hyped movie version of Randy Shilts' controversial best-selling novel about the rise of the AIDS epidemic, *And the Band Played On* (1993), which many preferred because it wasn't steeped in the sort of homo-ignorance that had undermined the Hanks movie.

Back in Britain, the early 90s produced some great gay-related movies, most notably Neil Jordan's unpredictable, unconventional, multi-Oscar nominated masterpiece, *The Crying Game* (1992), a sleeper hit that took America by storm.

In 1997 came Brian Gilbert's elegant account of the nineteenth-century playwright Oscar Wilde's fall from grace, with Stephen Fry perfectly cast as the flamboyant poet whose scandalous affair with a young aristocrat (Jude Law) enraged Victorian society.

Interestingly, a couple of years before Fry appeared as Oscar Wilde, a little British movie called *A Man of No Importance* (1994) had Albert Finney giving a sublime performance as Alfie Byrne, a bus conductor in 1960s Dublin who comes to terms with his homosexuality through an abiding love of Wilde, entertaining his passengers with the great man's poems.

More British-produced, gay-interest drama came in the form of Antonia Bird's melodramatic but still important *Priest* (1994), starring Linus Roache in an allegory-packed story written by the acclaimed TV writer Jimmy McGovern (*Cracker*). Wickedly sardonic and very moving, *Priest* explored a provocative checklist of religious taboos – celibacy, incest, sexual abuse and, of course, homosexuality.

Sean Mathias's harrowing concentration camp-set *Bent* was also released to great acclaim, in 1997. A powerful and moving film adaptation of Martin Sherman's award-winning stage play about three homosexual men's fight for survival in the face of persecution, it stunned audiences around the world.

Clive Owen, star of Sean Mathias' *Bent* (1997)

A lot of the British gay-themed films were comedies: Hettie MacDonald's coming-of-age drama *Beautiful Thing* (1995); Neil Hunter and Tom Hunsinger's fabulous date movie *Boyfriends* (1996); Paul Oremland's campy look at the Soho scene *Like It Is* (1998); and Simon Shore's youth-led *Get Real* (1998).

Meanwhile, over in Eastern Europe during the mid-90s, Czech Republic director Wikotor Grodecki was making a name for himself documenting the stories of real hustlers. His first two documentaries – *Not Angels But Angels* (1994) and *Body Without Soul* (1996) – detailed the fast yet fragile lives of teenage male prostitutes in the Czech Republic, following the Velvet Revolution. In both, the youths range in age from 14 to 19 and all hustle at the central train station and at clubs. They talk about why they hustle, what

Michael Urwin, Andrew Abelson and Darren Petrucci in *Boyfriends* (1996)

LIFE AFTER AIDS – THE 90s

> 'You know, pumpkins, sometimes it just takes a fairy.'
>
> Vida Boheme in *To Wong Foo*

> 'When a gay man has way too much fashion sense for a single gender, he is a drag queen.'
>
> Noxeema in *To Wong Foo*

> 'I'm the Latina Marilyn Monroe. I've got more legs than a bucket of chicken!'
>
> Chi-Chi in *To Wong Foo*

they really think about their clients (mainly foreign tourists), prices, dangers, their thoughts on AIDS, their fears (disease and loneliness), and how they imagine their futures. One Czech bar hustler explains in *Not Angels*: 'I think I am like body without soul... The body I sell but my soul is for someone else. My soul is the second me. I want to hustle and I'm not afraid my body will get infected... I want the money. The body has to sell itself but no one can sell the soul.'

Unsentimental and direct, the documentaries gave a real insight into the dark side of the tourist trade, a subject developed further later on in the decade, in Grodecki's compelling dramatisation of these two films, *Mandragora* (1997).

In the mid-90s, there was a noticeable shift in subject matter for gay filmmakers. Following on from the AIDS dramas and new queer movement, and in some ways an answer to it, gay cinema took a comedic turn for the rest of the decade, starting with a brief obsession with drag.

An aspect of gay culture previously seen in movies such as *Some Like It Hot* and *Tootsie*, drag was suddenly embraced by mainstream culture again with the 1994 release of Stephan Elliott's *The Adventures of Priscilla, Queen of the Desert*, and a year later with Hollywood's *Priscilla* rip-off *To Wong Foo, Thanks for Everything Julie Newmar* (1995).

After the release of *Priscilla* and *To Wong Foo* came *The Birdcage* (1996), Mike Nichols' slick update of *La Cage aux Folles* (1979), in which Robin Williams starred as the outlandish owner of a wild Miami Beach nightclub where his partner Albert, played by openly gay actor Nathan Lane, is the star attraction.

Aimed straight at the same Middle America targeted by *To Wong Foo*, *The Birdcage* was actually a bit better than that; by updating the setting of *La Cage* to Miami Beach, Nichols energised the film. Meanwhile, the performances – particularly the supporting roles – made *The Birdcage* genuinely entertaining.

Priscilla, *To Wong Foo* and *The Birdcage* – drag had truly been embraced by mainstream culture. And even before these three hits, remember that Robin Williams had already donned drag for much of his 1993 feel-good family comedy, *Mrs Doubtfire* – and was nominated for an Oscar for it.

More silver-screen gender benders came our way later in the 90s: Todd Haynes' controversial and explicit *Velvet Goldmine* took us on a journey into rock 'n' roll excess, back to the glam era of the stardust 70s where anything goes; even Clint Eastwood was getting in on the drag act with his movie *Midnight in the Garden of Good and Evil* (1997), in which the highlight of the piece was a black transvestite called Lady Chablis who rose above all the Dixie prejudice with lines like 'If your husband's a gyno, honey, he's all mine!'

As well as the American and British gay films of the decade, from the mid-to-late 90s, there was a veritable explosion of international productions that attracted attention.

From Taiwan came Ang Lee's *The Wedding Banquet* (1993), which won the Berlin Film Festival's top prize and succeeded in bringing gay-relationship issues to a mainstream audience.

Meanwhile, from the Philippines came Mel Chionglo's erotic and shocking *Midnight Dancers* (1994). Banned in its native country, it told the story of three brothers who work as exotic dancers and prostitutes in a Manila gay club.

China's entry in 90s gay cinema came from Zhang Yuan whose *East Palace, West Palace* (1996), about one long night in the life of a young gay writer (Si Han), made the official selection at Cannes.

Another critics' choice at the 1996 Cannes Film Festival was *Hamam: The Turkish Bath*, the first film from Ferzan Ozpetek, director of *Le Fate ignoranti*. An erotic drama, set in Istanbul, *Hamam* centred on a young Italian designer who inherits his aunt's Turkish steam bath, and, after becoming infatuated with the young son of the bath's caretaker, begins questioning everything about himself.

Turks lined up for blocks to see *Hamam* and it was even nominated to represent Turkey at the 1998 Academy Awards. But the film never had its night in Hollywood. Turkey's Culture Ministry overruled the independent film board, instead choosing a heterosexual romantic drama as the country's candidate for the Oscar for Best Foreign Film.

Meanwhile, during the same year, the official Academy Awards Best Foreign Film entry for Greece also happened to be gay themed. Like a Greek version of *My Own Private Idaho*, Constantinos Giannaris' *From the Edge of the City* (1998) took us to a little-known corner of Eastern European chaos: the sad lives of Athens' immigrant rent boys.

Canada's best 90s gay movie offering came in John Greyson's stylish and engrossing *Lilies* (1996). A complex adaptation of Michel Marc Bouchard's

Scenes from Mel Chionglo's *Midnight Dancers* (1994)

'Being a man one day and a woman the next is not an easy thing.'

Bernadette in ***Adventures of Priscilla, Queen of the Desert***

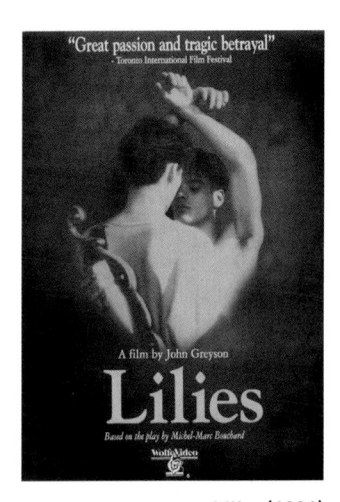

Lilies (1996)

play *Les Fleurette*, *Lilies* was an emotionally intense, suspense-laden tale of love, betrayal and revenge set in the early 50s. It won four Canadian Genie Awards (the equivalent of the American Oscars) including Best Picture, and won critical acclaim worldwide.

Germany, meanwhile, decided to ditch gay drama in the 90s, opting instead for some light-hearted gay-themed movies. *Regular Guys* (1996) took a tongue-in-cheek look at the complexities of relationships – gay, straight and somewhere in between – while *The Trio* (1998) had a father-and-daughter pickpocket team opening their arms, and hearts, to a young bisexual drifter, bringing him into their operations.

France also produced a few notable gay movies in the late 90s. *A Toute Vitesse* (1996) was a poignant study of a group of young French provincials – some from North Africa – falling in and out with one another; *Man is a Woman* (1998) had *Eurotrash* presenter Antoine de Caunes as a gay man living in Paris, deciding whether to take his uncle's bribe to get married, produce children and continue the family name; and *Drôle de Felix* (1999) centred around a 30-year-old HIV-positive gay man living in a small town in northern France, who decides to take a hitch-hiking trip to Marseilles to track down the father who abandoned him before he was born.

All these international, gay-interest films were well received in their native countries but, more importantly, also garnered some great reviews around the world.

The 90s was also a great period for the girls as well as the guys. At the start of the decade, many lesbians took the Hollywood-mainstream, female-buddy movie *Thelma & Louise* (1991) to their hearts, because Ridley Scott's 'pro-women movie' made it fairly clear viewers could look beneath the surface of the women's bonding. The film depicted female friendship and lesbian relationships but left those erotic feelings implicit. Lesbianism remained unspoken, although it's certainly a source of strength and inspiration.

Thelma & Louise charted the extraordinary tale of a housewife and a waitress (Susan Sarandon and Geena Davis) whose innocent weekend escape becomes an electrifying odyssey of self-discovery. The perfect casting of Sarandon and Davis made *Thelma & Louise* a movie for the ages, and Brad Pitt became an overnight star after his appearance as the con-artist cowboy.

> 'Man is least himself when he talks in his own person. Give him a mask and he'll tell you the truth.'
>
> Brian in ***Velvet Goldmine***

Many lesbians 'read between the lines' as they watched Thelma's transformation from ultra-femme to ultra-butch. In the closing moments of the film, the lesbian attraction between Louise and Thelma was finally expressed in a kiss on the mouth just before the leap to their death into the Grand Canyon.

Other films, such as *Aliens* (1986) and *Fried Green Tomatoes* (1991), also developed strong lesbian cult followings because they too left the sexuality of their female protagonists unmarked, available for lesbian appropriation.

The Hollywood blockbuster *Basic Instinct* (1992), however, with its lethal bisexuals and ice-pick murders, caused controversy amongst the lesbian community, for the very same reasons that earlier killer-lesbian films such as Russ Meyer's *Faster Pussycat! Kill! Kill!* had offended.

Paul Verhoeven's film was criticised for its stereotypes of man-hating lesbians and protesters cried 'misogyny' outside cinemas on its opening weekend. They felt it portrayed bisexuals as insatiable, untrustworthy and homicidal.

Equally furious was the response to the hit thriller *The Silence of the Lambs* (1990), directed by Jonathan Demme and written by Ted Tally, which equated homosexuality and transgenderism with insanity and murder.

Outspoken lesbian writer/activist Camille Paglia, however, has not only defended *Basic Instinct*, but called it her 'favourite film', even providing an audio commentary track on the DVD release. In fact, in the years since *Basic Instinct*'s release, many critics have re-evaluated the film. The lesbian film writer Judith Halberstam has noted how Catherine Trammell is quite the lipstick lesbian in control: 'I would rather see lesbians depicted as outlaws and destroyers than cosy, feminine, domestic, tame lovers.'

In 1996, the Wachowski Brothers (the men behind *The Matrix*) released their thriller *Bound* featuring Jennifer Tilly and Gina Gershon as partners in crime – and as lovers. A modern-day *film noir*, the plot centred around two lesbian ex-cons' plot to steal $2 million of Mafia money. Simultaneously violent, funny and suspenseful, *Bound* was placed on many critics' top-ten lists for 1996.

Another cutting-edge, lesbian-themed movie, *High Art* (1998), appeared two years later, starring the former Brat Packer Ally Sheedy, whose performance as Lucy Berliner, an enigmatic lesbian, drug-taking photographer won the Best Actress award at Cannes and some of the best reviews of her entire career. *High Art* was painful and thought provoking, a sincere love

Gina Gershon in the Wachowski Brothers' *Bound* (1996)

Jennifer Tilly in the Wachowski Brothers' *Bound* (1996)

Trisha Todd as Claire Jabrowski in Nicole Conn's *Claire of the Moon* (1993)

FERGUS:
'The thing is, Dil, you're not a girl.'

DIL:
'Details, baby. Details.'

from *The Crying Game*

story, as well as being a reflection on the nature of art. Above all it was a 'lesbian film' for which the lesbianism was integral but not part of an overriding agenda.

Later, in 1999, from lesbian filmmaker Kimberly Peirce, came the even more successful *Boys Don't Cry*, a film based on true events about the life of Teena Brandon. Hilary Swank's audacious and riveting performance shocked critics for the amount of raw emotion she brought to the character, a lesbian who transforms herself into a man under the name Brandon Teena, in order to gain acceptance in conservative rural Nebraska.

The film earned acclaim from mainstream and lesbian and gay critics, and Swank won both the Golden Globe and the Academy Award for Best Actress. Aside from these mainstream Hollywood forays into lesbiana, 'real' lesbian film also caught fire in the 1990s – *Claire of the Moon* (1992), *Go Fish* (1994), *Bar Girls* (1994) and *Everything Relative* (1996), to name just a few.

And, as lesbian cinema hit new heights, the comedian Ellen DeGeneres came out on her hugely popular TV show in April 1997. This led to a *TIME* magazine cover, and a wonderfully public relationship with actress Anne Heche. Both became outspoken activists, earning heaps of praise from the community and opening a lot of minds in the process.

In 1998, *Will & Grace* aired on US television and quickly became the most popular gay-themed network TV series since DeGeneres' *Ellen*. A landmark show which attracted worldwide mainstream attention, many episodes were, however, full of campiness (Jack in particular) and predictable white-yuppie characters. In fact, it's fair to say that the huge success of *Will & Grace* paved the way for a glut of trashy gay comedies into the late 90s and 2000s – but not just on TV.

It's ironic that the widespread acceptance of homosexuality, thanks to TV shows like *Will & Grace*, was actually, in some ways, detrimental to the quality of output found in late-90s gay film. Whereas Russell T Davies's groundbreaking British TV series *Queer as Folk* was rightly lauded for tearing up the TV rulebook and opening up the world's eyes to realistic gay culture, most other gay telly shows relied on gay stereotypes and trivialised gay romance. The media-friendly, camp stereotype propagated by Graham Norton, *Will & Grace* and later *Queer Eye for the Straight Guy* encouraged others to emulate this gay male figure and, by the end of the decade, there was a whole spate of light and fluffy gay comedy movies – such as *Billy's Hollywood Screen Kiss* (1998) and *Trick* (1999).

In *Billy's Hollywood Screen Kiss*, Billy announces at the outset, 'My name is Billy, and I am a homosexual.' He says he grew up in Indiana and now lives in Los Angeles, where he rooms platonically with a gal-pal named George. Billy is a struggling photographer who falls in love with Gabriel, a waiter and aspiring musician. Gabriel is probably straight but possibly gay or at least curious. With that in mind, Billy tries to get Gabriel to model for his latest project, while also trying to win his affections. Gripping stuff!

Meanwhile, in *Trick*, a variety of characters graced the screen – a selfish roommate, an irritating best friend, and a vicious, jealous drag queen, all of whom Gabriel, an aspiring writer, and Mark, a muscled stripper, had to contend with in their quest to find somewhere to be alone for the night. If you get a feeling you've seen it all before, it's because you have.

All fairly non-threatening, these films, in fact, were no more than extended versions of safe mainstream TV sitcom episodes. Even the *New York Post* dubbed Rose Troche's bland gay romp *Bedrooms and Hallways* (1999), '*Friends* meets Almodovar!' while *Village Voice* exclaimed, 'It's a gay-friendly *Friends*!'

Other offenders included *Broadway Damage*, *I Think I Do* and *In & Out*, all released in 1997. The main problem with these cute-boys-in-love flicks is that the characters they portray look like they were made by Mattel. They are all young, toned, white, cute, middle-class men with a token fag-hag clinging on.

We wouldn't be fascinated by a routine Hollywood love story simply because the leading characters were heterosexual; we'd want them to be something else besides – interesting, perhaps, or funny. But in the late 90s, many gay filmmakers seemed to follow the idea that gayness itself was enough to make a character interesting.

It isn't.

Film companies send emails and press releases to the gay press, urging critics to ask their readers to 'support' such gay-themed films on their release. But why should anyone buy a ticket to 'support' a film? And what message would it send to 'support' a gay film like *Trick* or *Billy's Hollywood Screen Kiss*? That gay people should have romantic comedies just as dim and dumb as the straight versions – although it's impossible to remember many recent straight films this cringeworthy.

> 'It's only love. What's everyone so scared of?'
>
> **Steven in *Get Real***

Kevin McKidd (Leo), Jennifer Ehle (Sally) and Tom Hollander (Darren) in a scene from Rose Troche's *Bedrooms and Hallways* (1999)

Director Rose Troche on the set of *Bedrooms and Hallways* (1999)

> 'If y'see my life as I do, y'realise it's been one big metaphor for that journey to the human state known as respect.'
>
> Lady Chablis in *Midnight in the Garden of Good and Evil*

The problem with these 'screwball comedies' and 'gay date movies' is that they're all too cute and sugary, annoyingly trashy, with trite stories. As gay director Gregg Araki memorably remarked a few years ago, 'Just because a movie is gay doesn't make it good. I'd rather go see fuckin' *Coneheads* than see most of them!'

Nevertheless, there were some interesting gay-related films made towards the end of the 90s. Thom Fitzgerald's *Beefcake* (1998) was a real gem, a film that looked at the 1950s muscle men's magazines that were supposedly popular as health and fitness magazines, but in reality were primarily purchased by the still-underground homosexual community. The combination of interviews with the stars of that lost era with re-enactments of the events leading to Mizer's trial, made for a heady mix of biography, fantasy and social history, as well as a voyeuristic look at the underlying homoeroticism that really sold *Physique Pictorial*.

Another wonderful re-telling of a past Tinseltown tale also hit the big screen in 1998. *Gods and Monsters* was certainly one of the high points of 90s gay cinema, picking up a string of top industry awards around the world – BAFTAs, Golden Globes and, at the 1999 Academy Awards, Bill Condon even picked up the Oscar for Best Screenplay Adaptation.

Sir Ian McKellen remarked: 'Over the last two decades there has been a considerable revolution in the treatment of gays and lesbians in plays and films. For too many years we were portrayed as villainous or stupid. I am proud to have been associated with *Gods and Monsters*, which boldly treated homosexuality as a fact of life, worthy of the same serious approach as any other aspect of human nature.'

In the 90s alone, three major actors had been nominated for the Best Actor Oscar while playing gay roles – Stephen Rea for *The Crying Game*, Tom Hanks for *Philadelphia* and Sir Ian McKellen for *Gods and Monsters*.

This strong standing left many wondering: *Who says gay men aren't mainstream?*

THE FILMS

POISON
(1991)

US, 85 mins
Director/Writer: Todd Haynes
Cast: Buck Smith, Edith Meeks, Larry Maxwell, Susan Norman, Scott Renderer, James Lyons, John R Lombardi, Millie White
Genre: Drama/ Horror

One of the most audacious and original American films in years, Todd Haynes' *Poison* was inspired by the works of Jean Genet.

A powerful and disturbing study of deviance, cultural conditioning and disease, the film comprises three segments, all separate but interrelated stories, shot in three strikingly unique cinematic styles. The three stories illustrate the lives of a people living outside the fringes of 'normal' society. There is 'Hero', the pseudo-documentary about a seven-year-old boy called Richie who kills his own father and flies away; 'Horror', a sci-fi spoof about a brilliant research scientist (Larry Maxwell) who discovers the source of the human sex drive but precipitates a frightening reaction; and 'Homo', about a prisoner who falls in love with a fellow inmate and becomes drowned in obsession, fantasy and violence.

As each compelling story is told, their themes become inextricably linked, and the tension intensifies, culminating in an explosive climax of unsettled emotions. The unifying thread is sex, the poison to which the title refers. In each of the three sections, sex is virtually synonymous with perversion, abuse, domination and disease.

Poison took certain liberties with Genet's work but it captured his spirit in a way that's rarely been equalled. In fact, it's difficult to imagine a more vivid, skin-crawling depiction of sexual loathing.

Haynes received funding from the National Endowment for the Arts for *Poison*, and on the American DVD commentary he states that the NEA funding was a great help because it allowed him the independence to carry out his vision without having to worry about satisfying commercial studio interests. Unfortunately, *Poison* was cited by right-wing campaigners (along with Robert Mapplethorpe) as a reason why NEA funding should be stopped. Under Bush, it was.

THE CRYING GAME
(1992)

UK, 107 mins
Director/Writer: Neil Jordan
Cast: Stephen Rea, Miranda Richardson, Forest Whitaker, Jaye Davidson
Genre: Political Thriller

Neil Jordan's *The Crying Game* (1992) was the British thriller that took America by storm. Starting off

Jaye Davidson as Dil

in art houses in major metropolitan areas, it quickly became a social phenomenon and broke all box-office records.

Though a superb blend of social statement and political thriller, interest in the film spread primarily because of a shocking 'secret' in the plot, causing it to move into the major mainline movie theatres. It was subsequently nominated for nine Academy Awards.

Jordan's film is set in London and Northern Ireland, and begins with the capture of a black English soldier by a group of IRA terrorists. One of the terrorists, Fergus (Stephen Rea), befriends the soldier, finding out about his exotic girlfriend Dil (Jaye Davidson) in London in the process. As events develop, the terrorist flees Northern Ireland and goes to London where he begins a relationship with the soldier's girlfriend. The film then explores their relationship as the terrorist is pursued by his former colleagues.

At the outset a simple story – and this movie could have simply been an interesting thriller – essential to its plot is a twist that catapults the film into the realm of social statement. The girlfriend, as it turns out, is not a girl at all, but a transvestite.

So it's impossible to ignore the fact that this film, like *Kiss of the Spider Woman* (1985) and Jordan's own *Mona Lisa* (1986), really tries to involve its audiences in understanding gay and lesbian sensibilities. Through a thrilling sexual mystery, *The Crying Game* exposes mainstream cinemagoers to an attractive fantasy of alternative sexuality. It's also a story of love in the time of AIDS with no reference to that terrifying subject.

Where Jordan's film distinguishes itself from many other gay-themed films, though, is in the fact its homosexuals are 'real' people with whose loneliness, hurts and fears anyone can sympathise. Dil misses his soldier/lover and yearns for Fergus's love, yet earns the audience's respect as a loyal, funny friend to Fergus when love turns out not to be an option.

Rather than preaching the 'victimisation' of homosexuals, or showing over-the-top glitzy gay lifestyles, *The Crying Game* is instead an admirable film with a politically correct message, the acceptance of gay love and openly gay identity. As if this wasn't enough, the film also comes complete with an astounding soundtrack, featuring the hypnotic title track performed by Boy George, as well as Lyle Lovett's version of *Stand By Your Man* and the classic Percy Sledge hit *When a Man Loves a Woman*. The screenplay is a triumph of clarity, particularly since the film's plot is so complicated, and the acting is also superb – no surprise then that *The Crying Game* was nominated for the Oscar for Best Picture.

Jaye Davidson (Dil) with Stephen Rea (Fergus)

MY OWN PRIVATE IDAHO
(1992)

US, 100 mins
Director/Writer: Gus Van Sant
Cast: River Phoenix, Keanu Reeves, James Russo, William Richert, Rodney Harvey, Udo Kier
Genre: Road Movie

When rumours began circulating around Hollywood that pin-up boys River Phoenix and Keanu Reeves would play gay hustlers in Gus Van Sant's next movie, hearts – male and female – began pounding. The rumours turned out to be true, unlike the tabloid reports that Reeves had married music mogul David Geffen at a secret ceremony in Hawaii.

My Own Private Idaho was soon hyped up as a 'mainstream' gay movie and really did deserve to become a cult classic of gay cinema. Made for two and a half million dollars, in 1991, it made around seven million dollars at the US box office. It also won several awards at film festivals around the world, mainly for Phoenix's performance (he won Best Actor at Venice), and for Van Sant's brilliant screenplay, tenuously based on Shakespeare's *Henry IV* plays, which further develops the themes and concerns of his previous two features *Mala Noche* (1988) and *Drugstore Cowboy* (1989).

Phoenix plays the lonely, narcoleptic Mike. He has never known his father, and his mother abandoned him when he was young, so he's not a very secure or well-adjusted individual. Living on the edge of destitution, he survives by working as a male prostitute, mainly servicing middle-aged men, although his clients range from a Capote-like compulsive who likes his bathtubs well scrubbed to a rich dame who likes her boys all at once.

Reeves is Scott, the brash eldest son of a wealthy family, who also works the streets in the Pacific Northwest. Despite their completely different backgrounds, they become friends. The pair spend time hanging with a ragged street family in a condemned building and, in a deliberate reworking of Orson Welles's Shakespearean *Chimes at Midnight*, they converse in bard-speak. In fact, Van Sant's cinematic references are extremely varied. Away from the Shakespearian stuff, the long empty roads and

River Phoenix in the arms of Keanu Reeves

landscapes recall James William Guercio's *Electra Glide in Blue* (1973), while Mike and Scott's entire journey is akin to Jon Voight and Dustin Hoffman's trip in John Schlesinger's *Midnight Cowboy* (1969).

Mike and Scott set out, in vain, on a search for Mike's mother, a journey that takes them to Idaho, then to Italy. Mike passes out regularly and is usually carried to safety and protected by Scott. Along the way, Mike's emotional attachment to Scott develops, but is rewarded only with friendship. In fact, Scott has no intentions of sticking with his friends once he receives his inheritance, due in a week. He plans to abandon his wanton lifestyle and become a respectable member of society at the very moment when his family least expects him to.

During his sleep Mike is visited by the vision of his mother who strokes his hair and tells him repeatedly, 'Don't worry; everything's going to be alright.' A close shot of his sleeping face then changes to show his face approaching orgasm as he receives oral sex from a client in Seattle. His passion is shown by salmon leaping, his orgasm by a shot of a wooden barn dropping and shattering on a desert landscape.

On their travels to Italy, they discover that Mike's mother has returned to the US long before but Scott begins a relationship with an Italian girl, deserts Mike and returns to Portland to claim his inheritance. A raw and sometimes shocking story of two guys' struggle to come of age and to terms with reality, *My Own Private Idaho* is a poetic film about desire and the desperate need to belong. It has remained one of the best-known films in American gay cinema, mainly due to the subsequent career successes of Van Sant and Reeves, and the enduring pop mythology of River Phoenix, who died of a drug overdose in 1993.

The film's final scene shows Mike alone on a road in Idaho in a narcoleptic state again; Scott is no longer there for him. Mike will never find what he's looking for. For him, real love, intimacy and lust combined are distant dreams, more accessible in sleep, perhaps, than in waking. But the film was never more tender or moving than the moment Mike confronts his love for Scott. His murmured plea, 'I really want to kiss you, man,' as they sit round a campfire, is nothing short of heartbreaking, a scene which helps make this a modern gay classic.

GRIEF
(1993)

US, 92 mins
Director/Writer: Richard Glatzer

Cast: Craig Chester, Illeana Douglas, Alexis Arquette, Kent Fuher
Genre: Comedy

Dubbed 'the out version of *Soapdish*', Richard Glatzer's first feature film, *Grief*, is a good example of 90s 'AIDS Cinema'. Released in 1994 to international acclaim, it's one of the sharpest gay indie films of the 90s.

Made on a micro-budget of just $40,000 and shot in ten days, *Grief* is a deeply heart-warming movie, full of humour (with jokes about semen stains, leprosy and circus lesbians!) but also full of compassion. Winner of awards at both the San Francisco Gay and Lesbian Festival and the Torino Festival, *Grief* deservedly became a cult hit and finally earned a DVD release in 2004.

The bittersweet comedy follows the frenzied and romantic antics of the outlandish staff of *The Love Judge*, a low-budget, daytime-TV show. Starring *Last Exit to Brooklyn*'s Alexis Arquette, *Swoon*'s Craig Chester, and Illeana Douglas from *Alive*, *Grief* centres on the show's writer, Mark (Chester), who is mourning his lover's death from AIDS and yet has a crush on a 'straight' co-worker Bill (Arquette), who sends back very mixed signals.

Director Richard Glatzer used to produce the TV show *Divorce Court*, so the film has a true sense of the absurdity of cheap television. Glatzer even throws in some amusing courtroom cameos, including Mary Woronov and Paul Bartel.

A decade after the film's release, Glatzer remarked: 'Funny how ten years on, the film already benefits from the patina of nostalgia. Big hair and bright fabrics were about to bite the dust. Courtroom shows would soon give way to reality TV. Protease inhibitors were just around the corner. I didn't realise when we were making *Grief* that we were capturing a very specific point in time, but we were.'

Nevertheless, the chief reason for *Grief* was so that Glatzer could make a film that examined his feelings about surviving the loss of his lover. Said Glatzer: 'That had been the lowest point of my life, and yet somehow I could only write about it comically. I'm not even sure if, at the time, I saw the film as a comedy. I think I felt I could coerce an audience into sharing my misery by enticing them with a few jokes. I do know that the only way I could address the film's eponymous subject was indirectly. To see Mark at home crying himself to sleep was impossible for me. Much better to glimpse his emotional distress fleetingly, while he cranked out trash TV.'

On this level, *Grief* digs deeper than comparable mainstream projects. Chester's character is extremely well rounded; not just another empty stereotype but more a great gay prototype. He's cold, jaded and bitchy on the outside but tender and vulnerable on the inside – and this double-edged performance really helps in the film's poignant finale.

PHILADELPHIA
(1993)

US, 125 mins
Writer: Ron Nyswaner
Director: Jonathan Demme
Cast: Tom Hanks, Denzel Washington, Antonio Banderas, Roberta Maxwell, Buzz Kilman, Karen Finley
Genre: AIDS drama

Jonathan Demme's weepy pic had sanctimonious Tom Hanks as Andy Beckett, a respected member of a prestigious legal firm. But within months of being promoted, he's out, a victim, he claims, of unfair dismissal. And this was one of the most controversial aspects of the film when it was initially released. While everybody knew it was about AIDS, the emphasis was on human rights and the rule of law – a David and Goliath struggle between a stricken individual and a powerful adversary. In fact, promotion for the film carefully avoided any reference to AIDS, using the slogan: 'No one would take on his case, until one man was willing to take on the system.'

The man who steps in to defend Beckett is black lawyer Joe Miller. He knows all about discrimination but his own deep-seated prejudice against homosexuals becomes one of the principal conflicts in the drama.

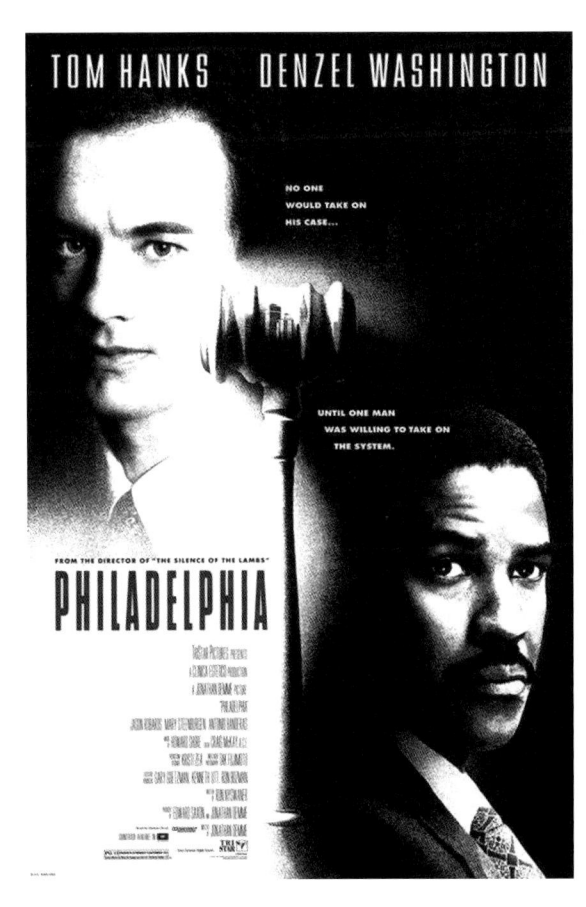

The film, however, reinforced stereotypes and was far too timid in its depiction of same-sex relationships. The role of Hanks' lover Miguel (Antonio Banderas) was drastically cut and any affection between the two characters is kept to a bare minimum, to the point where Banderas is only ever seen to kiss Hanks' hands. The pair don't even appear to have any gay friends. It seems the Hanks character has only ever made one mistake in his life. Other than that, he's the perfect guy with the perfect boyfriend and the perfect, supportive family and perfect, caring friends. Where a seedier character might earn less sympathy, viewers won't think Beckett 'deserves' his AIDS. Indeed, everything about the Hanks character is so wonderful and flawless that the movie lacks reality; it would certainly have been more interesting if its lead had some genuine flaws.

Nevertheless, there's no denying its popularity at the box office and it was no great shock when the lead role brought Hanks the first of two successive Academy Awards.

AND THE BAND PLAYED ON
(1993)

US, 144 mins
Director: Roger Spottiswoode
Cast: Matthew Modine, Lily Tomlin, Richard Gere, Alan Alda, Sir Ian McKellen
Genre: AIDS drama

And the Band Played On, an HBO TV movie, debuted in September 1993, not long after the release of the big-budget Hollywood AIDS movie *Philadelphia*. It is an account of the first efforts by medical researchers to identify and define the epidemic.

Matthew Modine delivers an excellent performance as the film's central character, a doctor who witnesses both the outbreak of the disease and its far-reaching social impact.

But the TV film is also remembered for its array of star cameo appearances including Richard Gere, Steve Martin and Phil Collins. Lily Tomlin is great as the cantankerous Dr Selma Dritz of the San Francisco Department of Public Health, on a righteous crusade, cruising the gay bathhouses, confronting the secret STD-doctors of the closeted elite, looking for solutions and providing the necessary outbursts. Sir Ian McKellen received an Emmy nomination for his performance as a San Francisco gay activist who campaigns for AIDS education at the cost of his lover.

Unlike *Philadelphia*, which simply shored up a bit of sympathy for a too-good-to-be-true victim, *And the Band Played On* decided to dole out the blame where blame was deserved. Ronald Reagan is the worthy villain, at the top of the bureaucracy heap, announcing an increase in defence spending as Modine scrapes away in his lab, looking for meagre funds for a new electron microscope.

And the Band Played On's screenwriters were highly astute at turning social arguments into real-

Sir Ian McKellen in scenes from *And the Band Played On*

istic and meaningful dialogue – always in character – and, unlike *Philadelphia*'s homo-ignorance and preachy tone, its passion and anger makes for a far more powerful and engrossing film.

THE ADVENTURES OF PRISCILLA, QUEEN OF THE DESERT
(1994)

Australia, 104 mins
Director/Writer: Stephan Elliott
Cast: Terence Stamp, Hugo Weaving, Guy Pearce, Bill Hunter
Genre: Road movie – musical comedy

The Adventures of Priscilla, Queen of the Desert is an extraordinary Australian road movie, extraordinary mainly for the amazing camp performances by the three, straight, leading actors.

Priscilla is about two drag queens (Anthony/Mitzi and Adam/Felicia) and a transsexual (Bernadette) who are hired to perform a drag show at a resort in Alice Springs in the remote Australian desert. The flamboyant trio are Hugo Weaving and Guy Pearce (as the two queens) and Terence Stamp (as the world-weary transsexual). They take a tour bus (called Priscilla) west from Sydney, across the enormous Outback – a journey full of bitchy banter and outrageous incidents. En route, it is discovered that the woman they've contracted with is Anthony's wife. Their bus breaks down, and is repaired by gruff mechanic Bob (Bill Hunter), a big fan from the past, who travels on with them. It's not long before our three favourite queens are performing their own inimitable version of 'I Will Survive'.

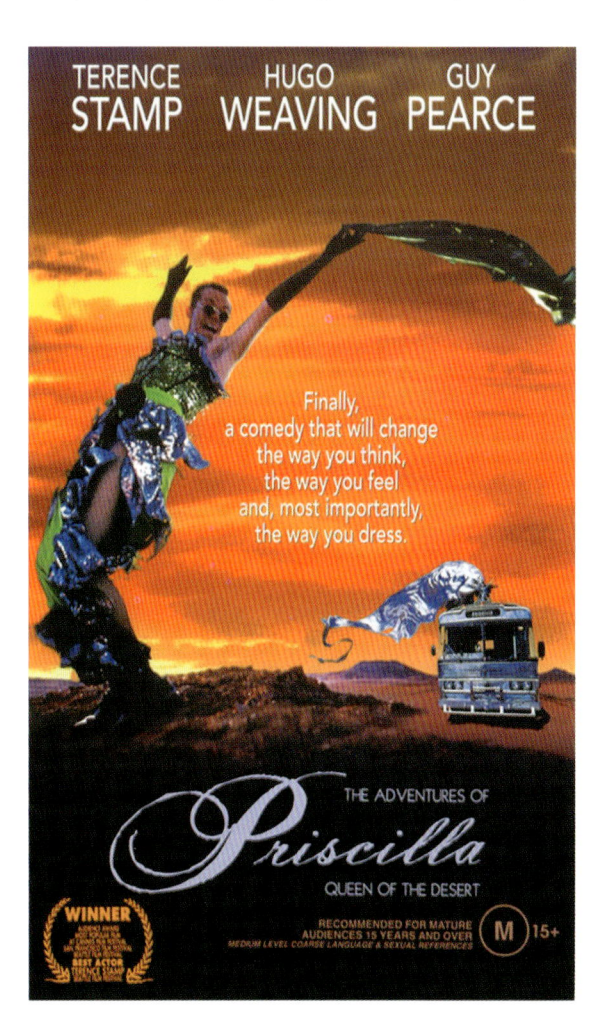

For all the tack and bitchiness, there are some really understated moments and emotional scenes, and lots of gay issues are explored. In one key development, Stamp is plunged into despair by the death of someone close to him and this is where the 60s British icon shines. He is totally credible and utterly dignified.

The three main characters – one gay guy, one bisexual and a transsexual – represent three highly segregated communities. And they all detest each other. Only the danger and hardship of the journey unite them. Viewers need to watch closely to pick up on the subtleties in this movie. In fact, viewing several times would help. In the end, Adam gets to fulfil his dream of climbing to the top of King's Canyon in a Gaultier frock, tiara and heels; Mitzi faces up to being a father; and Bernadette gets her man.

We are told Bernadette is an ex Les Girl. In fact, the inspiration for the film was Play Girls, the touring troupe of the acclaimed cabaret group Les Girls. This group achieved iconic status in Australia and featured Carlotta, the Balmain Boy who had Australia's first recognised sex-change operation. Australia was also one of the most loyal audiences for Abba, and Lasse Hallström's *Abba – The Movie* (1977) was filmed on their Australian tour. So in Australia at least, a cultural precedent had already been put in place for the mainstream acceptance of *Priscilla* on its release and thus provided the springboard for its international distribution and success.

Priscilla is a ready-made gay *cult* movie, complete with all of the vital ingredients, including countless memorable lines of dialogue, which include stabs at Abba – 'I've said it once and I'll say it again – no more fucking Abba'; 'What are you telling me – this is an Abba turd?' The camp 70s soundtrack is to die for – Abba, Village People, Ce Ce Peniston, Gloria Gaynor, M People; both originals and exclusive dance remixes. The movie even inspired some theatres to get into the spirit of things by hanging disco balls from the ceiling and flashing coloured lights when the 'Finally' dance played out on screen. In addition to the wonderful soundtrack, the gaudy costumes were fabulous and won a well-deserved Oscar.

Later, Hugo Weaving was also happy to play a gay man in Rose Troche's *Bedrooms and Hallways* (1998) and Guy Pearce, having shaken off his soap-star past, broke into Hollywood, with some very meaty roles in films like *Memento* and *LA Confidential*.

Interestingly, around the same time *Priscilla, Queen of the Desert* was released, the same country also brought us *Muriel's Wedding* (1994), a tale about a social misfit who copes with the screwed-up reality of small-town society by listening to Abba's 'Dancing Queen'. Sound familiar?

TO WONG FOO, THANKS FOR EVERYTHING, JULIE NEWMAR
(1995)

US, 104 mins
Writer: Douglas Carter Beane
Director: Beeban Kidron
Cast: Wesley Snipes, Patrick Swayze, John Leguizamo, Stockard Channing, Blythe Danner, Arliss Howard, Chris Penn

John Leguizamo as drag queen Chi-Chi

The success of the hit Aussie, drag-queen movie *Priscilla* resulted in a cash-in movie from Hollywood, *To Wong Foo, Thanks for Everything, Julie Newmar* (1995).

Producing a similar off-beat road movie about drag queens, this time it was Patrick Swayze, Wesley Snipes and John Leguizamo who were glamming it up. En route from New York to Hollywood for a drag-queen beauty pageant, the trio are forced to take an unwelcome detour. Stranded in the tiny Midwest town of Snydersville, the three make the best of the unfortunate situation as their glitz and glamour shake up the sleepy locals.

It's all flamboyant fun but, like most real-life drag queens, much of *To Wong Foo*'s material is old and tired and this Hollywood effort failed to tap into the same nerve that *Priscilla* did with its innovative subject matter and sensitive character portrayals. *Priscilla*'s campy trio were far more impressive in a film in which the glitz and glamour seemed far more stylish – less Hollywood and more appealing and believable to a gay audience. It's fair to say that *To Wong Foo* provides a point of comparison which can only reinforce *Priscilla*'s reputation.

BEAUTIFUL THING
(1995)

UK, 85 mins
Director: Hettie MacDonald
Writer: Jonathan Harvey
Cast: Meera Syal, Linda Henry, Martin Walsh, Glen Berry, Scott Neal, Steven M Martin, Andrew Fraser, Tameka Empson
Genre: Coming-of-age

Set during a long hot summer on a housing estate in South London, and released in 1995, *Beautiful*

Jamie (Glen Berry) cuddles up to Ste (Scott Neal)

Thing turned out to be one of the most tender love stories ever told on film. A story of sexual awakening, this urban fairytale depicts what it's like to be sixteen and in the throes of bashful first love. Hettie MacDonald's delightful debut feature charts a seemingly unlikely romance between two teenagers, from first nervous glances to ingenious use of Peppermint Foot Lotion!

Jamie, an unpopular kid who skips school to avoid games lessons, lives next door to Ste, a more popular athletic boy but who is constantly beaten up by his father and older brother. Jamie's mum, Sandra, offers refuge to Ste, who has to 'top-and-tail' with Jamie.

There are obvious issues covered, such as the boys' coming to terms with their sexuality and others finding out. But the film also details Sandra's unconditional love, loyalty and defence of Jamie and the fear of repercussion should Ste's family find out. The character of Sandra is extremely well rounded and we get a real sense of her dreams of promotion and desire to manage her own pub, and escape the estate, and of her new relationship with her hippie boyfriend Tony. Girl next door, Leah, is another great character. Having been expelled from school, she spends her time listening to Mama Cass records and tripping on a variety of drugs.

Glen Berry and Scott Neal as Jamie and Ste

Understandably, the film struck a chord with the gay community and there's undoubtedly a cult of *Beautiful Thing*. Those teenagers in particular who sent themselves deep into denial about their sexuality have taken the film to their hearts.

Looking at the numerous fan websites, *Beautiful Thing* chat-rooms and email discussion pages, it seems the movie has affected people most powerfully if they've had a hard time accepting themselves. One fan explained how the strongest reaction he heard came from a man he knew in his late 40s who came out recently to his wife and grown sons, straight after seeing the film. One other fan described how he'd been to London before but now planned to go to Thamesmead in the summer. 'Can you imagine,' he wrote, 'there'll be all these poofs walking around with maps looking for *Beautiful Thing* locations!' The same writer explained how he and his new boyfriend Andi – also a huge fan of the film – planned on putting together a tour plan, and maybe using it as an excuse for *BT* fans to meet sometime the following summer. Other sites include virtual tours of Thamesmead, with maps and photos.

Most film critics missed the groundbreaking nature of the film – and criticised the (deliberate) happy ending – saying it was unrealistic (unlike, apparently, *The Birdcage*). The film has, however, been taken up by many high-school teachers (mainly in the US) who play it to their classes to convey the message to both gays and straights that 'it's okay now'.

BENT
(1996)

UK, 100 mins
Director: Sean Mathias
Writer: Martin Sherman
Cast: Clive Owen, Lothaire Bluteau, Brian Webber, Sir Ian McKellen, Mick Jagger

When Sean Mathias's *Bent* was released in 1996, most critics agreed it was just as powerful and moving as the award-winning stage play upon which it was based. Both Fassbinder and Costa-Gavras wanted to film Martin Sherman's 1979 play about gay persecution under the Nazis, but it was theatre director Mathias who finally brought it to the screen.

Set amidst the decadence of pre-war, fascist Germany, it tells the story of three homosexual men's fight for survival in the face of persecution. The film opens with promiscuous partier Max (Clive Owen) and his flatmate Rudi (Brian Webber) enjoying a coke-fuelled evening's entertainment at a decadent club. Flamboyant dancers and circus performers revel with customers in various sorts of public 'debauchery', while a transvestite nightclub singer named Greta/George (Mick Jagger) warbles a tune about all the beautiful boys and the intoxicating nightlife.

But Nazi thugs are also out in Berlin that evening, the infamous Night of the Long Knives, and Max, who's picked up a man for the night has been followed back to his apartment. Stormtroopers burst in and kill his one night stand, as Max makes his escape.

Despite pleas from his uncle (Sir Ian McKellen), Max refuses to flee Germany unless he can get Rudi out with him.

The pair set off into the woods, only to be caught and shipped in a boxcar full of prisoners to the concentration camp at Dachau. Their time in the woods, which alternates between sheer terror and the gentle prayer of their love for each other, is handled well by director Mathias, as are the blindingly horrific events of the train ride. At one point, Max is forced to beat his lover to death then prove his manhood by having intercourse with a young girl who's been shot in the head.

En route, Max is befriended by a timid gay man named Horst (Lothaire Bluteau), who advises him not to acknowledge his lover if he wishes to remain alive. Following that advice allows Max to survive after Rudi is beaten to death. Later, by 'performing' with a young girl to convince the Nazis of his heterosexuality, Max is able to 'upgrade' his status from that of a homosexual (who must wear a pink triangle) to that of a Jew (who wears a yellow star).

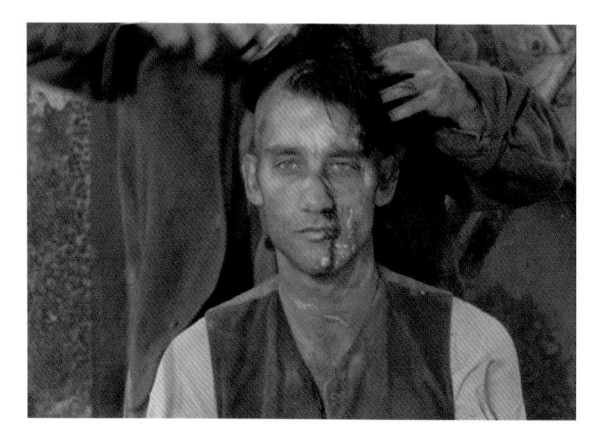

Clive Owen as Max in scenes from *Bent*

Within the confines of the camp, however, Max and Horst develop a secret love affair and through the most terrible torture they overcome the oppression. In one moving scene the two men take the opportunity to 'make love' to each other by describing various sex acts sotto voce while the guards look down on them as they pointlessly move rocks from one side of a quarry to the other. They're not allowed to touch or even look at one another but still manage to share this explicit imaginary sexual encounter. 'We feel we're human,' says Horst afterwards. 'They're not going to kill us.'

Max and Horst's secret love affair is as inspirational as it is emotional, and Mathias's film illustrates how the selfless love of one person for another can overcome oppression, even under the most extreme circumstances.

MANDRAGORA
(1997)

Czech Republic, 134 mins
Director: Wiktor Grodecki
Cast: Mirek Caslavka, David Svec, Miroslav Breu, Jiri Kodes, Karel Polisenksy, Pavel Skripal, Richard Toth
Genre: Sex industry drama

Sixteen-year-old Marek (Mirek Caslavka), a boy with an angelic face and a freshly stolen jacket, is about to embark on an adventure. He's run away from his life back home with an overpowering father and arrived at the main train station in the busy city of Prague.

He's immediately spotted by a man called Honza, who asks him if he wants to earn some quick cash. The boy is too naive to realise he's being set up as a prostitute. He is drugged and wakes in the room of a gay client who has just had sex with him. Shaken, he takes his payment from the man and returns to the train station where Honza demands his cut.

Marek meets David (David Svec who also co-wrote the film and won the Prize of the City of Setúbal for his performance), another street hustler. After befriending each other, they decide to become pimps themselves by combining their money together to purchase a handful of young men. When that fails, they turn to petty crimes. With each step forward Marek and David take, they find themselves at least three steps back. In the end, Marek is addicted to drugs, sick from AIDS, and maggots and worms eat away at his skin while he sits at the base of a public toilet. He slashes his leg with a knife, unaware that his father who has come in search of him is just a mere two feet away in another stall.

In less than a year (and within 135 minutes – the running time of this film) Marek has become a street prostitute, a drug addict, a porn star, and worse of all – a statistic. He ends up just one of the hundreds of young men who flock to Prague each year in search of freedom – only to end up trapped.

Director Wiktor Grodecki, who had previously made *Not Angels But Angels* and *Body Without Soul* – two documentaries which influenced *Mandragora* – used real-life prostitutes and a non-professional cast to depict the despair and tragedy that infects so many young adults in Prague.

He ends this dramatisation by showing yet another young man getting off a train in Prague. He, like Marek and countless others before him, steps off the platform and proceeds to walk down the stairs and through the tunnel that will perhaps lead him to Honza or someone like him.

In case you're wondering about the film's title, *Mandragora* (also known as Mandrake) is a plant from North Africa, a plant that has been described as 'having magic power to heal a great variety of diseases, to induce a feeling of love, affection and happiness'. According to East Indian folklore, it was also thought that Mandragora grew under the gallows from the sperm of hanged men.

Although the acting is good and the lighting and sets are all well done, ultimately, *Mandragora* is marred by Grodecki's heavy hand. The pathos is laid on rather too thick and, at 134 minutes, the film is far too long to sustain such a one-dimensional approach.

GET REAL
(1998)

UK, 110 mins
Director: Simon Shore
Writer: Patrick Wilde
Cast: Ben Silverstone, Brad Gorton, Charlotte Brittain, Stacy Hart
Genre: Coming-of-age

Following the success of *Beautiful Thing* (1995), British gay cinema produced another excellent film, accessible to all audiences, in the shape of

Get Real (1998), which tells the story of a teenage boy who has become sexually active at 16. As Roger Ebert memorably remarked in his review at the time: 'When straight teenagers do it, it's called sowing wild oats. When gay teenagers do it, it's hedonistic promiscuity.' The film obviously offended many but the point is that most teenagers have sex. Some are gay. Fact.

Ben Silverstone plays Steven Carter, a 16-year-old who lives in leafy, stuffy Basingstoke. Although comfortable with his sexuality, he knows neither his parents nor schoolmates are ready for the news. Until, that is, he forms an unlikely relationship with John Dixon (Brad Gorton), star athlete and all-round school hunk. Wary of damaging his cool image, John insists the romance remains secret, although Steven finds this easier said than done.

Charlotte Brittain plays Steven's next-door-neighbour Linda, the only person who knows he is gay. Much of the humour in the film comes from the scenes between these two characters. Steven's cover as well as confidante, she even faints at a wedding when he needs to make a quick getaway.

There is also Jessica (Stacy A Hart), an editor on the school magazine, who likes Steven a lot and wants to be his girlfriend. He wants to tell her the truth, but lacks the courage. Then the relationship with John helps him to see his life more clearly, to grow tired of lying, and he writes an anonymous article for the magazine that is not destined to remain anonymous for long.

Like *Beautiful Thing*, Simon Shore's feature argues that we are as we are, and the best thing to do is accept that. The gay themes are handled with an admirable lack of fuss and this is far better made than most of Hollywood's recent straight teen love weepies.

LIKE IT IS
(1998)

UK, 95 mins
Director: Paul Oremland
Writer: Robert Gray
Cast: Roger Daltrey, Dani Behr, Ian Rose, Steve Bell
Genre: Romantic drama

Aimed at the audience that made a success of *Beautiful Thing*, another British movie about gay youth, *Like It Is* was released in 1998, adding a class-conflict dimension by pairing a London record producer with a working-class boxer.

In this sexy drama, set around London's gay club world, we follow the two young men as they fall in love, despite enormously different backgrounds. Steve Bell gives an unforgettable performance as Craig, the Blackpool fighter who is struggling with his sexual identity; Ian Rose plays the ultra-cool urbanite Matt who knows everybody; and Roger Daltrey (of The Who) is wickedly funny as Ian's bitchy gay boss Kelvin.

Daltrey steals the whole movie. He's like one of those flesh-eating villainesses in a Disney animation feature – overwrought, campy and full of

Roger Daltrey, Ian Rose and Steve Bell

malice. A deliciously unscrupulous record company and club impresario, this vicious old queen's regular collagen injections and steady diet of fresh young boys keep him trim and ever ready. For laughs, it seems, he tries to draw a wedge between the two young lovers. Also trying to keep them apart is Matt's roommate Paula (Dani Behr), a singer who resents Craig's intrusion.

What's most interesting about *Like It Is*, is the nature of the relationship between Matt and Craig. Unusually for gay screen romances, their courtship is slight. Matt, who is described as a 'serial shagger', works for Kelvin and meets Craig on an out-of-town trip, but their attempt at sex reveals that Craig has some issues to work out regarding his homosexuality. Craig earns money boxing in illegal bare-knuckles fights, but soon moves down to London to seek out Matt; but the fast-paced world of the druggy club scene is a bit out of Craig's league.

Like It Is offers an enjoyable and positive look at gay life and has a welcome, realistic feel. It's romantic, honest, and, above all, entertaining.

GODS AND MONSTERS
(1998)

US, 106 mins
Writer/Director: Bill Condon
Cast: Sir Ian McKellen, Brendan Fraser, Lynn Redgrave, Lolita Davidovitch

One of the most critically acclaimed gay-interest films of the late 1990s, *Gods and Monsters* was the winner of several awards including the Oscar for Best Adapted Screenplay.

Bill Condon's film is a tribute to the controversial life of the eccentric genius, James Whale, who died in 1957. The director of *Frankenstein* and 20 other films of the 1930s and 40s, was openly gay at a time when homosexuality in Hollywood was discreetly concealed.

The film stars Sir Ian McKellen in a sublime performance as the white-haired Whale, who is portrayed as a dapper gent and amateur artist prompted by failing health into melancholy remembrance of things past. Flashbacks of lost love, World War I battle trauma, and glory days in Hollywood combine with Whale's present-day attraction to a newly hired yard worker (Brendan Fraser) whose hunky, Frankenstein-like physique makes him an ideal model for Whale's fixated sketching.

Sir Ian McKellen (as James Whale) with Brendan Fraser (as Clayton Boone)

The friendship between the handsome gardener and his elderly gay admirer is by turns tenuous, humorous, mutually beneficial and, ultimately, rather sad – but to Condon's credit Whale is never seen as pathetic, lecherous or senile. Equally rich is the rapport between Whale and his long-time housekeeper (played with wry sarcasm by Lynn Redgrave), who serves as protector, mother, and even surrogate spouse while Whale's mental state deteriorates. Flashbacks to Whale's filmmaking days are painstakingly authentic (particularly in the casting of look-alike actors playing Boris Karloff and Elsa Lanchester), and all of these ingredients combine to make *Gods and Monsters* (executive produced by horror novelist-filmmaker Clive Barker) a touchingly affectionate film that succeeds on many levels.

THE ACTORS AND DIRECTORS

TODD HAYNES
Writer/Director
1961–

Openly gay, experimental filmmaker Todd Haynes burst upon the scene two years after his graduation from Brown University with his now-infamous 43-minute cult treasure *Superstar: The Karen Carpenter Story* (1987). Seizing upon the inspired gimmick of using Barbie and Ken dolls to sympathetically recount the story of the pop star's death from anorexia, he spent months making miniature dishes, chairs, costumes, Kleenex and Ex-Lax boxes, and Carpenters' records to create the film's intricate, doll-size mise-en-scène. The result was both audacious and accomplished as the dolls seemingly ceased to be dolls, leaving the audience weeping for the tragic singer. Unfortunately, Richard Carpenter's enmity for the film (which made him look like a selfish jerk) led to the serving of a 'cease and desist' order in 1989 and the film has never surfaced since.

Haynes' award-winning first feature, *Poison* (1990), was inspired by the prison writings of Jean Genet, and recalls Werner Fassbinder's unrestrainedly gay *Querelle*. Steeped in obsession, violence and rape, it was not for the faint of heart, prompting walkouts at its 1991 Sundance Film Festival screening and cries of outrage from right-wing critics.

Haynes' next film, *Safe* (1995), was a very different project, the story of a woman suffering from a breakdown caused by a mysterious virus. She ends up in a strange clinic called Wrenwood, a new-age retreat for those who are 'environmentally ill', and even leaves her husband and stepson to try and find salvation there. Many thought the whole film was a metaphor for the AIDS virus. Considered to be an outstanding work, it was voted by many critics as their best film of the year.

Haynes took a highly personal look at the British glam-rock scene of the early 70s with *Velvet Goldmine* (1998), his biggest and most accessible film yet. Dazzlingly surreal with a vibrant glam-era soundtrack, it puts ordinary period filmmaking and time-capsule musicology to shame.

In *Far From Heaven* (2002), Haynes revisited, with little nostalgia, the almost forgotten genre of the domestic melodrama. Drawing from the 'women's films' of the 1950s, he cast Julianne Moore as a 1957 Connecticut housewife and mother who finds out one day that her idyllic suburban life is a lie once she realises that her husband is having a homosexual affair. Haynes explodes the mythical shell of innocence enveloping films from the 50s and warns us that many of the period's most confining concepts of sexuality and the rigid pursuit of complacency and stability are as alive and volatile today as they were in yesteryear's precautionary tales from suburbia.

Haynes' latest film *I'm Not There* (2007) explores the world of Bob Dylan, where six characters embody a different aspect of the musician's life and work. 'The film is inspired by Dylan's music and his ability to re-create and re-imagine himself time and time again,' according to key producer, Christine Vachon. Featuring Heath Ledger, Richard Gere, Christian Bale and Cate Blanchett, it's the first biographical feature project to secure the approval of the pop-culture icon.

SIR IAN McKELLEN
Actor
1939–

Long considered one of the finest British stage actors, Sir Ian McKellen has defied the conventional wisdom that being openly homosexual would either pigeonhole you or destroy your career. Since his 1988 decision to come out during a BBC radio broadcast, he has not only been knighted for his services to the theatre (in 1991) but found himself an unlikely movie star.

Joining the National Theatre in 1965, much of McKellen's work was on the stage, where he played a variety of roles from the Shakespeare canon. But he became an international star for two contemporary parts. In 1979, he created the role of Max, a gay man who pretends to be Jewish when he is shipped to a concentration camp, in Martin Sherman's groundbreaking *Bent*. The following year, McKellen took the role of Salieri, the jealous rival of Mozart, in Peter Shaffer's fine *Amadeus*. Recreating the latter on Broadway only increased his stature, which was capped when he won a Tony Award for the role.

Although he has continued to appear on stage throughout the world, post-*Amadeus* McKellen found himself in demand for film and television roles.

Spurred by legislation that prohibited local authorities from promoting 'homosexual causes', McKellen disclosed his gayness on a 1988 BBC radio broadcast. While it made headlines in the United Kingdom and spawned much conjecture that he would be typecast in future parts, the actor confounded his critics by undertaking the role of John Profumo, a politician brought down by a notorious heterosexual sex scandal in the 60s in *Scandal* (1989). Fully embodying a manly character, the actor demonstrated that his own sexual orientation was immaterial to his abilities as a performer.

Beginning to become more active in gay-related causes, he recreated the role of Max in a one-night-only staging of *Bent* that led to a 1990 revival, accepted the role of AIDS activist Bill Kraus in the HBO movie *And the Band Played On* (1992) and devised his one-man show *A Knight Out*, which he often performs as a benefit fund-raiser.

Following a well-received supporting performance as Russian Czar Nicholas II in the HBO drama *Rasputin* (1996), McKellen accepted the smaller role of Freddie, who attempts to help Max escape from the Nazis, in the feature version of *Bent* (1997). The next year, as he approached his 60s, McKellen's undeniable triumph was playing James Whale, the expatriate British film director best known for his *Frankenstein* horror films, in Bill Condon's superlative *Gods and Monsters*. McKellen found numerous parallels between their lives. Both hailed from the same area of England, both started their careers on stage as actors and both were homosexual, which informed his deeply moving characterisation and helped him nab an Oscar nomination.

More recently, McKellen has played Patrick Stewart's evil rival Magneto in *X-Men* (2000), and in the same year signed on to play the wizard Gandalf in Peter Jackson's eagerly anticipated *Lord of the Rings* trilogy. Giving another stellar performance, alternately charming and commanding, he earned rave reviews and numerous award nominations for his portrayal, as well as the hearts of fans for his dedication to the role. Making another subset of fans equally happy, McKellen reprised the role of the villainous Magneto for the comic-book sequels *X2* (2003) and *X3* (2006).

McKellen is, arguably, the most famous gay actor in the world, recently named the most influential gay man in Britain, having topped the Pink List. But he's more than just a household name. One of the founders of Stonewall in the UK, a charitable organisation which tries to influence legal and social change in regard to gays and lesbians, McKellen has sought to use the power of his celebrity to fight homophobia and anti-gay discrimination around the world. He spoke out in 1988 against the United Kingdom's homophobic legislation known as Section 28, and he continues to speak out today against intolerance everywhere. 'Twenty years ago,' he says, 'the only stories you ever read in the newspapers were entirely negative. Gay people were only treated as news items if some sensation had occurred. That really has changed, at least in the UK, and it would be a very brave newspaper these days that only treated gays and lesbians as a matter of sensation.'

As for Hollywood, McKellen maintains it's still very difficult for a gay actor to be open about their sexuality. Speaking to afterelton.com in 2006 he said, 'My agent in London counselled me against coming out when I did and I'm sure that still happens in Hollywood. Yes, I'm sure the advice to young actors is, "Don't come out, [or] you'll never be a young film star playing romantic roles."'

McKellen continued: 'I was disappointed... when Tom Cruise took someone to court on the grounds that to even suggest or lie that he, Tom Cruise, had had gay sex experiences was detrimental to his career because he would no longer be convincing playing the sort of parts that he plays on film. That is such palpable nonsense. It shows a very innocent, ignorant view of what acting is and what an audience knows about actors.

'There is no confusion in the audience's mind when they see an actor playing a part. You might as well say that the point at which Tom Cruise got divorced and became a single man he could never in the future be convincing as a married man on film. It doesn't make sense. Or that an actor who wears a wig is not convincing because we all know he is bald. It really doesn't work like that. He should've been called on that. I'm not interested in whether Tom Cruise is gay or not. Whether he's lying or not is a matter none of us can judge. But that he should say that if he were thought to be gay, he could no longer ever be taken seriously playing heterosexual parts, it doesn't work like that. Otherwise, I wouldn't keep playing all these heterosexual parts I keep getting offered.'

GUS VAN SANT
Writer/Director
1952–

Gus Van Sant's poetic yet clear-eyed excursions through America's seamy, skid-row underbelly have yielded some of the more potent independent films of the late 1980s and early 90s. 'I guess I'm interested in sociopathic people,' he has stated, 'in life and in my movies.' With art-school training in painting as well as film, Van Sant worked in commercials before entering the film industry by making small personal films that played the festival circuit, notably in highbrow gay and lesbian venues. Openly gay, he has dealt unflinchingly with homosexual and other marginalised subcultures without being particularly concerned about providing positive role models.

Van Sant's first feature, *Mala Noche* (1986), is a dreamy black-and-white rumination on the doomed relationship between a teen Mexican migrant worker and a liquor-store clerk. Made for about $25,000, it won a Los Angeles Film Critics Award as the best independent/experimental film of 1987.

Drugstore Cowboy (1989) chronicles the exploits of a rootless druggie (Matt Dillon) and his 'crew' who survive by robbing West Coast pharmacies. Lyrically shot, and boasting superb performances from Dillon and co-star Kelly Lynch, the film marked Van Sant as a director of considerable promise.

Van Sant's 1991 feature, *My Own Private Idaho*, based on his first original screenplay, starred River Phoenix as a narcoleptic male prostitute whose search for home and family takes him from Portland, Oregon, to such disparate locales as Idaho and Italy. Keanu Reeves plays his well-heeled companion of the streets and son of the local mayor.

After *Idaho*, the trades buzzed that Van Sant would make his Hollywood studio debut as the director of *The Mayor of Castro Street*, based on Randy Shilts' book about San Francisco's assassinated, openly gay city supervisor Harvey Milk. Oliver Stone was set to produce and Robin Williams reportedly wanted the lead. The project eventually fell apart due to the creative differences between Van Sant and Stone over the screenplay.

Van Sant returned to familiar territory – another indie road picture centring on an outsider (budgeted at $7.5 million), *Even Cowgirls Get the Blues* (1994), adapted from Tom Robbins' 1976 cult novel about a young woman whose outsized thumbs make her a formidable hitchhiker.

Next came Van Sant's *To Die For* (1995), his first major studio project. The film was inspired by the true story of a high-school teacher who seduced her teenage lover into murdering her husband. A modest commercial success, it was a critical hit for everyone involved, particularly its star Nicole Kidman who portrayed the media-obsessed careerist who romances Joaquin Phoenix into murdering Matt Dillon.

That same year, Van Sant served as executive producer on one of the more controversial films of 1995 – Larry Clark's *Kids*, a 'vérité'-styled drama about the sex and drug habits of a group of middle-class Manhattan teens. Some found the work profound, while others found it profoundly troubling for its 'exploitive' use of young actors.

As a follow-up, Van Sant returned to the director's chair to make *Good Will Hunting* (1997), about an underachiever (Matt Damon) on the road to self-destruction who finds unlikely aid from several people, including a therapist (Robin Williams) and his best friend (Ben Affleck). Written by Damon and Affleck, it's well crafted, if somewhat predictable.

The feature's success, however, moved Van Sant further toward mainstream Hollywood, and with new-found clout he opted to direct a shot-by-shot 1998 remake of Alfred Hitchcock's 1960 classic *Psycho*, a curious career move which left film purists fuming and audiences unmoved.

Van Sant achieved some slight redemption with his next effort, *Finding Forrester* (2000), a conventional but mostly effective tale (despite a white patriarchal undercurrent) in which a reclusive author (Sean Connery) mentors an inner-city poetry prodigy (Rob Brown).

Returning left of centre, Van Sant re-teamed with Matt Damon and Ben Affleck's brother Casey, who co-wrote and starred in *Gerry* (2002), a highly unusual film in which two young men named Gerry are stranded and hopelessly lost during a hiking expedition. It put Van Sant squarely back on the road to more personalised and experimental filmmaking.

The arresting and remarkable *Elephant* (2003) is an abstract exploration of the contrast between banality and violence in American life, and stubbornly refuses to embrace any sort of conventional narrative. Named for the aphorism about the problematic pachyderm in the living room that's so big that it goes ignored, the star-less *Elephant* follows students at a Portland high school until violence erupts, delivering Van Sant's take on the murders that took place at Columbine High School. It earned Van Sant the Palme d'Or at the Cannes Film Festival, as well as a Best Director award and the Cinema Prize of the French National Education System.

More recently, Van Sant made *Last Days* (2005), a Seattle-set, rock 'n' roll drama about a musician whose life and career is reminiscent of Kurt Cobain's, and then *Paranoid Park* (2007) based on a novel by Blake Nelson and set in and around an infamous Portland skate park where a teenage boarder accidentally kills a security guard. The elliptical narrative of *Paranoid Park* was enhanced by an amazing sound mix, excellent skate scenes and impressive cinematography by Christopher Doyle. The young cast was recruited on MySpace and the film deservedly won the special 60th Anniversary Prize at Cannes.

Van Sant's latest film to go into production, *Milk* (2008) is about Harvey Milk, the San Francisco supervisor and first openly gay, elected official in the US, who was assassinated in 1977. Bryan Singer had been developing his own Harvey Milk project, working with his *Usual Suspects* writing partner Christopher McQuarrie, but in the end, Van Sant got there first, signing Sean Penn for the title role.

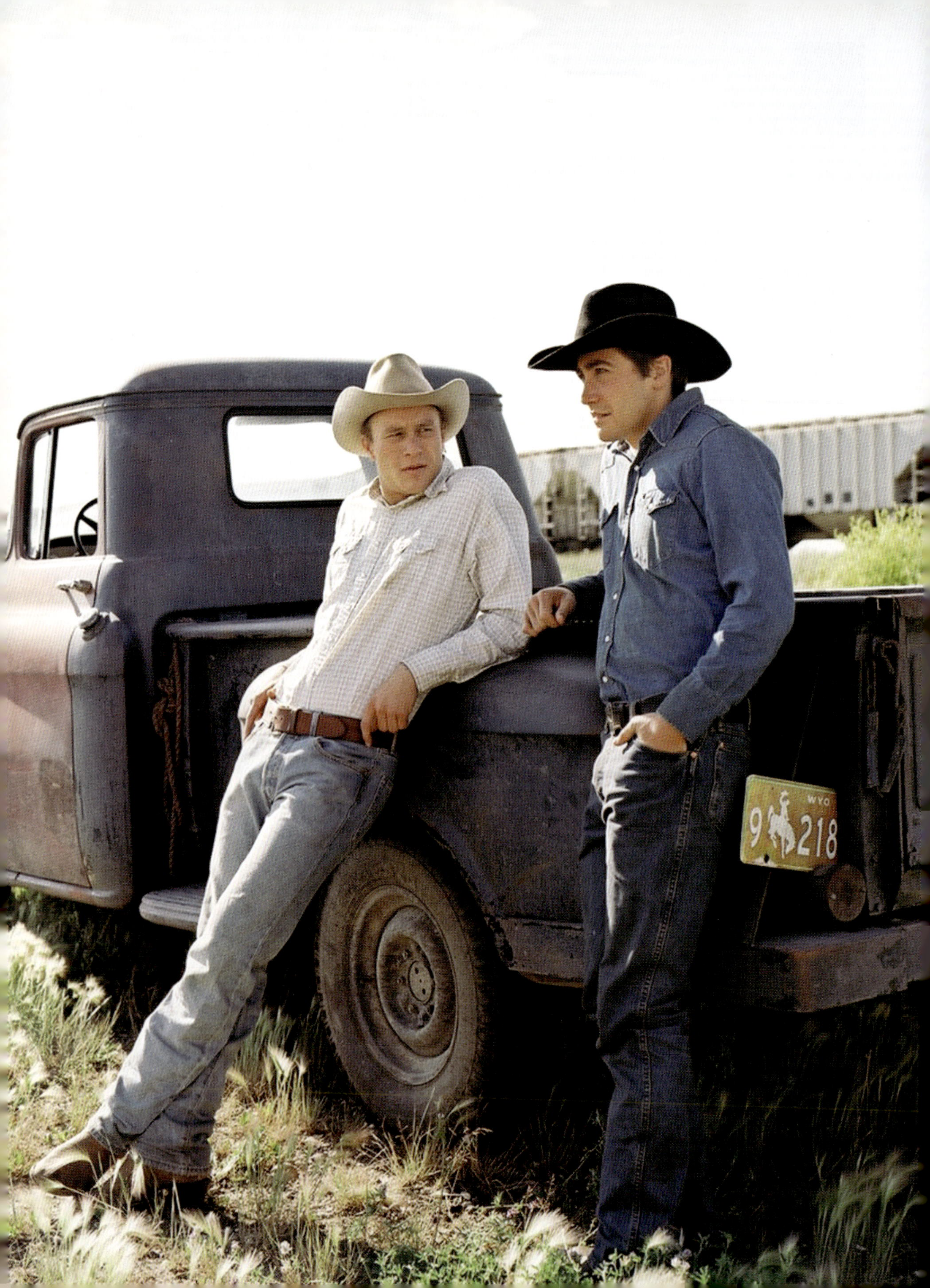
WYO
9 218

HOLLYWOOD GOES GAY – 2000s

'People get fucked up working at K-Mart. People get fucked up working in Hollywood. It's called the adult film industry. If you're going to work in it, you'd better be an adult.'

Silver in *The Fluffer*

Although the 1990s ended on a high note with quality films such as *Gods and Monsters* (1998) and *Beefcake* (1998), they were still released amongst a host of dubious sit-com-style gay comedies. Unfortunately, early into the new millennium, many gay filmmakers were still partying like it was 1999, and along came a load more 'heartwarming' gay-life-is-a-blast pics.

The decade began with *The Broken Hearts Club* (2000), another sunny light comedy about a group of guys who were all friends and just happened to be gay. Marketed as a 'gay *Big Chill*' or a 'gay *Diner*', it was clear from the outset that originality would not be its selling point. It was, however, talked up at Sundance because of the way the film apparently played down gay 'issues'. And there were lots more equal-opportunity offenders early on in the decade.

All Over the Guy (2001) was one dreadful entry in the glut of gay romantic comedies. *Under One Roof* (2001) was another, but with a more erotic slant, that revolved around a Chinese-American mama's boy who wants 'to dip his chopstick in the rice bowl' of a lanky Indiana slacker boy. *Police Academy*-star Steve Guttenberg appeared in the long-awaited but disappointing film adaptation of gay writer James Kirkwood's dark comedy, *P.S. Your Cat is Dead* (2002), while ageing British actor Roger Moore popped up in another American gay-themed 'comedy', *Boat Trip* (2002), playing a flamboyant gay man who propositions Cuba Gooding Jr and Horatio Sanz, two straight men looking for romance who are mistakenly booked on to a gay cruise. Talking about the movie, Moore recently admitted: 'I sort of went back into the

Heath Ledger and Jake Gyllenhaal in *Brokeback Mountain*

closet to do it. Half the actors I've worked with have been gay while pretending that they weren't – so I imagined I was them.'

Nevertheless, we all know subtle and sensitive films about sexual politics are not usually made in Hollywood and *Boat Trip* was the usual garish, often offensive, adult comedy. The negativity is pretty constant, with gay men portrayed in the usual, stereotypical manner, and we see a variety of cross-dressers, old queens, men in dog collars, and Gooding mincing about, screeching noisily and donning drag for the cabaret; all of which only feeds into the film's underlying homophobia.

Friends and Family (2002) was another one-joke comedy, although not as negative as *Boat Trip*, about a gay couple who are also working as hit men for the Mafia. Then came the soap-opera schlock of *200 American* (2003), about an advertising executive who falls for a hustler, and *Danny in the Sky* (2003), yet another eye-candy comedy that boasts a story about a pretty boy who wants to be a model and escape from his gay dad, only to end up a stripper at gay club. A year later came *Eating Out* (2004), a 'screwball comedy' about a hunky straight guy pretending he's gay to get a date with a woman who only likes to hang out with gay men. The twisted, reunion rom-com *Adam & Steve* (2006) followed, and then came *Another Gay Movie* (2006), a spoof about four high-school graduates' mission to lose their anal virginity any way they can. A kind of gay *American Pie* or *Porky*'s, it featured all the toilet humour and crass behaviour to boot. Very un-PC, with pure, unadulterated, in-your-face gay jokes from start to finish, it was popular because of its raunchy scenes and gorgeous cast.

More recently, 2007 saw the release of Adam Sandler's comedy film, *I Now Pronounce You Chuck and Larry*, the latest in this long line of gay-themed 'wacky' mainstream comedies, about two, semi-homophobic firefighters pretending to be a gay couple to receive partnership benefits. A massive international hit, in the US the film knocked *Harry Potter and the Order of the Phoenix* from the number-one spot at the box office. But the movie is packed full of the usual Adam Sandler, *Wedding Crasher*-type fat jokes and crass comedy.

Sandler's co-star Kevin James defended the film, telling WENN: 'We screened it for gay-rights group GLAAD (the Gay & Lesbian Alliance Against Defamation) because we certainly didn't want to offend anybody in any way.

The main reason of this movie is really just to make people laugh and that's all we wanted to do. These guys are idiots in a way. They learn tolerance, what it's about, and what happens when they have to pretend to be this way. That's basically it, but we're certainly not trying to tell people how to live their lives in any way, shape, or form.'

In reality, people should expect crass and offensive comedy from Sandler. Quite simply, it's what he does. After delivering 90 minutes of gay stereotypes, *I Now Pronounce You Chuck and Larry* tries to turn itself around into a full defence of gay rights and an applause of gay culture by the end, even boasting appearances by Lance Bass and Richard Chamberlain, but by this point it's all far too late. The film spends too much time revelling in the prejudice and ignorance of its small-minded characters, and the closing scenes in support of gay rights are simply designed to undermine much of the preceading homophobic bigotry and offer the film moral redemption.

Whatever the case, to rain on Sandler's parade, the makers of *Chuck and Larry* were accused of plagiarism by the producers of Australian film *Strange Bedfellows* (2004), who thought the plot of *Chuck and Larry* was all too familiar. Shana Levine, one of the producers of the Aussie film, said legal action was being considered after expert analysis of the two scripts found striking similarities. *Strange Bedfellows*, starring Paul 'Crocodile Dundee' Hogan and Michael Caton, was a comedy about a widowed businessman who weds his widowed friend in order to take advantage of new tax breaks. It was certainly very similar and had the same matey vibe running throughout, the same rather corny, clichéd comedy and the same warm undercurrent, which crept up on the audience at the end.

By the end of 2007, it was quite satisfying to hear the nominations for the worst films of the year announced. Not surprisingly, *Chuck and Larry* made it to the Golden Raspberry Awards shortlist, nominated in eight categories including Worst Film and Worst Actor (Adam Sandler).

But away from these inconsequential fluffy movies, some filmmakers were getting down to the nitty-gritty. As the new millennium lit the horizon in a glow of possibility, more subtle, cutting-edge works began to emerge. Everything from *Punks* (2000), Patrick-Ian Polk's comedy of life among African-American gay men; *Before Night Falls* (2000), Julian Schnabel's biopic of the late gay Cuban author Reinaldo Arenas; Curtis Hanson's *Wonder Boys*

AUNTY: 'What are you drinking?'

SEAN: 'Bourbon and coke'

AUNTY: 'The very drink Tallula cried out for on her deathbed!'

Aunty and Sean in *The Fluffer*

(2000), with Robert Downey Jr bedding Tobey Maguire; *By Hook Or By Crook* (2001), Harry Dodge and Silas Howard's lesbian/transgender buddy film; and Moises Kaufman's *The Laramie Project* (2001) which recounted the horrific 1998 bashing death of young gay man Matthew Shepard in the small Wyoming community, dubbed the 'hate capital of America.'

In fact, *The Laramie Project* was particularly groundbreaking in its style, mixing real news reports with actors portraying friends, family, cops, killers and other Laramie residents in their own words. Kaufman's film followed Matthew's visit to a local bar, his kidnap and beating, the discovery of him tied to a fence, his death and funeral, and the trial of his killers. It was a harrowing, moving and hugely important monument to a dark day in recent history that we should never forget.

Michael Cuesta's *L.I.E.* was another quality release. An unsensationalised drama of intergenerational gay love, it emerged a critical winner at Sundance in 2001. The film had Brian Cox in the role of Big John Harrigan, a guy who feels the love that dares not speak its name, but expresses it by seeking out adolescents and bringing them back to his pad. But John is an even-tempered, funny, robust old man who actually listens to the kids' problems (as opposed to their parents and friends, who are too caught up in the high-wire act of their own confused lives). He'll have sex-for-pay with them only after an elaborate courtship, charming them with temptations from the grown-up world. Undoubtedly a powerful, intensely moving drama, Brian Cox, speaking on its release, was right to be proud to be part of it: 'It's a rites-of-passage story that any 15-year-old would identify with,' he explained. 'It's about sexual awakening and whether one is gay or straight. This film is meant to unsettle and, I think, that is what drama at its best does. At its best, it throws questions at you. At its best, it puts things into the ring for debate. That's why I am very proud of this film.'

Based on a play by Daniel Reitz, *Urbania* (2000) was another gay-interest gem discovered at Sundance. Jon Shear's dark psychological thriller had a wonderful sense of style and toyed with audience expectations, treading the thin and often ambiguous line between the real and imagined. The main storyline centres on Charlie (Dan Futterman), a gay man who has recently suffered through the traumatic end to a meaningful relationship. Charlie pines for his ex, making rambling, pleading phone calls to answering machines

> 'I think you are just like James Bond except James Bond doesn't go around blowing boys.'
>
> **Howie in *L.I.E.***

and languishing in his now-too-big bed, his hand lingering on the empty pillow beside him. He roams the rainy downtown streets encountering urban legends come to life everywhere, from the lady who microwaves her poodle to the man who gets a nasty surprise the morning after a one-night-stand. In *Urbania*, it's difficult to tell the truth from sorrowful, wishful-thinking fantasy. And that's probably the point.

Big Eden (2000) wasn't anywhere near as dark as *Urbania* but it attracted as much attention, winning the audience awards at just about every gay and lesbian film festival there is. Thomas Bezucha's film cast Arye Gross as Henry, an artist living in New York but still carrying a torch for the guy he had a crush on in high school. When his grandfather has a stroke, Henry returns to his Montana hometown, Big Eden, where he rediscovers friends he hasn't seen in years. His high-school crush has since married, had children and divorced – and seems ready to take some very different steps with his life.

Eric Schweig and Arye Gross in *Big Eden* (2001)

Writer-director Bezucha made sure he deviated from the elements that typically punctuate gay films: 'The thing that infuriates me or is offensive to me about the attitudes of distributors or the industry is they so underestimate the breadth of gay experience and the types of films gay people want to see about themselves. That was really important to me in terms of making this film – gay people come in all shapes, all sizes, all colours. If you looked at the history of gay cinema in the last few years you wouldn't know that. You'd think everybody was about 20 years old and goes to the gym three times a week. I really wanted to reverse that notion and see the kinds of people I know on the screen – people who are close to their families, or go to church, or work with children and have relationships with straight people – to show that gay people are *just* like everybody else.'

Bezucha succeeded in his mission to tell a more true-to-life gay story. His uniquely American fable is more than just a crowd-pleaser with pretty mountain location scenery – it's a genuinely funny and moving romantic comedy, without a single syrupy moment.

The Fluffer (2001) was another American indie that got people talking. A triangular story of obsessive love set against the backdrop of the adult-video industry, the film featured cameos from a number of figures in the adult-entertainment industry, including Ron Jeremy, Chi Chi LaRue, Karen Dior,

Scott Gurney in *The Fluffer* (2002)

HOLLYWOOD GOES GAY – 2000s **157**

Zach Richards, Derek Cameron, Chad Donovan, Thomas Lloyd, Jim Steel and Cole Tucker.

Meanwhile, John Cameron Mitchell's transsexual rock musical *Hedwig and the Angry Inch* (2001) appeared with a cult status already established. Beginning life in 1997 as an Off-Broadway musical, *Hedwig* tells the story of an East German boy named Hansel who grows up gay, falls in love with a US master sergeant and wants to go to America with him. The master sergeant explains that, as Hansel, that will be impossible, but if the lad undergoes a sex-change operation, they can get married and then the passport will be no problem ('To walk away, you gotta leave something behind'). Filmed with ferocious energy, it was no surprise when the movie quickly spawned a small *Rocky Horror*-like cult following, with midnight screenings, or 'shadowcasts', where fans dress up as the characters and sometimes act out the dialogue or talk back to the screen.

Another quirky release came in the form of a 'mockumentary', *Showboy* (2002), with cameos by Whoopi Goldberg, Siegfried & Roy, Alan Ball and the cast of the television series *Six Feet Under*. The movie centres around a closeted guy called Christian Taylor who is talked into being the subject of a British television documentary series about English writers working in Hollywood. It won Best Directorial Debut at the British Independent Film Awards and Best Film at the Milan International Film Festival.

Everett Lewis's 2002 *Luster*, a film about the lives of a group of friends in the queer punk scene, impressed many filmgoers, as did Brad Fraser's *Leaving Metropolis*, a Canadian drama about a gay man and a married heterosexual man who fall in love.

Happy Birthday (2002) was another indie drama of intense poignancy and emotional power that won praise from critics and audiences. Taking some ensemble tips from Robert Altman, Yen Tan's film traces the lives of five people who share the same summer birthday. Jim, a gay, overweight telemarketer (for a weight-loss programme) faces his self-esteem issues. Ron is a minister who preaches about conversion but practises watching gay porn whenever he can. Javed, living in the US with a gay-porn actor, faces deportation as a Pakistani and condemnation from his Islamic family. Kelly, a young lesbian, weathers a breakup with her lover and considers an earlier unrequited love. And Tracy, an Asian lesbian, goes back in the closet when her mother visits.

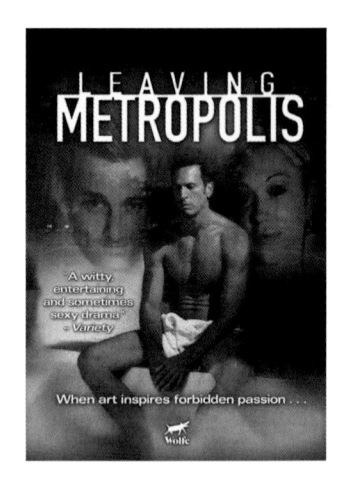

Shot on DV, Tan's black-and-white movie is remarkably filmic, much of it framed in stark, wide shots. It was different because it successfully captured a diverse group of people at various stages of their gay lives in a way that many gay films have not been able to accomplish.

Also appearing in 2002 was acclaimed director Todd Haynes' most mainstream movie to date, *Far From Heaven*, for which he re-created a 1950s weepie, depicting a gay man coming to terms with his sexuality. The film, starring Julianne Moore and Dennis Quaid, was nominated for four Academy Awards and over a hundred other major awards around the world. It won seventy-one.

Stephen Daldry's *The Hours* (2002) was also nominated for lots of Oscars. Based on the novel of the same name by out, gay author Michael Cunningham, the film explored the parallel lives of three women from different eras (played beautifully by Nicole Kidman, Julianne Moore and Meryl Streep), all in some way dealing with underlying suppressed homosexuality. Most praise was heaped upon Kidman for her role as Virginia Woolf, who is in the middle of writing her book *Mrs Dalloway* in 1923 England, coming to the realisation of her lesbianism and fighting her pure despair of life. Kidman walked away with the Best Actress Oscar. The film's second strand is set in 1951 Los Angeles where Laura Brown (Julianne Moore), a pregnant housewife, is planning for her husband's birthday, but is preoccupied with reading Woolf's novel. Meanwhile, in 2001 New York, Clarissa Vaughn (Meryl Streep) is a lesbian publisher planning an award party for her friend, an author dying of AIDS (Ed Harris, nominated for Best Actor in a Supporting Role). Taking place over one day, all three stories are interconnected through *Mrs Dalloway*: one is writing it, one is reading it and one is living it.

In 2003, Christopher Munch tackled a rather difficult subject area in his movie *Harry and Max*, about two brothers who are also lovers. Harry is a 23-year-old, ex-boy-band member whose solo career is drying up while Max is his 16-year-old brother whose music career is on the rise. A lot of hype surrounded the film, which premiered at Sundance, mainly because the two main characters are supposedly based on Nick Carter of the Backstreet Boys and his brother Aaron Carter, though this was never confirmed or denied by the film's makers. Unfortunately, what could have been a serious, interesting look at a controversial subject turned out to be so amateurish and full of psychobabble, it was utterly disappointing.

Also in 2003, playwright Tony Kushner adapted his political epic *Angels in America*, about the impact of AIDS on the gay community, for the quality TV network HBO. The result was one of the most thought-provoking, visually beautiful pieces of work ever seen. The drama encompasses so much: it's a story about loneliness, friendship and family, biological and chosen; about sexual, racial, religious, ethnic and political identity; about life in the Reagan era and living with – and dying from – AIDS. Tony Kushner's writing is, as always, exceptional, and Mike Nichols' direction impeccable. There are eight flawless principal performances, and a Michelangelo-like team of production designers. Originally shown as a miniseries on American television, *Angels in America* has subsequently played at festivals as an epic, continuous piece. On DVD, the miniseries' episodes are divided into chapters which can be watched continuously without interruption.

Rodney Evans' *Brother to Brother* (2004) was another interesting work, a drama about the struggle of being young, black and gay. An ambitious film, comparing and contrasting post-millennial gay angst in the black community with the audacious sensibilities of the Harlem Renaissance, it seemed to have the same urgency of those early 90s, new queer movies. With a bigger budget and a sharper focus, it might have fared better.

Meanwhile, *Latter Days* (2004), a rather unique, unexpected love story between a West Hollywood party boy and a closeted, gay Mormon missionary, was sweet and sexy but more ambitious than most of the early-2000s fluffy romance flicks, as was Miles Swain's epic romance *The Trip* (2004).

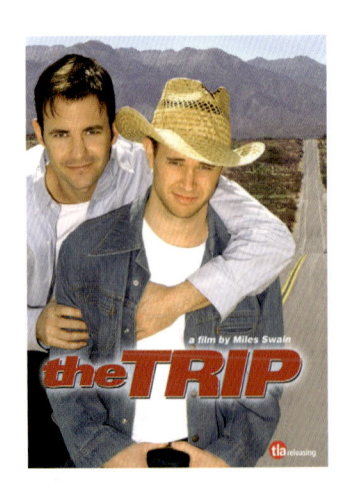

The Trip told the love story of two very different gay people – an activist called Tommy and a closeted journalist called Alan – over a 30-year span, from the 60s to the 80s. Whereas most recent gay rom-coms have had little substance, *The Trip* had attitude and took a few more risks. Interspersed among the scenes are documentary sequences of the highlights and lowlights of the gay-rights movement: Harvey Milk's rise and fall, Anita Bryant's infamous anti-gay crusade, Gay Liberation and AIDS. It's the kind of gay social history that has rarely been attempted in film.

A 'gay party culture' movie seemed to emerge in the new millennium too, with various films set in the sex-and-pecs, music-and-steroid world of the party scene – where drugs flow and inhibitions fall away on the sweaty dance floor. Circuit parties are usually held in major cities like Los Angeles and Miami, or resort destinations such as Fire Island and Palm Spings, attracting thousands of people. Created in the 1990s, ostensibly as fundraisers for gay and AIDS organisations, in time these parties took on their own identities as weekend-long extravaganzas and gay men would travel from one to the next, creating their own subculture. Dirk Shafer's *Circuit* (2001) was a sizzling saga of life inside this sexy and dangerously seductive area of the gay world. With actual circuit-party footage and mounds of glistening and chiselled flesh, the pulsating film focused on a character called John, a gay Midwestern policeman who has moved to Los Angeles to experience the freedom that circuit parties offer. Guided by a beautiful but ageing hustler who lives only for his next high, John realises that although many find pleasure, escape and healthy recreation in this fast-paced world, others are not so lucky. Passionate about the filmic potential of circuit parties, Dirk Shafer knew the world intimately: 'Because circuit parties started out as AIDS fundraisers, I knew it was a controversial, provocative subject matter to depict on film. I wanted to show both sides of the circuit phenomenon – the light and the dark side. When Gregory Hinton and I developed the story, we initially aspired for the edge of *Boogie Nights* and *Trainspotting*. Later we decided that too strident a portrayal wasn't fair to the majority of gay men who attended. Circuit parties can be many things to many people, as the film depicts…'

The key to the success of *Circuit* was the filmmakers' ability to film at actual circuit parties, opening the movie up to some thrilling visuals. A year after *Circuit* premiered, documentary makers Stewart Halpern and Lenid Rolov went a step further with their true-life film *When Boys Fly* (2002), which followed a group of men to the Palm Springs White Party. After a series of auditions, four men were selected who had varying degrees of experience in the circuit. The cameras then followed them and their friends as they experienced the full range of the scene's highs and lows, from creating friendships to suffering drug overdoses. The groundbreaking film offered a true insider's view of a world that few actually see.

Both *Circuit* and *When Boys Fly* dared to show what modern gay life is all about, warts and all, and was a welcome change from all the feel-good, romantic fantasies and love stories that would never happen in a million years.

> 'Greetings, Prophet! The great work begins! The Messenger has arrived!'
>
> **The Angel in *Angels in America***

> 'I have sex with men. But unlike nearly every other man of whom this is true, I bring the guy I'm screwing to the White House and President Reagan smiles at us and shakes his hand.'
>
> Roy Cohn in
> **Angels in America**

The filmmakers responsible for *Circuit* and *When Boys Fly* were telling real stories. They were trying to tell the *truth*.

In Britain, it was left to television dramatists to come up with realistic depictions of the current UK, gay, party-hard lifestyle. Rikki Beadle-Blair's *Metrosexuality* (2001) was a hip, energetic series that offered up a vivid take on the sexual and mating dilemmas of today. Meanwhile, Russell T Davies's second series of *Queer as Folk* (2000) continued a story more important than most on our movie screens, that of Stuart and Vince, two Canal Street regulars just starting to think about where their lives may be going. The excellent follow-up to Davies's original landmark series was darker, had more of an edge and seemed even more grounded in the realities of modern gay life than the earlier episodes. *Queer as Folk 2* spoke more emotional truth than any recent narrative film about gay life and, if the two-parter is watched back to back, it stands alone as a feature of its own.

Another film based around party culture saw Macaulay Culkin's return to the screen after a nine-year absence. In *Party Monster* (2003), he played fresh-faced Michael Alig, the real-life gay king of New York's 'Club Kids', a group of young, costumed, party-obsessed carousers who ruled the city's nightlife in the late 80s and early 90s. The film explored how Alig rose to fame, launched his own magazine and music label, then fell into a drug-fuelled downspin and eventually murdered his live-in dope dealer.

As well as fact-based thrillers, various documentaries were made during this decade: *Southern Comfort* (2000), an account of love and death among trans people; *Trembling Before G-d* (2001), which detailed stories of lesbian and gay Orthodox and Hasidic Jews; *The Cockettes* (2001), a lively history of the seminal San Francisco performers; and *Andrew and Jeremy Get Married* (2004), an intimate portrait of two Englishmen from vastly different social backgrounds dealing with the 'ups and downs' of their eccentric relationship.

This decade also saw some notable lesbian-interest films. Set in Paris and starring two of France's most exciting new actresses, *The Girl* (2000) was a gorgeously realised, modern *film noir*, following a spiralling affair between the film's narrator – a beautiful painter (Agathe de la Boulaye) – and a nightclub singer who she calls The Girl (Claire Keim). Sande Zeig's film was a fascinating look at obsessive love, as was Lea Pool's *Lost and Delirious* (2001), a story about the friendship of three schoolgirls and how they experience life and love together at a private college. Based on the novel *The Wives of Bath* by Susan Swan, the story is about a love deeper than sexuality; it's about the quest for real, true love, a theme which is obviously close to the director's heart.

Benzina (2001) was another moody, modern, lesbian *film noir*, following the story of two lovers living in a remote petrol station, with their blissful lives giving way to desperation and the need to escape. While *Benzina* was a kind of *Thelma & Louise* meets *Bound*, Sharon Ferranti's *Make a Wish* (2002), on the other hand, was more *Friday the 13th*. In the tradition of classic slasher films, this movie revolved around a group of lesbian ex-lovers camping in Texas and had all the blood, gore and suspense you'd expect in a horror movie.

By far the most mainstream and successful lesbian-interest movie, however, came in the Hollywood studio-produced *Kissing Jessica Stein* (2002), a sharp rom-com about two women so fed up with the dating scene that they decide to go out with each other. It's not really about lesbian lifestyles but it's a fairly witty take on change, risk and romance. Let down slightly by its general sit-com tone, like *Friends* and *Will & Grace* it's set in a glossy New York world; but the film had its merits and came with the same feel-good factor as other female-focussed dramas such as *Fried Green Tomatoes* (1991) and *The Joy Luck Club* (1993). Interestingly, the two women who starred in *Kissing Jessica Stein* (Jennifer Westfeldt and Heather Juergensen) also wrote the screenplay.

Another romantic, lesbian-themed comedy of the fluffiest kind was *Puccini for Beginners* (2005), Maria Maggenti's long-awaited follow-up to her 1995 indie hit *The Incredibly True Adventures of Two Girls in Love*. Once again a comedy set in Manhattan, it was about a neurotic writer who has simultaneous affairs with the male and female halves of a recently split couple. Like *Kissing Jessica Stein*, there was nothing particularly original going on, and the laughs were often minor. Borrowing from the devices of vintage Woody Allen, the result was more a cutesy, sitcomised jaunt through the Big Apple, *L-Word* style.

Maria Maggenti's ***Puccini for Beginners*** (2005)

More recently, *The Gymnast* (2007) was a runaway hit on the LGBT festival circuit, capturing the Jury Award for Best Feature at New York's NewFest, the Audience Award for Best Feature at Frameline (San Francisco's queer

Ned Farr's *The Gymnast* (2007)

film festival) and the Grand Jury Award at Outfest in Los Angeles. In fact this lesbian-interest movie – which can be enjoyed by anyone – was the winner of more than 20 awards at gay (and straight) film festivals worldwide. The feature-length directorial debut from Ned Farr, it's the story of 40-something Jane (Dreya Weber of *Lovely and Amazing*), who's trapped in a lifeless marriage, working as a massage therapist and forever lamenting an accident which nixed her potential as an Olympic hopeful. That is, until she begins training for a Vegas-style revue with a beautiful Korean gymnast named Serena (Addie Yungmee). With standing ovations from most audiences, as the emotional final scenes play out over the end credits, it's clear that *The Gymnast* has been simply one of the best, and most well-received, lesbian-interest movies of recent years.

British cinema began the decade with some interesting gay-themed movies. Originally made by the Scottish Television Network, *Forgive and Forget* (2000) was a love-triangle drama that finally emerged as a full-length theatrical release. Starring Brit-packers John Simm, Laura Fraser, Steve John Shepherd and Meera Syal, the story centred around long-time best friends David (Shepherd) and Theo (Simm) who find their relationship strained when Theo falls for a woman and moves in with her. David is forced to face his biggest secret – he's gay.

Forgive and Forget played out its story without relying on major stereotypes (here, the gay guy is a plasterer), which made it all the more powerful; a film which both gay and straight audiences could relate to.

Movies set in the criminal underworld have invariably been suffused with homoeroticism and *Endgame* (2000) was no exception. A moody, stylish and sex-charged British thriller, it starred Daniel Newman as Tom, a rent boy kept in style by sado-masochistic gangster George Norris (Mark McGann). Sucked down into a nasty scheme involving drugs, money and protection by Norris's connection with a crooked gay cop Dunston (John Benfield), things turn nasty rather quickly for Tom in Gary Wicks' fast-paced thriller. With a striking soundtrack and excellent acting, *Endgame* is one of the better gay gangster thrillers released in the last decade.

A rent-boy plot strand also featured in *A.K.A* (2002). Set in Thatcher's Britain, it was the gripping story of Dean (Matthew Leitch), a shy, working-class lad from Romford, kicked out by his abusive father. The film, based on a

> 'We won't die secret deaths anymore. The world only spins forward. We will be citizens. The time has come.'
>
> Prior Walter in *Angels in America*

true story, followed Dean's move to London and a new life of deception and duplicity, rent boys, toffs, artists, Champagne and coke. Duncan Roy's film was a mesmerising study of the British class system, a modern day *Pygmalion*. It also garnered the director a BAFTA nomination.

Meanwhile, from Ireland, came *Cowboys and Angels* (2003), a drama about life in the big city, centred around gay boy and straight boy, though here it's all out in the open. The movie has Shane (Michael Legge), a shy civil-service worker, moving into a Limerick apartment with Vincent (Alan Leech), a gay fashion-school student who goes out to clubs and picks up guys on a regular basis. Vincent goes all Queer Eye on his awkward flatmate, trying to help him adapt to his new surroundings, starting with a makeover. Another film that should be praised for its non-issue treatment of sexuality, *Cowboys and Angels* took an important step towards movies where 'straight' and 'gay' don't matter so much as 'relationships'.

Also from Ireland, in 2003, came a rather different approach to a gay-themed movie. Offensively funny, politically incorrect and in your face, *9 Dead Gay Guys* told the story of Kenny (Glenn Mulhern) and Byron (Brendan Mackey), two Irish lads who'd moved to London in a bid to hit the big time. But the straight mates end up hustling for beer money at the local gay pub and before the end of the film there are nine dead locals. A dark comedy in the John Waters tradition, there's little to offend; connecting with both gay and straight audiences, it's a good example of a crossover movie.

In Canada, *Leaving Metropolis* (2002), adapted from his stage play *Poor Superman*, marked the directorial debut of screenwriter Brad Fraser. It's the story of David (Troy Ruptash), a successful gay artist who falls in love with a married 'straight' guy. Within this erotic exploration of the fluid nature of sexuality and gender identity, *Leaving Metropolis* features a scene-stealing performance by Thom Allison as David's transgendered, HIV-positive friend and roommate Shannon. The film fared well at festivals around the world.

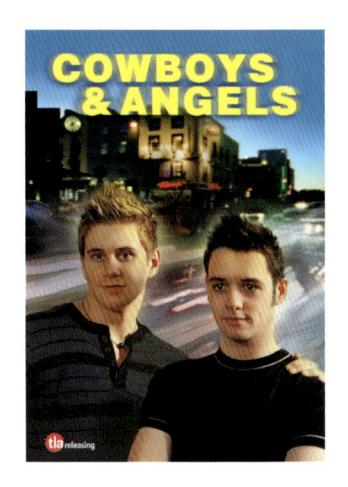

Whole New Thing (2005), also from Canada, was the winner of 11 awards at lesbian and gay film festivals around the world. Set in a remote part of Nova Scotia, it's a funny, intelligent take on teenage sexuality, centring around 13-year-old Emerson (Aaron Webber), home-tutored all his life by his hippie parents and now finding it hard to fit in at his local high school. An openly gay English teacher (Daniel McIvor) tries to give the boy some helpful advice, but is totally unprepared for a daring (and dangerous) response. Despite the subject matter, director Amnon Buchbinder made a film of admirable purity and one full of heartache.

Thailand produced a couple of intriguing gay-interest movies in the early part of the decade. *Iron Ladies* (2001) was a lively and often hilarious comedy about an all-gay volleyball team who, against all odds, make it to the national championships against increasing opposition. Queeny and camp, an uplifting gay classic, the film would be almost too heartwarming if it weren't a true story. The largest-grossing Thai film of all time, it was no surprise when director Youngyooth Thongkongthun recently made a sequel about how the characters in *Iron Ladies* met, and how they would later reunite for another volleyball tournament.

Also from Thailand came *Beautiful Boxer* (2003), a warm, funny, action-packed film about the experience of being transgender, based on the true story of Nong Toom (Asanee Suwan), a poor boy from rural Thailand whose only hope of raising the money to pay for a sex-change operation was to enter the ring as a professional kickboxer. He subsequently won fight after fight, humiliating his macho opponents in the process.

South Korea has only recently taken homosexuality off its list of 'unacceptable social acts', and soon after this conservative country picked a gay-themed production as its Foreign Language Film submission for the Oscars. *King and Clown* (2005) was a surprise hit in South Korea, selling over 12 million tickets. Lee Joon-ik's film is set in the court of a mad king and centres around a love triangle involving an attractive young jester.

Staying with Asian cinema, *The Blossoming of Maximo Oliveros* (2006) was a great film from the Philippines by first-time director Auraeus Solito. Winning the 2006 Teddy award at the Berlin Film Festival, Solito pulled off an assured and delightful work, set in the backstreets of Sampaloc, a poor district of Manila, with the lead character Maximo a self-confident 12-year-old boy with a penchant for dressing up and a clear sense of his own gay identity. Sashaying around the neighbourhood with no problems, helping his widowed father and two brothers run the household, Maximo soon falls in love with a young policeman, and the scene is set for a dramatic conflict of loyalties. This bittersweet tale of adolescence captured the hearts of audiences around the globe, managing to handle the notion of prepubescent sexual

Ekachai Uekrongtham's
Beautiful Boxer (2003)

Auraeus Solito's ***The Blossoming of Maximo Oliveros*** (2006)

anxiety with intelligence and unflinching honesty. Solito's film revealed a style of gay life rarely explored on the screen, and for that it was rightly praised.

Israel produced a winner too – in *Yossi & Jagger* (2003). Originally produced for Israeli cable TV, this tender drama tells the story of two Israeli soldiers who fall in love while serving in a remote military outpost on the Israeli-Lebanese border. Commanders Yossi (Ohad Knoller) and Jagger (Yehuda Levi, one of Israel's biggest heartthrobs) develop an intensely romantic connection, which is unknown to almost all of the base's other occupants and visitors. Although gays have been allowed to serve in the Israeli military since 1985, the film showed how homophobia still manages to permeate society on all levels. Featuring a stirring, heart-wrenching climax, *Yossi & Jagger* ended up a theatrical box-office smash at home and was one of the most emotionally moving gay films of 2003.

French cinema produced a string of gay-themed films this decade. *The Closet* (2001) was French farce in the tradition of Molière: a man pretends to be something he's not, people begin treating him differently, his lie escalates out of all proportion and comedy ensues. Frances Veber's film centred around François Pignon (Daniel Auteuil), a sweet-natured if slightly dull, divorced accountant who discovers that the best way to save his job and appear more interesting to his workmates is to pretend he's just come out of the closet – even though he's straight. Starring alongside Auteuil was Gérard Depardieu, playing the office manager, a rugby-playing brute, forced to swallow his homophobic views and explore his feminine side. Boasting some sharp satire, lampooning current political correctness, Veber's comedy played merry havoc with sexual politics and the social commentary built to an unashamedly feel-good climax.

Originally created for French television, Fabrice Cazaneuve's 2001 film *You'll Get Over It* (*A Cause D'un Garcon*) covered all the bases of a contemporary coming-out story: the lying, the betrayal, the shock and the locker-room homophobia. Set in a suburban Paris high school, the drama follows popular athlete, Vincent, who, constantly struggles with the secret of his homosexuality, runs off to Paris for a rendezvous with an older man, while back at home a strict code of silence is in effect. Unfortunately, Cazaneuve's film didn't really have anything unique to distinguish it from other coming-out or coming-of-age dramas.

Novelist-playwright Christophe Honore stepped into filmmaking in 2002 with *Close to Leo*, a sensitive and realistic look at a rural family coping with AIDS. Intriguingly, the story was told from the point of view of the curious and precocious 12-year-old Marcel (Lespert), who knows his family is keeping something from him. Honore's film is energetic and extremely honest, and contains some superb performances; it deservedly became an international festival classic.

Son Frère (2003) was Patrice Chéreau's film about two estranged brothers, brought together when one is diagnosed with a rare blood disease. Reunited, they go on to learn about life, love and acceptance, amidst all the taboos often tackled in many French art-house films: incest, homosexuality, suicide, infidelity and male nudity to name but a few. Adapted from a novel by Philip Besson, the film was an unsettling and unusual affair, consciously slow and sombre, in the director's words: 'A film about bodies, about the degradation of one body, about how one faces change.'

Patrice Chéreau's **Son Frère** (2003)

France seems to have embraced digital-video technology wholeheartedly, and *Ma Vie* (2002), by the directing duo Olivier Ducastel and Jacques Martineau, who made the gay road movie *Drôle de Felix*, is one example. Their film, about a teenager's sexual awakening, is structured like a video diary, with 16-year-old virgin Etienne (Jimmy Tavares) making confessions to the camera. The format isn't an easy one to get used to, as events take shape very subtly but the directors struck a careful balance between improvisation and directorial control, deliberately avoiding turning the film into a parody of 'reality TV'.

A few years later, Ducastel and Martineau's next gay-interest film *Cockles and Muscles* (2006) was much more light-hearted. A pleasurable comedy of love and sexual identity, it was a tale of the intricacies of modern French family life, set in a seaside resort on the Côte d'Azur. A holidaying family – husband and wife Marc and Béatrix, their teenage son Charly and his friend Martin – set themselves up for a string of sexual revelations, all served with oodles of saucy French humour and moral tolerance. The film culminated in what writers Olivier Ducastel and Jacques Martineau call a 'number of blissful unions and song', a truly spectacular camp ending. It was all good fun, though nowhere near as interesting as earlier Ducastel and Martineau films.

Also from France, and certainly worth a mention, is the documentary *Beyond Hatred*, released in 2006. French doc-maker Olivier Meyrou spent time with the family of François Chenu, a gay man murdered by three skinheads in 2002, and through conversations with François' parents, schoolteacher Jean-Paul and hospital caregiver Marie-Cecile Chenu, the family's chain-smoking female lawyer and others, the main facts of the case emerge. The point of the film was not to explore the homophobic attack itself, but its aftermath. The Chenu family's feelings are all documented, as they evolve from anger and despair toward an almost saintly recognition of how the killers' own deprived backgrounds led them to this horrible act. The father of one of the killers, an alcoholic who tried to destroy evidence, and another attacker's aunt, were also interviewed and treated with the same even-handed sympathy by the filmmakers, helmer Meyrou and his crew, who were invisible throughout, in classic vérité style, and refused to spell things out via explanatory subtitles or narration.

Most recently from France, Franck Guerin's *Un jour d'été* (*One Day in Summer*) (2007) tried too hard to cover a number of genres: a coming-of-age movie, a family drama, a tale about the loss of a friend. It's a rather unfocused muddle of a movie, about the death of a soccer goalie named Mickaël (Théo Frilet) and what subsequently happens to his small town. Other directors, such as Christophe Honore, have fared better (*Close to Leo* is just one example).

From Italy came an occasionally moving if ultimately familiar soap opera, *La Fate Ignoranti* (2001), a film from Italian-Turkish director Ferzan Ozpetek, who directed *Hamam: The Turkish Bath* (1997). The film concerned a man's secret gay life uncovered by his grieving widow and, although it was quite refreshing, it was altogether too fluffy.

Ferzan Ozpetek's **La Fate Ignoranti** (2001)

The Best Day of My Life (2003) became a box-office hit in Italy when it opened. Christina Comencini's film is a portrait of a rich Roman family: matriarch Irene (Virna Lisi) and her grown-up children – two daughters Sara (Margherita Buy) and Rita (Sandra Ceccarelli) and a gay son Claudio (Luigi Lo Cascio). Almost everyone is forced to confront love, sex and fidelity in what was a compelling story of three generations and their moral choices. The film became the surprise winner of the Grand Prix of Americas, the top prize at the Montreal World Film Festival.

Romance has radiated throughout the various Spanish entries in gay cinema this decade. *Km. 0 – Kilometer Zero* (2000) took its title from a popular meeting place in Madrid's central plaza, the Puerta del Sol, and follows a series of chance meetings, missed connections and mistaken identities that give way to erotic interludes, sexual escapades and romantic couplings. From a fresh-faced aspiring director involved with a prostitute, to a gay dance instructor whose computer sees more action than he does, to an older woman seeking a male escort for the first time, *Km. 0* is fast-paced, inventive and stylish – but not quite Almodovar.

Meanwhile, the famous Spanish director Ventura Pons chose to film his 2002 movie *Food of Love* in English, with an English cast, even though the entire production was Barcelona-based. His meticulous adaptation of David Leavitt's novel *The Page Turner* was a highly moving account of an inexperienced gay teenager who falls for an older concert pianist and won rave reviews at the Berlin Film Festival.

Cesc Gay's stunning Spanish coming-of-age story *Krampack* (2001), cut from similar cloth as *Beautiful Thing* and *Get Real*, detailed the sexual awakenings and experimentations of two teenaged boys during a summer holiday on the sun-baked Spanish coast. The virginal boys, Dani (Fernando Ramallo) and Nico (Jordi Vilches), spend time with two girls of their age, but Dani's feelings for his best friend are clouded with unspoken desire, and when the occasional night-time 'krampack' (mutual wank) fails to satiate Dani's appetite, the friendship slowly drifts apart. Writer-director Gay thankfully refused a happy-ever-after ending, opting for a more ambiguous conclusion.

Also from Spain, in 2003, came the comic and darkly romantic thriller *Bulgarian Lovers*, the film that marked the long-awaited return of the pioneering Spanish gay filmmaker Eloy de la Iglesia. With its themes of love, money and lust, the film was an almost surreal journey through the life of the loveable Daniel (Fernando Guillén Cuervo), a wealthy, spoilt, middle-aged but attractive businessman whose ordered life is thrown into a tailspin when he meets Kyril (Dritan Biba), a sexy, muscular beauty with a charmingly cute smile and a covert life.

German cinema produced the melodramatic coming-out tale *Summer Storm* (2005), set at a summer rowing camp in idyllic countryside where a talented teenage oarsman, Tobi (Robert Stadlober), is struggling with his

Marco Kreuzpaintner's **Summer Storm** (2005)

feelings towards best friend and team-mate Achim (Kostja Ullmann). A kind of German *Beautiful Thing*, Marco Kreuzpaintner's film covered old territory in lessons on sexual tolerance and the importance of being true to one's desires; unfortunately it chose to end on a calculatedly uplifting climax, to the beats of a rather naff cover version of 'Go West'.

The Aussie film *Tan Lines* (2006) also contained plenty of shots of buff, shirtless guys in tight trunks but, unlike *Summer Storm*, its story was subtle, surreal and intriguing. Something a bit different. Set on the sun-drenched beaches of Australia, *Tan Lines* was a sexy but angst-ridden coming-of-age romance about a cute teen called Midget Hollow (Jack Baxter), who wanders through life riding big waves and partying with surfer boys. This 'gay surf movie' had passion, love, laughs, sex and drugs set against the backdrop of the Pacific Ocean. Although not a perfect indie movie, it had flashes of originality from British-born director Ed Aldridge, one of them the religious images of popes and saints hanging in the bedroom who come to life in Midget's mind, bicker in Italian and tease him about his sexuality. 'There's enough sperm in those sheets to make the washing machine pregnant!' says one pope. Aldridge's film had relatable characters without pretension or affectation, and, thankfully, no predictable Hollywood happy ending or tacky soundtrack.

Yet Hollywood too can go gay without resorting to tacky soundtracks. 2005 saw the release of *Brokeback Mountain*, Ang Lee's epic, passionate and beautifully executed 'gay western' about two young men – a ranch hand and a rodeo cowboy – whose 20-year bond to each other proves stronger than either of their marriages. Based on a novella by Pulitzer Prize-winning author Annie Proulx, with a screenplay co-authored by Pulitzer-winner Larry McMurtry, it starred Jake Gyllenhaal and Heath Ledger.

After the flop of *Alexander* (2004) – which its director, Oliver Stone, attributed to the fact that America was 'not ready to accept a romance between two men' – many assumed it would be a long time before we saw another gay love story aimed at a mainstream audience. But Ang Lee knew better. Set against the sweeping vistas of Wyoming and Texas, his film followed the two men's first meeting in the summer of 1963, and their subsequent lifelong connection, their relationship's complications, joys and tragedies providing a testament to the endurance and power of love.

'My body may be a work-in-progress, but there is nothing wrong with my soul.'

Bree in *Transamerica*

Brokeback Mountain had opened at the end of 2005, a few weeks before Christmas, but, in fact, the whole of that year had been an amazing 12 months for gay-themed cinema and countless films with prominent gay characters.

One of the twentieth century's most celebrated – and most flamboyant – gay figures, writer Truman Capote, was played by Philip Seymour Hoffman in *Capote* (2005). The writer was shown with his male lover in the film, and described as having fallen in love with one of the two convicts whose story he told in the fact-based novel *In Cold Blood*. A few months after *Capote* was made, production on *Infamous* (2006) began, in which the iconoclastic author was played by little-known British actor Toby Jones, accompanied by a star cast including Sandra Bullock, Gwyneth Paltrow, Sigourney Weaver, Hope Davis and Jeff Daniels.

Ultimately though, it was the earlier Hoffman film that got all the attention, which is a shame because *Infamous* is arguably *Capote*'s equal; also focusing on the writer's relationship with convicted killer Perry Smith, it dwells more on Capote's high-toned New York social circle, and contains humorous scenes in which straight-laced Kansans' jaws drop as they react to the flamboyant and unabashedly gay cosmopolitan writer in their midst.

A disturbing and challenging question was posed by director John Baumgartner in his 2005 debut *Hard Pill*. If you could take a pill to make you straight, would you? This provocative independent movie starred Jonathan Slavin, in a star-making, tour-de-force performance, as Tim, an unhappy gay man who decides to volunteer for a pharmaceutical study of a pill that's said to turn homosexuals straight. Examining issues of sexuality, medical ethics, and relationships of all stripes, *Hard Pill* is one of the best indie movies of the last few years: a refreshingly honest and often emotionally scathing look at what a 'cure' for homosexuality might actually mean in the everyday lives of gay men.

Other gay-interest movies of 2005 included *Kiss Kiss Bang Bang*, which had Val Kilmer as a gay police detective pursuing, and then teaming up with, straight petty criminal Robert Downey Jr. Meanwhile, *The Dying Gaul*, directed by *Longtime Companion* screenwriter Craig Lucas, centred around a gay writer who turns the story of his lover's death from AIDS into a haunting screenplay, before being told by a Hollywood producer it will never be made unless he changes the gender of the dying character. Make the lovers

Douglas McGrath's **Infamous** (2006)

Craig Lucas's **The Dying Gaul** (2005)

heterosexual, says the executive, and I'll cut you a check for $1 million, here and now. 'Americans hate gays', he says.

And the mainstream gay-interest movies kept on coming. The heart-warming British comedy *Kinky Boots* (2005) told the truth-based story of how a provincial shoe factory on the brink of collapse resurrected itself by switching from making Oxfords for civil servants to stiletto-heel boots for cross-dressers. There was also a cross-dressing director character in the film version of *The Producers* (2005); a prominent gay character featured throughout *Mrs Henderson Presents* (2005); and a lesbian couple, a transvestite and a gay man were central characters in *Rent* (2005), Chris Columbus's film version of Broadway's rock-musical sensation.

Breakfast On Pluto (2005), based on the novel by Patrick McCabe, told the story of Patrick (Cillian Murphy) who, growing up in 1960s Ireland, quickly realises he's not quite like all the other boys. With an unusual fondness for sequins and eyeliner, Patrick, soon calling himself Kitten, escapes the disapproving townspeople and sets off for London in search of love, and his long-lost mother.

Equally as touching, *Transamerica* (2005) featured Felicity Huffman playing a pre-op, male-to-female transsexual about to have surgery to become a woman when she discovers that, years earlier, she fathered a son, who's now a gay hustler in New York. She becomes his guardian on one very complicated cross-country trip that had audiences captivated. A remarkable film about transsexuality, *Transamerica* was a moving story of people seeking a sense of purpose in their lives, and finding someone understanding to share it with.

All of the films discussed here from 2005 were popular at the box office but it was *Brokeback Mountain* that proved a defining film in gay cinema history. Ang Lee's movie quickly became a cultural phenomenon and everyone – from Christians in Middle America to builders in working-class Britain – had something to say about it. Chat-show hosts – David Letterman and Jay Leno in the States and Graham Norton and Jonathan Ross in the UK – parodied it endlessly, as did newspapers and magazines, including one issue of the *New Yorker* which had George Bush and Dick Cheney as the *Brokeback* heroes on its cover. The Christian brigade found it all morally offensive, some cinema chains in certain US states banned the film and the usual groups of gay-haters organised protests.

> 'God, I wish I knew how to quit you!'
> **Jack Twist in *Brokeback Mountain***

> 'I got a boy. Eight months old. Smiles a lot.'
> **Jack Twist in *Brokeback Mountain***

> 'These people spend all night sucking cock and eating ass, and then hit the buffet claiming they're vegan.'
>
> Justin in *Shortbus*

Back in the real world, however, critics heaped praise on *Brokeback* and millions of cinemagoers packed out theatres to watch the gay love story. Not surprisingly, the film led the posse of gay-themed movies in the Oscars race; and 5 March 2006 is the date that goes down in history as the 'Gay Oscars' with Hollywood actively ushering in the 'year of the queer'.

Six awards had already gone to movies with gay or transgender characters at the Golden Globe Awards, with *Brokeback* roping in four, making it the firm favourite for Tinseltown's top honours. However, despite its run of success at the Globes and the BAFTAs, *Brokeback* failed to win as many Oscars as hoped. The film received eight nominations but was beaten to Best Picture by *Crash*. Neither Jake Gyllenhaal nor Heath Ledger took home gongs, although Best Director went to Ang Lee.

Historically, the film with the most Oscar nominations almost always wins Best Picture. *Brokeback* had the most nominations, but didn't receive the award, so most critics in the press took the line that the movie was 'snubbed' or described it all as 'an upset'. Although this was nothing new. Tom Hanks won Best Actor for *Philadelphia*, as did William Hurt for *Kiss of the Spider Woman*, but both films failed to break into the best-picture pack.

So perhaps Hollywood isn't really all that tolerant or progressive. And it's worth remembering that not a single one of the actors who played those characters was actually gay, but straight actors who 'dared' to take on gay roles. If straight actors can play gay parts, why can't it work the other way around?

The fact that directors and producers have very few high-profile, out gay actors to choose from is an entirely separate debate, and has more to do with agents and executives telling their clients not to come out for fear of 'disappointing' fans, and it's also down to the closeted actors who choose to go along with this advice. There are few, if any, A-list US movie stars who are openly gay for fear of compromising their careers as leading men and ladies, and who knows how long they'll remain in Hollywood's closet. If they're good-looking, and credible as romantic leads or action heroes, probably a very long time.

Openly gay British actor Sir Ian McKellen remarked, in 1992, to a reporter for the American magazine *Out*: 'There's not one [leading actor] in your country. Not one. It's odd, isn't it? It's the one area of American life where there are no openly gay people.'

Recently, the *Lord of the Rings* star told closeted actors that their craft would improve if they were open about their sexuality: 'I became a better actor, and my film career took off in a way that I couldn't have expected. You can't lie about something so central to yourself without harming yourself. That's why I can say to other actors: if you really want to be a good actor and a successful one, and you're gay, let everybody know about it.'

McKellen also believes those actors who choose not to come out are sending a 'dreadful message' to their audiences: 'It is extremely sad, but no major actors are happy to say they are gay. They are doing it and cannot be happy with themselves.'

Until very recently, former A-lister Jodie Foster frequently came under attack by gay-rights groups for not talking openly about her sexuality, but in December 2007 she finally chose to 'out' herself as a lesbian by publicly thanking her 'beautiful Cydney who sticks with me through all the rotten and the bliss' during a Hollywood awards ceremony. The only surprising thing about it was all the fuss it created. Everyone had known for years that Ms Foster was gay and in a happy relationship.

We already have a few openly gay actors whose work hasn't been affected by their coming out, and it's fair to say that most people really don't seem to care if Sir Ian McKellen, Antony Sher, Simon Callow or any of the other luminaries of the theatre are gay. But they're character actors, not sex symbols. Could any A-list star who is currently marketed as a sex symbol come out today? Probably not, which is depressing.

Rupert Everett is one of the few out-and-proud gay men in Hollywood, but he has recently been confined to playing homosexual roles or dressing up in drag. He himself claims to have lost major roles because of his sexuality.

Indeed, many out gay actors play camp supporting roles: the gay best friend, the camp comedy character and so on. But to actually have an openly gay actor playing James Bond? No chance.

In the pop world, after George Michael's outing in America, his record sales plummeted. So it's a real, legitimate fear for agents of actors and other pop stars to protect their clients and keep their sexuality a secret.

Researching a Channel 4 documentary about gay Hollywood, the author Paul Burston stated: 'I was overwhelmed at the amount of closeted gay people in the industry that work against the gay community. And it's often gay

TOBY:
'Did you know that the Lord of the Rings is gay?'

BREE:
'I beg your pardon.'

TOBY:
'There's this big, black tower, right? And it points right at this huge burning vagina thing, and it's like the symbol of ultimate evil. And then Sam and Frodo have to go to this cave and deposit their magic ring into this hot, steaming lava pit. Only at the last minute, Frodo can't perform, so Gollum bites off his finger. Gay.'

from *Transamerica*

casting agents that tell gay actors that there isn't a job for them, because they don't want to be seen as being associated with that person. There are a lot of people who have a vested interest in keeping the closet firmly locked and that includes gay people in the industry. The only way this can change is if people take a stand because otherwise it will be like this forever.'

Following the success of *Brokeback Mountain* and other studio-funded gay-themed films, mainstream filmmakers have undoubtedly been more at ease working within the gay-cinema genre. *Boy Culture* (2006), a romantic drama about the lives of a male escort and his two sexy roommates, proved a commercial and critical success, as did *The Walker* (2007), which features Woody Harrelson as gay Carter Page III, a social butterfly of Washington's political elite who entertains wealthy wives of a certain age.

Shortbus (2006) came courtesy of *Hedwig and the Angry Inch* director John Cameron Mitchell. A subversive yet refreshingly funny and sexy gay-interest movie, it was funded by Universal Pictures and dubbed 'the most sexually explicit film to go on general release'. The story follows various emotionally challenged, New York City characters trying desperately to navigate the comic and tragic intersections between sex and love in and around a modern-day polysexual underground salon called Shortbus.

In the wake of *Brokeback*'s success, producers have also dusted off old scripts, returning to gay projects that were previously overlooked or stuck in development. Among these was an adaptation of an old 70s novel by Patricia Nell Warren, *The Front Runner*, about a same-sex affair between a male track coach and a member of his team. Paul Newman bought the film rights to the book more than 30 years ago, but the project remained dormant for decades. Post-*Brokeback*, however, producers began talking it up again as a possible big-budget movie and many Hollywood gossip sites started trying to link A-list actors to the main roles. The casting chat around Hollywood was that Brad Pitt had expressed interest in playing a gay role, possibly the role of the coach in *The Front Runner*.

The hype around the Patricia Nell Warren project seems more recently to have calmed down but other gay-themed films have been given the go ahead, including *I Love You Phillip Morris*, with Jim Carrey as a married prisoner who falls in love with another inmate, played by Ewan McGregor. The film itself if based on a true story (and book), which traces the plight of convict

Steven Russell, whose love for Morris motivated his escape from prison four times, once by using a green pen and a bucket of water to change his prison outfit into what looked like surgical scrubs, another time by faking his death from AIDS and signing his own death certificate. Morris eventually got out, but Russell's escapades landed him a 144-year sentence.

Another high-profile film to go into production in 2008 was Gus Van Sant's *Milk* (2008). With a script by Dustin Lance Black, the much-anticipated biopic stars Sean Penn as Harvey Milk, the first prominent American political figure to be elected to office on an openly gay ticket back in the 70s. So loved was he that his brutal and homophobic assassination by ex-policeman Daniel White sparked the biggest riots in gay history.

After signing Penn, Van Sant stated: 'I think what we have to do is get across a sense of the period, the political climate and the social climate. We want to show a world that is almost unshakable, unless you had a documentary camera on the Castro [in San Francisco] in 1977. So we're trying to capture the flavour of something that is very elusive.'

Van Sant beat the likes of Oliver Stone and fellow, openly gay director Bryan Singer, who had both been developing their own Harvey Milk projects. Singer's *The Mayor of Castro Street* had a script by *Usual Suspects* writer Christopher McQuarrie, but was delayed in pre-production. Van Sant stepped in, got Penn on board and beat them to it.

It took 30 years but thankfully Hollywood filmmakers have finally got around to documenting the event which shaped contemporary gay politics in the States.

Over the decades, gay cinema has reflected the community's journey from persecution to emancipation to acceptance. Politicised dramas like *Victim* in the 60s, *The Naked Civil Servant* in the 70s, and the AIDS cinema of the 80s have given way to films which celebrate a vast array of gay lifestyles.

Gay films have undergone a major shift, from the fringe to the mainstream, and the rise of gay imagery in TV and cinema has undoubtedly loosened the stays of straight society. Many gay films were so mired in issues of coming out, discrimination and AIDS that they left little room for fun, but times have changed and gay politics evolved. Four decades on from the legalisation of homosexuality, there's certainly cause for celebration over what's been achieved in the representation of gay life on screen. And the argument

'New York is where everyone comes to get fucked.'

Tobias in Shortbus

> 'You boys sure found a way to make the time pass up there.'
>
> Joe Aguirre in
> **Brokeback Mountain**

was never *just* about 'positive images' but images of all kinds. The gay community had been sorely underrepresented in Hollywood, decade after decade, but the taboo has slowly faded and films now more accurately portray our diverse society.

It's a few years since the late 90s pink explosion that brought us all those loud-and-proud, *Will & Grace*-style, gay movie characters, and now that the glitter has settled, it's good to see films such as *Brokeback Mountain*, *Breakfast on Pluto* and *Shortbus* achieving well-deserved, worldwide success and acclaim. With so many gay-interest movies being released by mainstream studios, a Saturday night out at the movies is almost beginning to feel like an evening at a gay film festival. Indeed, by the mid-2000s, many of the best gay films around were on general release, being embraced and cherished by both gay and straight audiences. Anyone looking for a gay movie only need check the film listings in their daily newspaper.

However, it's worth remembering that it's only relatively recently that filmmakers and studios have begun to represent the diversity of gay life. There's still a way to go before total industry and audience acceptance of gay-themed cinema, and the early chapters in this book should provide a timely reminder that not so very long ago we really didn't have it this good.

THE FILMS

THE FLUFFER
(2001)

US, 95 mins
Directors: Richard Glatzer, Wash Westmoreland
Writer: Wash Westmoreland
Cast: Scott Gurney, Michael Cunio, Roxanne Day, Taylor Negron, Deborah Harry
Genre: Porn Industry drama / coming-of-age

(fluff-er, n): One who offers ego reinforcement; one who provides the necessary stimulation for a male porn star to perform

A fluffer is responsible – by hand or blow – for keeping a porn star erect. It's a job description that was begging to be made into a movie, and Richard Glatzer and Wash Westmoreland did just that.

A self-taught filmmaker, Wash Westmoreland directed his first film, *Squishy*, in 1995. It was entirely funded by tips made while working at a New Orleans jazz club. The film's unique and provocative stance made it an underground hit at many film festivals. Moving to Los Angeles, Westmoreland had the original idea to make *The Fluffer*, a story of unrequited love set within the modern-day, gay-porn industry. Having no experience of that world, however, he decided first to do some research, and got a job directing gay porn. In just two years, not only did he write *The Fluffer*, but he managed to take the porno world by storm. His movie *Naked Highway* swept both the 1998 GV Guide and Adult Video News awards shows, receiving an unprecedented 15 awards, including Best Movie, Best Director, Best Screenplay, Best Cinematography, and Best Sexual Performance. One of Westmoreland's porn films, *The Devil's Bottom*, was the first-ever adult film, gay or straight, to be included on the *LA Weekly* Best Films of the Year list. Westmoreland co-directed *The Fluffer* with his long-term partner Richard Glatzer (*Grief*).

Boogie Nights is the standard against which any film about the porn industry will be measured. A more modest effort than Paul Thomas Anderson's film, *The Fluffer* is nevertheless a winner and repudiated Anderson's sentimental idea that porn performers and filmmakers are like family. This comes far closer to portraying the reality of the porn industry: the general tedium of life on set, the cheap porn sets, the cost cutting and the cynical outlooks. Bitterly funny, this multi-layered film subverts various narrative strands – porn-industry satire, unrequited love and obsession – and ultimately emerges as an intelligent coming-of-age odyssey.

The story centres around three main characters: Johnny Rebel (Gurney), a gay-for-pay porn star;

Michael Cunio as Sean McGinnis

Sean McGinnis (Cunio), the young, naive, adventurous and pure wannabe filmmaker who's moved to LA to pursue his dream; and Rebel's girlfriend Julie Disponzio (Day), also known as Babylon, the most fiery of the dancers at the strip club, Leggs.

The film opens with a quirky, porn-like twist of fate. On a trip to his local video store to rent his favourite Orson Welles movie, Sean somehow ends up with a copy of *Citizen Cum*.

Westmoreland's porn-industry training is put to good use in the opening sequence of *Citizen Cum*, which is dreamlike and highly erotic, despite avoiding any explicit images. This serves to fetishise Johnny Rebel from the outset. Interestingly, after this mesmerising initial sequence, the porn film sequences and shoots from then on are shown up for what they really are: an unromantic world of sterile, cheap and mostly ridiculous scenarios (pool-cleaner seduction, barnyard orgy), with corny titles such as *Tour de Ass* and *Tranny Get Your Gun*.

Intrigued by *Citizen Cum* and, in particular, the rippling muscles of star Johnny Rebel (Gurney), Sean hunts down the production company, which has Rebel under exclusive contract. He soon gets a job interview at Men of Janus (because 'Janus was the Roman god of entrances and exits'), where vandals frequently erase the 'J' from the sign on the front door, and signs up for some work in order to meet the star. Sean's love of arty compositions soon disqualifies him from camera duties. But as Johnny tends to require stimulation between takes, Sean is deployed instead as a 'fluffer', responsible for ensuring that the leading man is properly prepared for his explicit close-up. Sean is smitten, but the oblivious hunk is strictly 'gay for pay', living a heterosexual life off screen. Johnny is happy to use Sean's services, and to be turned on by having Sean tell him how much he adores his body, but is so self-absorbed he doesn't notice that the young man is in love with him.

While Sean is completely obsessed with the icon Johnny Rebel, Babylon deals with his day-to-day reality. Sean and Babylon find it more and more difficult to cope with their roles and dealing with the inhabitants of the porno underworld. In this slippery city of dreams, both try to cling to their self-respect as they go down on their knees. Babylon dreams of having Johnny's children but Johnny only loves himself, living for money, drugs and attention – from both women and men.

Largely about obsession, *The Fluffer* is also about humiliation. Sean is very attractive, yet nervy and vulnerable. The poster for Andre Techine's sensitive gay drama *Wild Reeds* on his rented apartment wall marks him as a sensitive, introspective film lover, as does the fanatical monologue he delivers on the obsessive themes of *Vertigo* at an industry party when he's wired on crystal meth. 'Total porn,' he exclaims. He has taken direct action by actually getting himself a job at Johnny Rebel's workplace, but he still can't get to the man he desires. He can't get close; can't break through the barrier of the glass screen, whether that be to the erotic images inside his TV screen or into the mirror that Johnny vainly gazes into.

Sean begins a romance with another guy called Brian (Josh Holland), but his heart is never in it and the relationship falls apart once it becomes obvious that all Sean can think about is Johnny. Sean even goes to Babylon's strip-joint and pays her to give him a lap dance and confess intimate secrets about Johnny, including how he tastes and smells.

Sean's own self-loathing and relatively closeted life is traced back – via black-and-white flashbacks – to traumatic childhood abuse. His current emotional status is mirrored by the clock on his kitchen

Michael Cunio (centre) has a **Graduate** moment in **The Fluffer**

wall, whose arms have been frozen at 9.29 AM since he frantically dislodged its batteries to work the remote pause button during *Citizen Cum*. The frozen clock remains a motif throughout the film, until a new clock far away finally chimes for Sean, relieving him of his crisis.

Johnny's dramatic fall from grace (he kills a producer and gets Sean to drive him to Mexico) results in Sean realising how dangerous he really is. He knows he can't stay on his knees forever. Completely heartbroken, he just about finds the courage to move on, as does Babylon. Johnny keeps on running.

The solid supporting cast features Robert Walden (*Lou Grant*) as a porn entrepreneur, Deborah Harry as a strip-club manager and Adina Porter as a lesbian who's into gay-male porn. X-rated actors Cole Tucker and Ron Jeremy also show up briefly in cameos. Taylor Negron and Rich Riehle put in two of the film's finest performances as two directors. Their jaded reactions to everything, and particularly Riehle's repeated complaints about excessive artiness in Sean's filming, offer some great comic moments.

The film's punk soundtrack is superb. Gay porn director Chi Chi La Rue makes a cameo appearance leading a spirited rendition of the Joan Jet song 'Cherry Bomb' while the closing credit scroll is accompanied by the Buzzcocks' brilliant 'Ever Fallen in Love'. Perfect!

Interestingly, at the time of release, the filmmakers devised a 'Fluffer Manifesto' which stated the following: fluffer aims to get the verb 'to fluff' into the dictionary by the year 2003; fluffer salutes all people who have ever been brave enough to work in the adult industry; fluffer acknowledges the tacit compliance between the worshipper and the worshipped; fluffer feels the most interesting areas of sexuality lie between definitions; fluffer sees the adult industry as exploitive only in the same way that all industries are exploitive; fluffer champions feminine aspects of sexuality; fluffer champions masculine aspects of sexuality; fluffer rails against the hypocrisy of censorship; fluffer acknowledges the link between random childhood experience and adult sexuality; and fluffer believes there is no line between art and pornography.

The Fluffer is edgy and compelling. Westmoreland and Glatzer's hypnotic film is one of the coolest gay-themed pictures ever made. That title got butts on seats. But those who went to see the film back in 2001 were treated to a truly rich and rewarding story. If you missed out then, buy the DVD…

L.I.E.
(2001)

US, 97 mins
Director/Writer: Michael Cuesta
Cast: Brian Cox, Paul Dano, Bruce Altman, Billy Kay, James Costa, Tony Donnelly
Genre: Teenage drama

Critically acclaimed as one of the top ten films of 2001, Michael Cuesta's *L.I.E.* is an intense and unsettling drama about the relationship between a middle-aged man and a 15-year-old boy.

The film opens with an arresting image: a teenager is walking precariously along the railings of a footpass, with traffic thundering past underneath. His voiceover intones, 'There are the lanes going east, there are lanes going west, and there are lanes going straight to hell.'

Set in a leafy suburban town just off exit 51 of the Long Island Expressway (the acronym of the title), Cuesta's film focuses on young Howie Blitzer (Dano), a troubled teen whose mother has recently been killed in a car accident on the notorious road.

His father (Altman) is a shady contractor with little time for his son, and so, with no emotional support, Howie begins ditching school and hooks up with an impoverished kid called Gary (Kay) who turns tricks on the expressway and burgles houses to fund his planned escape to California. There's a close bond between the two kids and an erotic undercurrent that hints at Howie coming to terms with his own sexuality. But the chance for this relationship to develop is cut short when they're caught breaking into the house of Big John Harrigan (Cox), a former Marine and well-respected member of the community.

It's at this point that *L.I.E.* enters darker territory. Although the Vietnam veteran seems very well connected with the local cops and the staff at school, it transpires that he also enjoys the company of young boys. After Big John approaches them about the robbery, Howie discovers an alluring secret that binds his friend and the ex-Marine. Howie's dad is then arrested for using unsafe building materials and so Howie is virtually abandoned, leaving the way for Big John to step in as paternal figure and predator.

The ambiguity of the Big John role was always going to cause controversy, but Cox – who deliv-

Billy Kay as Gary (left) and Paul Dano as Howie in ***L.I.E.***

ers one of his finest performances – catches the troubling complexity of a man who simply can't be written off as a stereotype. The actor plays him with a mixture of smooth-talking malevolent charm and genuine sympathy. So, while we are never allowed to forget he is a sinister, predatory figure, we also see a man battling his inner demons as he forges an unlikely friendship with the boy.

L.I.E. in no way excuses Big John's past actions but it does suggest that life is more equivocal than most tabloid headline writers would have you believe.

It could so easily have been a deliberately shocking, exploitative piece of cinema; instead, *L.I.E.* is a fantastic example of an American indie with subtle writing and direction, and a superb performance from Brian Cox. Of course, not surprisingly, the censors rated it as NC-17 in the US and opted for a 15 certificate in the UK. Yes, the film concerns teenage boys and an older man who preys on them sexually. But it's handled responsibly, without gratuitous nudity or lingering shots. In fact, it could even provoke vital discussions between teens and parents, which an NC-17 rating prevents.

Meanwhile, studio pics like *American Beauty*, in which Kevin Spacey fantasises over the underage Mena Suvari, sneak through with just an R rating.

But that's the hypocrisy of censors and the ratings system. A shame, because Michael Cuesta's film deserves a wider audience.

HEDWIG AND THE ANGRY INCH
(2001)

US, 95 mins
Director/Writer: John Cameron Mitchell
Cast: John Cameron Mitchell, Michael Pitt, Miriam Shore, Stephen Trask, Rob Campbell
Genre: Comedy musical

Hedwig and the Angry Inch, a *Rocky Horror Picture Show* for the 90s, had director-star John Cameron Mitchell in the title role of Hedwig, the East German refugee and failed pop star.

Born a boy named Hansel whose life's dream is to find his other half, Hedwig reluctantly submits to a sex-change operation in order to marry an American GI and get over the Berlin Wall to freedom.

The operation is botched, leaving her with the aforementioned 'angry inch'. Finding herself high, dry and divorced in a Kansas trailer park, she pushes on to form a rock band and encounters a lover/protégé in young Tommy Gnosis (Michael Pitt), who eventually leaves her, steals her songs and becomes a huge rock star and totally rich and famous. What else can Hedwig do but stalk him from gig to gig?

Hedwig and the Angry Inch shadows Tommy's massive stadium tour, performing in near-empty restaurants for bewildered diners and a few die-hard fans. But somewhere between the crab cakes and the crap motel rooms, between the anguish and the acid-wash, she pursues her dreams and discovers the origin of love.

The overall effect is of a journey: following this character through a traumatic but often exhilarating search for his identity. This may sound like every other homosexual coming-of-age story, but Mitchell gives it a very universal feel and makes sure to skirt the more embarrassing stereotypes that many gay-themed films often succumb to.

Mitchell retains the excitement of the off-Broadway theatre version, upon which it's based, by singing the musical numbers live on camera. You even get the audience sing-a-long section, complete with on-screen lyrics and a bouncing ball to keep everybody in time.

The action is interspersed with Emily Hubley's quirky animations, particularly during the musical numbers. These are extremely effective during the ballad 'The Origin of Love', in which Hedwig recounts a story from childhood about the creation of men and women.

This eccentric musical-comedy-drama is packed with wigs, 70s-style songs, lashings of eye shadow and bouffant hair, plus a generous helping of sharp one-liners. Audacious, funny and totally fabulous. Made for a paltry $6 million, it's a brilliant triumph and a victory against big-budget, big-star pap.

FAR FROM HEAVEN
(2002)

US/France, 107 mins
Director/Writer: Todd Haynes
Cast: Julianne Moore, Dennis Quaid, Dennis Haysbert, Patricia Clarkson, Viola Davis
Genre: 1950s-set drama

Far From Heaven revisits the almost forgotten genre of the domestic melodrama. Drawing from the 'women's films' of the 1950s, particularly those of director Douglas Sirk, Todd Haynes' re-working of *All That Heaven Allows* casts Julianne Moore as Connecticut housewife and mother, Cathy Whitaker. She's set up in a dream, portfolio house with a fine upstanding husband, Frank (Quaid), and two kids.

Set in the fall of 1957, the melodrama begins when Cathy is returning home from a day of errands. Her husband is expected home for a dinner engagement. There's only one problem – no one has heard from Frank all afternoon.

What begins as a curious snapshot of 1950s American values is soon transformed into a tangle of competing conflicts. Cathy discovers that her idyllic suburban life is a lie as she realises that her husband is having a gay affair. Trouble is, when Cathy finds solace in her formidable black gardener, Raymond (Haysbert), tongues start to wag, and she is faced with choices that spur hatred and gossip within the community.

Frank goes to a doctor for 'treatment', and his confession is heartbreaking. He says that he 'can't let this thing, this sickness, destroy my life. I'm go-

Dennis Quaid and Julianne Moore in a scene from *Far From Heaven*

ing to beat this thing'. We pity him because we realise that such a feat is impossible, and unnecessary, but Frank does not possess that knowledge.

Haynes spends a lot of time exploring these ideological tensions and contradictions concerning gender, sexuality and race that define the 50s melodrama and highlights the confining concepts of sexuality alive in yesteryear and today. Its themes are relevant, valid and important, whether in the context of the 50s or today.

Haynes reminds us that homosexuality was seen as a disease; blacks were openly marginalised and humiliated; kids were often left to their own devices while busy parents ran cocktail parties; and white women with black men caused a public outcry. All this, we already knew and, of course, a lot of this still goes on, but because the film deliberately lacks irony, it still has a genuine dramatic impact. Indeed Haynes believes his film has a lot to say about today, not just life in the 50s.

'It's a very sad story. Sadly, it's a story that really could be told today in America. Basically it's about these people, who look amazing, sound amazing, and move like none of us do, but who are ultimately very fragile people. They don't tear down the walls of their society. They ultimately succumb to the pressures of their society, and in that way they're more familiar than a lot of film subjects are – they're really more like us.'

Julianne Moore, back with Haynes after their previous collaboration *Safe* (1995), is superb as dutiful housemother Cathy Whitaker and was nominated for the Best Actress Oscar. Dennis Quaid is equally impressive as Cathy's tortured husband. Director Todd Haynes has created a stunning film, every frame steeped in deliciously gaudy Technicolor. A truly moving view of an intolerant time, *Far From Heaven* is a near perfect homage, and serves as proof that Haynes is one of America's finest living directors.

LUSTER
(2002)

US, 92 mins
Director/Writer: Everett Lewis
Cast: Justin Herwick, Shane Powers, Barry Wyatt, Pamela Gidley, Willie Garson, Jonah Blechman
Genre: Punk Scene

In a time when gay characters are now successful, clean-cut and fit into mainstream society (*Broken Hearts Club/Will & Grace* etc), Everett Lewis (*Skin and Bone/An Ambush of Ghosts*) sets his film in the 'queer' punk scene of recent Los Angeles and fashions his lead character as a skateboarding poet and fanzines producer. His name is Jackson and he's embracing LA's 'queer core' movement, completely at odds with the mainstream gay and lesbian community.

Waking up after an orgy is only the beginning of an unforgettable weekend for Jackson (Justin Herwick), who thinks he's in love with Billy (Jonah Blechman). He met Billy at an orgy, but Billy just wants to be friends. Enter Jackson's hunky cousin Jed (Barry Wyatt) who is in town for the weekend. Jackson lusts after him, but you're not supposed to have sex with your cousin – right?

Then there is Derek (Sean Thibodeau), a 'normal' fag who claims he knew the minute he laid eyes on him that Jackson was 'the One'. Well, Jackson isn't interested; falling in love at first sight is bullshit – or is it? To complicate matters further, it seems that Sam (Shane Powers), Jackson's best friend, may not be straight after all. And when Sonny (Willie Garson from *Sex and the City*), a closeted rock star, asks Jackson to help write lyrics for his next album, things really begin to spin out of control.

Set in a world of wacky artists, cute alternative guys and a rock star with twisted sexual habits, *Luster* is a wildly entertaining, gritty and charming look at a queer boy's adventures in lust, sex – and maybe even love.

A defining element of *Luster* is its soundtrack, which is a virtual 'Who's Who' of queer rock, led by Pansy Division. Other featured bands include Extra Fancy and Action Plus. Likewise, Jackson's poetry is actually the work of famed edgy gay poet Dennis Cooper. The film opens with lines from Cooper's acclaimed 'David Cassidy Then'.

ANGELS IN AMERICA
(2003)

US, 352 mins
Director: Mike Nichols
Cast: Al Pacino, Meryl Streep and Emma Thompson along with Mary-Louise Parker, Jeffrey Wright, Justin Kirk, Ben Shenkman, Patrick Wilson and James Cromwell, with performances by Michael Gambon and Simon Callow.
Genre: Fantasy/Political

Al Pacino as Roy Cohn in the epic **Angels in America**

In 2003, Mike Nichols (*The Graduate/The Birdcage*) made *Angels in America*. Adapted by Tony Kushner from his own Tony- and Pulitzer Prize-winning play, this epic drama, which features an extraordinary cast led by Al Pacino, was actually made for TV.

A two-part, six-hour movie event for HBO, *Angels in America* was lauded as a truly defining screen event and, as well as Pacino, featured other Academy Award- winning actors, Meryl Streep and Emma Thompson along with Mary-Louise Parker, Jeffrey Wright, Justin Kirk, Ben Shenkman, Michael Gambon and Simon Callow.

A sweeping film event, Nichols' epic and intimate drama explores the politics, morality and search for hope in the story of six interconnected characters and an Angel, in the complex and turbulent world of New York in the late 1980s.

Angels revolves around two very different men with AIDS, one fictional, one fictionalised. The almost-real character is the controversial and legendary lawyer, Roy Cohn, played by Pacino. Cohn is a fictional re-creation of the infamous American conservative ideologue who died of AIDS in 1986 and personifies all the hypocrisy, delusion and callousness of the official response to the plague. Nothing shakes his riveting lack of empathy: Cohn explains to his doctor (James Cromwell) how he is not a 'homosexual', he is a man who has sex with men, because a homosexual could not get the president on the phone (or, 'Better, the president's wife'), but Roy Cohn can. Therefore, Roy Cohn is not a homosexual. Then he bullies the doctor into diagnosing him with liver cancer instead of what he actually has, AIDS. Even on his deathbed, he fights with his gay nurse (Wright) and taunts the woman he helped put to death, Ethel Rosenberg (Streep, in one of three major roles).

The other patient facing the spectre of AIDS is Prior Walter (Kirk), who experiences dreamlike visitations by a prophet-seeking Angel (Thompson) and is deserted by his self-pitying lover, Louis (Shenkman). Louis moves on to Joe Pitt (Wilson), a Mormon lawyer whose own closeted homosexuality and sexual repression cause his marriage to his Valium-addicted wife (Mary-Louise Parker) to unravel and brings his mother (Streep again) to New York.

Spanning the extremes of comedy and tragedy, love and betrayal, life and death, *Angels in America* is a journey through the landscape of despair and hope that defines America at the end of the twentieth century.

Although an amazingly angry piece, Kushner's screenplay somehow manages to reach beyond that anger toward understanding. Indeed, that's what makes Prior's final prophecy all the more moving. 'This disease will be the end of many of us, but not nearly all... We will not die secret deaths anymore. The world only spins forward. We will be citizens. The time has come.'

Shortly after its television premiere, *Angels in America* garnered five Golden Globe Awards, leading all winners and winning in every category in which it was nominated. The wins included the awards for Best Actress (Meryl Streep); Best Actor (Al Pacino); Best Supporting Actress (Mary-Louise Parker); and Best Supporting Actor (Jeffrey

Wright). *Angels* also swept the board at the 2004 Emmys.

The network that aired *Angels* – justifiably proud – declared the drama 'not TV, it's HBO' – but this *is* TV, as it can be and should be more often. It is proof that TV producers as well as indie filmmakers *can* have faith in audiences to watch gay-related drama.

BROKEBACK MOUNTAIN
(2005)

US, 134 mins
Director: Ang Lee
Writers: Larry McMurtry, Diana Ossana (based on a story by Annie Proulx)
Cast: Heath Ledger, Jake Gyllenhaal, Randy Quaid, Anne Hathaway, Michelle Williams, Roberta Maxwell
Genre: Western

Nominated for eight Academy Awards, *Brokeback Mountain* was the gay-themed movie that captivated audiences around the world. A huge mainstream success, and quite simply a masterpiece, this landmark film was proof that times really were changing.

Hollywood, which had always been apprehensive about depicting homosexuality, finally got behind a powerful gay love story, a film about two cowboys who unexpectedly fall in love while working together one summer in 1963.

Of course, the trashier end of the media dubbed it 'the gay cowboy movie', 'the queer *Gone with the Wind*' and, as American chat-show host Jay Leno put it, 'the Western that puts the poke in cowpoke'. Meanwhile, amidst all the media fuss, gay groups celebrated the recognition and spotlight the film threw on the homosexual community, which had long been underrepresented in mainstream cinema. Here was by far the most uncompromising and unapologetic gay-themed drama ever made for a wide release by a major Hollywood studio with big-name stars.

An epic love story set against the sweeping vistas of Wyoming and Texas, Ang Lee's tragic and moving film is based on the 31-page novella by Pulitzer Prize-winning author Annie Proulx. In the opening scenes, we meet wannabe rodeo star Jack Twist (Jake Gyllenhaal) and ranch-hand Ennis Del Mar (Heath Ledger), two 20-year-old strangers meeting for the first time.

Ranch boss Joe Aguirre (Randy Quaid) hires the pair to herd sheep up on Wyoming's scenic Brokeback Mountain. The more outgoing Jack initiates a friendship with Ennis, and one cold evening invites him into his tent, where, huddling together for warmth, their awkward embrace leads them to stumble into a sexual act and sends their relationship in a new direction.

The next few weeks on the range prove a confusing time for the pair. They may claim that they 'ain't queer' but there is no denying their love for one another. As Proulx wrote in the original short story: 'They never talked about sex, let it happen, at first only in the tent at night, then in full daylight with the hot sun striking down, and at evening in

Heath Ledger as Ennis and Jake Gyllenhaal as Jack

the fire glow, quick, rough, laughing and snorting, no lack of noises, but saying not a goddamn word except once Ennis said, "I'm not no queer", and Jack jumped in with "Me neither".'

Both men agree there would be no harm in continuing a physically intimate relationship. 'Nobody's business but ours,' reasons Jack. And so, when their first summer together passes, the two men go their separate ways: Jack back to Texas, where he marries Lureen (Anne Hathaway) and has a son; and Ennis back to Washakie County, where he marries his fiancée Alma (Michelle Williams) and raises two young daughters.

But they can't forget one another. Eventually, the pair are reunited when Jack pays Ennis a visit. The meeting gives way to a passion that becomes regularly recharged in an annual rendezvous, which they explain away to their wives as 'hunting trips', which continue over the next 20 years. The two men hate the fact they have to live a lie and often, when they meet, there is a sense of love so frustrating it often manifests itself in physical violence. While Jack harbours dreams of a life together, the tight-lipped Ennis is unable to bring himself to even consider something so revolutionary. So Lee's film becomes increasingly heart-wrenching, with neither man able to make a total commitment to the other.

This beautiful portrait of regret and wasted chances has some heartbreaking closing scenes and praise must go to Roberta Maxwell for her small but memorable role as Jack's deeply understanding mother at the end of the film. The grief-ridden woman knows what kind of relationship her son had with Ennis. But so too does her homophobic husband (Peter McRobbie), who has obviously made mother and son's lives hell. So when the mourning Ennis arrives at their home, her face says it all. This emotionally crushed woman, under the nose of her mean husband, in just a brief few looks and words, conveys her sympathy and understanding. Ennis enters Jack's room, and we just know who has preserved it, in one of the few gestures of love and respect tolerated under the father's cruel, relentless, queer-hating nastiness.

Larry McMurtry and Diana Ossana's screenplay is a marvel of an adaptation; all the literary flavour remains and it is magnificently visualised. Lee and the gifted cinematographer Rodrigo Prieto (*Amores Perros*) transform Proulx's terse prose into ravishing cinematic poetry. With little dialogue, they create a whole world that can be read eloquently and movingly on the faces of the actors.

Ledger and Gyllenhaal deliver emotionally charged, remarkably moving performances in *Brokeback Mountain*. They are exceptional leads – both mesmerising and devastating. Gyllenhaal is the more self-accepting and open of the pair, his pain continually registering in those beautiful but oh-so-sad eyes. He brings extra dimensions to a character that could have so easily just been a cute pretty-boy type. Ledger, meanwhile, with his drawling accent and the slightly slovenly posture, catches all of his character's pent-up torment, delivering a portrait of an emotionally repressed man both undone and liberated by his feelings. Director Ang Lee called Ledger a young Brando and it seems certain this brilliant actor's untimely death at the age of 28 will elevate him to cult status akin to that of James Dean.

Speaking to *Attitude* magazine just before the film's UK release, Ledger stated: 'If I never get another part because I chose to play a gay character in a gay movie, then fuck Hollywood.'

Before his death in 2008, Ledger went on to star as The Joker in Christopher Nolan's latest *Batman* instalment and as one of the Bob Dylan characters in Todd Haynes' star-studded *I'm Not There* (both 2007). Gyllenhaal, meanwhile, starred in the offbeat hit *Jarhead* (2005) and featured alongside Gwyneth Paltrow and Anthony Hopkins in John Madden's *Proof* (2006).

Just as Tom Hanks went on to an Oscar-filled career following his gay role in *Philadelphia* (1994), it looks likely the same will now happen with Gyllenhaal. Yet despite winning a string of BAFTAs and Golden Globes, despite the rave reviews and the film's undeniable worldwide success, *Brokeback Mountain* scored eight Academy Award nominations (including Gyllenhaal for Best Supporting Actor and Heath Ledger for Best Actor), but only won three – Best Music Score, Best Director and Best Adapted Screenplay.

A group of disgruntled fans even formed an alliance to overcome the loss of the Best Picture Award by running an advertising campaign to highlight their shock. One internet blogger Dave Cullen collected $26,000 from over 600 people in the week following the Academy Awards for an advertisement in daily *Variety* suggesting that *Brokeback Mountain*, which was named Best Picture through 'unprecedented consensus' in other ceremonies, should have also won the Oscar.

Mr Cullen said: 'We wanted to send a message, there was a lot of fear involved here.' The group placed similar statements in *Entertainment Weekly* and the *New York Times*. *Newsweek* revealed that most of the donors were gay men who saw a win for the film as a step forward in the battle for equality and felt they lost because of homophobia.

But Oscars aren't everything and who cares if there's still a homophobic wind blowing through the Hollywood hills? Back in the world of sanity, *Brokeback Mountain* had flipped a switch. Everyone was talking about it. Inside theatres, audiences were mostly made up of straight people who took the story on its own terms. Customers of the mainstream website Lovefilm.com ranked the embrace between Jake Gyllenhaal and Heath Ledger as the sexiest screen kiss of all time. The supposedly controversial clinch beat other famous silver-screen kisses from romantic classics including *Gone with the Wind* and *Dirty Dancing* and began to suggest that the straight world had moved beyond simple 'tolerance'.

Even the scenic setting of the gay romance became a talking point, with travel agencies around the world offering holidays to Fort Macleod in Southern Alberta, Canada, which was passed off as Wyoming in the film; tours aimed at all sexualities.

A few months after *Brokeback*'s release, Diana Ossana, the film's co-screenwriter, said she felt it was changing hearts and minds: 'People come in with these preconceived notions of the film but after they see it they can't stop thinking about it. They'll tell me, "You know, I never really thought about gay men and their lives. I always tried to avoid it, but I really felt bad for those guys. I didn't know they felt the way that we do."'

So, it wasn't only gay groups celebrating the film's release. Ang Lee's film had crossover appeal. Save for the usual gay-hating Christians and Catholics who found it 'morally offensive', mainstream audiences chose to embrace it, as reflected in the box-office returns and DVD sales. There is, quite simply, no doubt that *Brokeback Mountain* is the biggest breakthrough gay film of all time.

TRANSAMERICA
(2005)

US, 103 mins
Director/Writer: Duncan Tucker
Cast: Felicity Huffman, Kevin Zegers, Fionnula Flanagan, Jon Businoff, Elizabeth Peña
Genre: Transgender-interest

Hilary Swank picked up an Oscar for playing a cross-dresser – and Felicity Huffman narrowly missed out on one for doing the same thing in Duncan Tucker's *Transamerica*.

Leaving the glamour of *Desperate Housewives* behind, Huffman makes a surprising diversion with this offbeat film as she turns in an impressive performance as an uptight, pre-operative, male-to-female transsexual named Sabrina Bree Osbourne (née Stanley), who's awaiting gender-reassignment surgery.

Bree holds down two jobs and saves every penny so that she can pay for that one last operation that will make her a woman at last, and she's convinced that her entire life has been leading up to this moment. But just a week before the final op she receives a sudden telephone call from New York informing her of the arrest of a son she wasn't aware even existed.

Toby (Kevin Zegers), apparently her wayward teenage son, must be the product of a somewhat clumsy sexual encounter 17 years ago when she was a man. At first, Bree is happy to ignore this reminder of her one and only sexual experience as a man, but then her therapist (Elizabeth Peña), realising she needs to resolve her feelings about being a parent, refuses to approve her for surgery until she has gone to the New York jail and faced her child.

Bree flies from Los Angeles to the Big Apple, bails Toby and they end up on a road trip across the country. Instead of revealing the truth, however, she ends up masquerading as a do-gooder missionary worker ('I'm from the Church of the Potential Father!'), determined to convert reprobates to Jesus. Initially, Bree sees no reason to clear up the misunderstanding.

Convinced Bree really is a Christian missionary, Toby is quite open about the fact he's actually a teenage hustler with a moderate drug problem. He even informs her of his intention to become a porn star on the west coast, which brings out plenty of motherly instincts in the worried cross-gender father. So the two end up embarking on a bizarre road trip back west, with Bree trying to get home in time for her operation, and Toby aiming for life in Hollywood as a gay porn star. It's also a trip which sees Bree flailing in her attempts to tell

Felicity Huffman as Bree in *Transamerica*

Toby the truth about who she is and what she once was, but, as the trip goes on, she starts to come to terms with being a parent and finally begins to feel comfortable in her own skin.

Transamerica is a quirky film and there's much to admire. Writer/director Duncan Tucker gets the balance between comedy and drama just right as he gently squeezes Bree's various revelations to Toby onto the screen. Tucker doesn't focus too much on Bree's gender or her operation – that is just a side issue to her relationship with the son she never knew she had. All in all, the film is an emotional portrait of a highly dysfunctional family, a family which is connecting. It's also a film which constantly drags the audience back from the brink with laugh-out-loud funny moments. It's beautifully shot, and played to a great country-and-western soundtrack.

A fine supporting cast, in this small but rich film, includes Fionnula Flanagan as Bree's hilariously overbearing mother, and Grant Monohon as a hitchhiking hippy. There's also a touching scene with Graham Greene as Calvin Manygoats, a Native American who has taken a shine to Bree. 'There's things about her she's not telling you,' Toby teases. 'Every woman has a right to a little mystery,' replies Calvin.

But it's Huffman who really shines, with her vocal inflections, make-up, and acting skills perfectly combining to give a convincing performance. She deserves every award she's received for her role in *Transamerica*.

CAPOTE
(2005)

Canada/US, 114 mins
Director: Bennett Miller
Writer: Dan Futterman
Cast: Philip Seymour Hoffman, Catherine Keener,

Philip Seymour Hoffman as Truman Capote

Bruce Greenwood, Clifton Collins
Genre: Biopic

Bolstered by an Oscar-winning performance by Philip Seymour Hoffman in the title role, Bennett Miller's *Capote* ranked highly among the best films of 2005. A finely crafted biopic, it recounts an historic chapter in American history and, in the process, captures the unravelling of a truly gifted mind.

Adapted from Gerald Clarke's acclaimed biography by actor/screenwriter Dan Futterman, this mercilessly perceptive drama concentrates on the seven-year period during which the openly gay author Truman Capote wrote his groundbreaking book, *In Cold Blood*, the 'non-fiction novel' that was immediately acclaimed as a literary milestone.

On the night of 14 November 1959, in Holcomb, Kansas, a farmhouse was broken into by the criminals Perry Smith (sensitively played by Clifton Collins, Jr) and Richard Eugene Hickock (Mark Pellegrino), who expected to get $10,000. With the policy of 'no witness', the murderers killed the entire family.

At the opening of the film, the clean, flat plains and deserted farmhouse in Kansas play in direct contrast to Capote's own frantic life in New York.

The idiosyncratic author reads about the tragic murder of the Clutter family in the morning paper and a couple of quick phone calls later, convinced he's on to something, heads south to write a piece for the *New Yorker*. He is escorted there by his friend and fellow author Harper Lee (Catherine Keener), herself about to publish a masterwork, *To Kill a Mockingbird*. Honest and completely committed to keeping Capote focused, she grounds the film, while serving as the author's research assistant during his investigation of the cold-blooded killings.

Somehow, the soft-spoken, eccentric Capote manages to earn the trust of local authorities, most notably reserved KBI agent Alvin Dewey (Chris Cooper). When the two killers are caught and returned to Kansas to await trial, he helps get their execution delayed by arranging extensive interviews with the prisoners, now determined not only to write his *New Yorker* article but also to use the topic to write a book.

Capote bonds with the pair but especially with Perry Smith, a quiet and articulate man with a troubled history. It is obvious Capote has fallen for him. As he works on his book, his intense emotional bond with Perry in part prompts him to help the prisoners to some degree. However, the pressure of this connection threatens to push an already fragile Capote into the darkest recesses of himself.

The author needs closure for his book, which only an execution can provide.

Exceptionally opportunistic, Capote borrows Smith's personal journals for his research because, he says, 'I don't want the world to see you as a monster.' Sometimes abandoning Smith and Hickock for months at a time, he comes and goes in their lives, leaving the pair desperate and confused.

Understandably, the conflicts and the mixed motives for both interviewer and subject make for a troubling experience, but Capote's main priority is to try to finish the book that he is convinced will shock the nation and change the course of writing forever.

With Lee by Capote's side, serving as his quiet voice of conscience, we see the many faces of a writer who grew too close to his subjects. The interactions between Hoffman and Collins lead to poignant scenes of great emotion, in particular when the author refuses to pay Smith a visit until just before his execution, and Capote crying, 'I did everything I could,' when clearly he did not.

So *Capote* is a film that asks if a great work of art is worth the cost of a couple of human beings. In the case of Truman Capote, the events of his later life created further intrigue when, unable to write anything to rival *In Cold Blood*, he penned a similar fictitious tale, *Handcarved Coffins*, then passed it off as fact.

Hoffman's tender portrayal of the writer is a remarkable achievement. He slips into the skin of Capote perfectly, allowing viewers to experience his inner turmoil for themselves. Couple this performance with Bennett Miller's overall vision, and intimate direction, beautifully realised by his technical collaborators (especially director of photography Adam Kimmel and production designer Jess Gonchor), and you have a truly great film.

A year after Hoffman won an Oscar for his role as Truman Capote, another Hollywood film about the eccentric author emerged. *Infamous* (2007) had little-known English actor Toby Jones in the Capote role, alongside new James Bond star Daniel Craig portraying killer Perry Smith, and Sandra Bullock as Harper Lee. Despite the starry cast, however, this other take on the life of Capote didn't fare as well.

SHORTBUS
(2006)

US, 102 mins
Director: John Cameron Mitchell
Cast: Sook-Yin Lee, Paul Dawson, Lindsay Beamish, PJ Deboy, Raphael Barker, Jay Brannan, Peter Stickles, Justin Bond
Genre: Tragicomedy

In early 2003, *Hedwig* director John Cameron Mitchell sent out an open casting call for his new film, at the time called *The Sex Movie Project*. 'We avoided agents and stars – stars don't have sex,' explains Mitchell. 'I'd envisioned a year-long workshop process, and stars don't generally do that either. Instead, we solicited interviews in various alternative periodicals inviting anyone who was interested – experienced actors or not – to go to our website, read about what we were trying to do and send in audition tapes.'

Over half a million people visited the website, and nearly 500 people, mostly from North America, sent in tapes. Some talked to the camera, some made short films, some sang songs, some jerked off. Forty people were called to the main audition and eventually Mitchell chose the actors that would appear in *Shortbus* (2006), a series of vignettes about highly sexed and sexually frustrated New Yorkers, all of whom find some kind of salvation at an underground club.

That venue is based on Brooklyn's D.U.M.B.O. club. Called Shortbus in Mitchell's film (a reference to the shorter yellow buses that are provided for less-able/special-needs kids in New York), it is 'a salon for the gifted and challenged', a mad nexus of art, music, politics and polysexual carnality. As one character dryly notes in what must surely be thought of as the film's signature line, 'It's just like the 60s, only with less hope.'

At Toys in Babeland, a sex shop in lower Manhattan, sales increased 30 per cent in the wake of 9/11, according to the *New York Observer*. A year later, the number of babies born in the city's hospitals was up 20 per cent. These statistics form the background for *Shortbus*, which is set against the electrical brown and black-outs that afflicted Manhattan shortly after the 9/11 atrocities.

Among the residents of Bush-exhausted New York City are Jamie (PJ DeBoy) and James (Paul Dawson), a gay couple looking to open up their relationship with young ex-model Ceth (Jay Brannan). Caleb (Peter Stickles) is a voyeur who stalks James and Jamie. Sophia (Sook-Yin Lee) is a sex therapist who can't orgasm. And then there's Dominatrix Severin (Lindsay Beamish) who's never had a relationship. Meanwhile, the flamboyant 'Mistress of Shortbus' (Justin Bond) provides multiple instances of comic relief.

Mitchell has created a film in which the characters and script were developed through group improvisation, inspired by the disparate techniques of John Cassavetes, Robert Altman and Mike Leigh. It is full of sex – real people having actual sex – in various gender permutations. Extremely sexually graphic (the film begins with an eye-opening montage of a man attempting to give himself a blowjob), *Shortbus* also includes one of the funniest gay threesomes ever committed to camera, a three-way which involves the singing of the Star-Spangled Banner into an anus!

In another scene, a young man being disciplined by a whip-wielding dominatrix accidentally ejaculates all over a Jackson Pollock-esque expressionist painting, his fluid merging with the picture's splattered brushstroke style until the two blend entirely.

However, whilst the orgies and ejaculations might be the reason the film has attained so much notoriety, it is fair to say that the sex is never gratuitous. 'I believe sex is sacred,' says Mitchell, 'but it's not being respected by the America cinema. The true perversion to me is crushing it and hiding it... This is an act of resistance.'

'I decided to make a New York-style, emotionally challenging comedy that would be sexually frank, thought provoking and, if possible, funny,' he explains. 'It would not necessarily seek to be erotic; instead, it would try to use the language of sex as a metaphor for other aspects of the characters' lives.'

Indeed, Mitchell and his cast juggle the sex, scathing humour and drama with incredible acuity. Most audiences will quickly get past the naked bodies – refreshingly not at all traditional, Hollywood airbrushed gloss – to focus on the people underneath.

As each character's plot develops, the viewer sees a similar melancholy bulldozing its way into these seemingly disparate lives. They are a fragile bunch and their club becomes as much a sanctuary as a pleasure dome. They focus on sex as a way of getting through to each other, and of getting in touch with themselves.

Eventually, the film rides to a delicious climax, one of the most generous and sweet in memory. 'Our demons are our best friend; we all get it in the end,' goes the song. And that pretty much goes for the film, too. As all of the characters converge at Shortbus, the city's lights fail, plunging everyone into moments of self-reflection. Then the lights across Manhattan come back on and regenerate, symbolic of all those troubled relationships reconnecting. Just as MC Justin Bond says in the film, everyone is trying to find that right connection.

THE ACTORS AND DIRECTORS

RICHARD GLATZER & WASH WESTMORELAND
Writer/Directors
1966– (Westmoreland)
Unknown (Glatzer)

Richard Glatzer and Wash Westmoreland (aka Wash West) are a formidable partnership – writing, producing and directing impressive drama for the gay audience and beyond.

Born in Leeds, in the UK, in 1966, Westmoreland graduated in Politics and promptly moved to the US, where he met his long-time partner Richard Glatzer, and made his first short film, *Squishy Does Porno!* (1994).

Glatzer's first feature film *Grief* was released in the same year, 1994, to international acclaim. Winner of awards at both the San Francisco Gay and Lesbian Festival and the Torino Festival, *Grief* also made a huge impression at the Berlin, Toronto and Sundance festivals. *Sight and Sound* magazine called *Grief* 'a deeply likeable movie ... [that] well deserves the cult status for which it seems destined'.

Originally intending to become an academic, Glatzer got his PhD in American Literature from the University of Virginia. His first script was optioned by Jay Presson Allen (*Marnie/The Prime of Miss Jean Brodie*) and he worked with her on two scripts that were eventually sold to Disney.

Glatzer also produced the US television series *Divorce Court* on which much of *Grief* was based, and collaborated with Tim Hunter on the fact-based TV drama *Anatomy of a Hate Crime* (2001) which centred on the brutal 1998 murder of Matthew Shepard, an openly homosexual college student in Wyoming, by two homophobic, trouble-making teens and their co-conspirator girlfriends. It was the incident which prompted an outcry of support for the Shepard family and tougher hate-crime laws by liberal activists, but also support for Matthew's killers by religious leaders and homophobic activists.

During these years, Westmoreland was directing stunning and successful gay-porn films. Often considered one of the most innovative and daring directors of gay pornography, directing under the names of Wash Westmoreland, Bobby Dazzler and Bud Light, his titles include *Naked Highway*, *The Hole* and *Seven Deadly Sins: Gluttony*. It was this experience in the adult-film industry that helped him to conceive his first feature as director.

In partnership together, Westmoreland and Glatzer made the controversial feature *The Fluffer* (2001), which follows Sean, a young filmmaker whose obsession with 'gay-for-pay' porn actor Johnny Rebel leads him to become his cameraman and then his 'fluffer'. As *Out* magazine put it, *The Fluffer* was 'everything you hoped *Boogie Nights* would be'.

The two also worked together on the documentary *Gay Republicans*, about the dilemma faced by gay Republicans in the face of President Bush's opposition to gay marriage.

More recently, the pair co-wrote and directed the 2006 Sundance Film Festival Grand Jury Prize and Audience Award–winning film *Quinceañera*. Marketed as *Echo Park, LA* in the UK, the film's original Spanish title refers to the Mexican tradition of holding a huge party to celebrate a girl's fifteenth birthday. In the movie, as Magdalena's birthday approaches, her simple, blissful life is complicated by the discovery that she is pregnant. Subsequently kicked out of her house, she is taken in by Tomas, her great-granduncle and Carlos, her outcast gay cousin. Westmoreland and Glatzer's film offers an enlightening insight into the racial, class and sexual tensions of a working-class Mexican LA neighbourhood in transition.

ANG LEE
Writer/Director
1954–

Taiwanese director Ang Lee was one of the first Chinese-born directors to find critical and commercial success on both sides of the Pacific. Born in 1954, he studied at the National Taiwan College of Arts in 1975 and then went to the United States, where he studied theatre directing at the University of Illinois and film production at New York University.

After winning awards in the mid-80s for his NYU student films, Lee spent the next few years working mainly on screenplays, eventually making his directorial debut in 1992 with *Pushing Hands*, a comedy about the generational and cultural gaps in a Taiwanese family living in New York.

His next film, *The Wedding Banquet* (1993), further explored these themes but through a gay New Yorker who stages a marriage of convenience to please his visiting Taiwanese parents. The film met with widespread acclaim, winning a Golden Bear at the Berlin Film Festival and a Best Director prize at the Seattle Film Festival, as well as Golden Globe and Academy Award nominations.

Lee followed up *The Wedding Banquet* with *Eat Drink Man Woman* (1994), another tale of generational differences, and then his mainstream Hollywood Jane Austen adaptation *Sense and Sensibility* in 1995. It won numerous awards for both Lee and its star Emma Thompson. After adapting Rick Moody's novel *The Ice Storm* for the big screen, Lee next tried his hand at Civil War drama with *Ride with the Devil*, which featured great performances from Jonathan Rhys Myers, Jewel Kilcher and Jeffrey Wright.

Crouching Tiger, Hidden Dragon (2000) was the intriguing fantasy that would eventually become the highest-grossing foreign-language film ever released in the US earning 14 Oscar nominations and 16 British Academy Award nominations. In the event, Lee's film actually earned four Oscars including Best Foreign Language Film, Best Director at the Golden Globes, and four British Academy Awards including Best Director.

Ang Lee is not gay but he's included in this book for his contribution to gay cinema. Already earning respect amongst gay-interest film fans for *The Wedding Banquet*, in 2005 he directed the monumentally acclaimed *Brokeback Mountain*, starring Jake Gyllenhaal and Heath Ledger. The film's sensitive and epic portrayal of a thriving romance that

EVERETT LEWIS
Writer/Director

Since his debut with *The Natural History of Parking Lots*, a 1991 Sundance award-winner, Everett Lewis has made films that celebrate a gay world populated by punksters, slackers and skinheads that hasn't been seen since the 'queer cinema' of the late 1980s.

'I am impatient with many "gay films", which seem to be rehashing issues and genres that are tired or exhausted,' says Lewis.

Lewis's most important film to date has been *Luster* (2002), a no-budget piece of grunge, and an irreverent and funny take on the clashing forces of unrequited love and overpowering lust. The film follows a blue-haired, skateboarding lyricist through the punk-rock world of Los Angeles. A tragi-comedy of bad manners, the film features the poetry of Dennis Cooper, music by Pansy Division and lines like 'So what's your opinion of Foucault's theory on sexuality?'

Talking about *Luster*, Lewis stated: 'I wanted to take a picture of the LA gay arts scene. It was important to me to present a world where being gay was normal. It's the straight man in the movie who is ultimately suicidal. I think the most difficult part of the film was trying to capture a certain moment in youth when the dividing line between callow and heartfelt is so very narrow and constantly shifting. That's a difficult and dangerous place to dwell for too long, and I hope we pulled it off.'

Lewis followed up *Luster* with *FAQs* (2005), an offbeat film and a touching and frustrating look at gay-bashing victims, and the bashers themselves. In fact, *FAQs* was kind of an action movie – *Death Wish* for the gay audience, but with the Charles Bronson character replaced with a gun-toting,

survives between two Wyoming cowboys in the 1960s was praised as both elegiac and grounded. Lee's deft handling of material that simultaneously drew on the established themes of classic cinema and pioneered completely unexplored territory in mass media could not have been more exalted and Lee won a Golden Globe for Best Director of a Motion Picture, as well as an Academy Award for Best Direction. The film also picked up Golden Globe awards for Best Motion Picture Drama, Best Screenplay and Best Original Song in a Motion Picture, and another Oscar for Best Original Score.

On *Brokeback Mountain*, Ang Lee commented, 'I believe everybody has a flip side: the cowboy with the homo, the tough guy with the sensitive... Love is more complicated than our culture categorises it. Everybody is a universe.'

muscular, black drag queen taking back the streets and the night. An interesting concept, and one that works very well.

JOHN CAMERON MITCHELL
Director/Writer/Actor
1963–

While on a plane flight in 1994, John Cameron Mitchell started talking with the only other passenger not watching the in-flight film, composer Stephen Trask. They would later collaborate on what was to be the actor's most influential role – the transsexual, East German rock singer Hedwig of *Hedwig and the Angry Inch*. However, it would take them some three years to fully realise the project, during which Mitchell appeared in the short-lived Fox sitcom *Party Girl* and honed his directorial skills with various stage productions.

In 1997, when *Hedwig* debuted, no one anticipated how successful it was to become. When it was re-staged the following year, *Hedwig* received rave reviews and Mitchell went on to play the role in the West Coast premiere of the show before developing the material as a feature film at the Sundance Screenwriters Lab.

His film version premiered at the 2001 Sundance Film Festival and proved an instant hit, taking home the Audience Award as well as the directing award for Mitchell.

After *Hedwig*, Mitchell executive-produced the documentary film *Tarnation* (2005) and directed the eternally camp Scissor Sisters' video *Filthy/Gorgeous*, which was banned from American MTV for its explicitly sexual content. After these quirky distractions, in 2006 Mitchell released the feature *Shortbus*, which was presented out of competition at the Cannes Festival. Full of real gay sex, the film obviously shocked quite a few people.

Tellingly, Mitchell was brought up in a strict Catholic, military environment where sex was 'the scariest thing imaginable'. That closeted youngster quickly morphed into one of today's hottest directors who has come to regard sex as 'the nerve endings of people's lives'.

'Sex is always tied solely to trauma,' he explains. 'It's almost seen as a cliché, just not worth it. And you know, it isn't only tied to trauma! Like in *Shortbus*, sex is not the problem. The characters don't shy away from it.

'I have seen so few films in which the sex felt really respected by the filmmaker. Hollywood too often shies away from it or makes adolescent jokes about it. Sex is only connected to the negative because people are scared of it. There is such a reluctance to address sex as an inherent part of the human experience in this country. The true perversion to me is crushing it and hiding it.'

With *Shortbus*, Mitchell has created something remarkably different – an emotionally challenging story that is both sexually frank and very funny.

Mitchell's most recent film *Oskur Fishman* is an eagerly anticipated surreal fairytale, supposedly reminiscent of *The Wizard of Oz*.

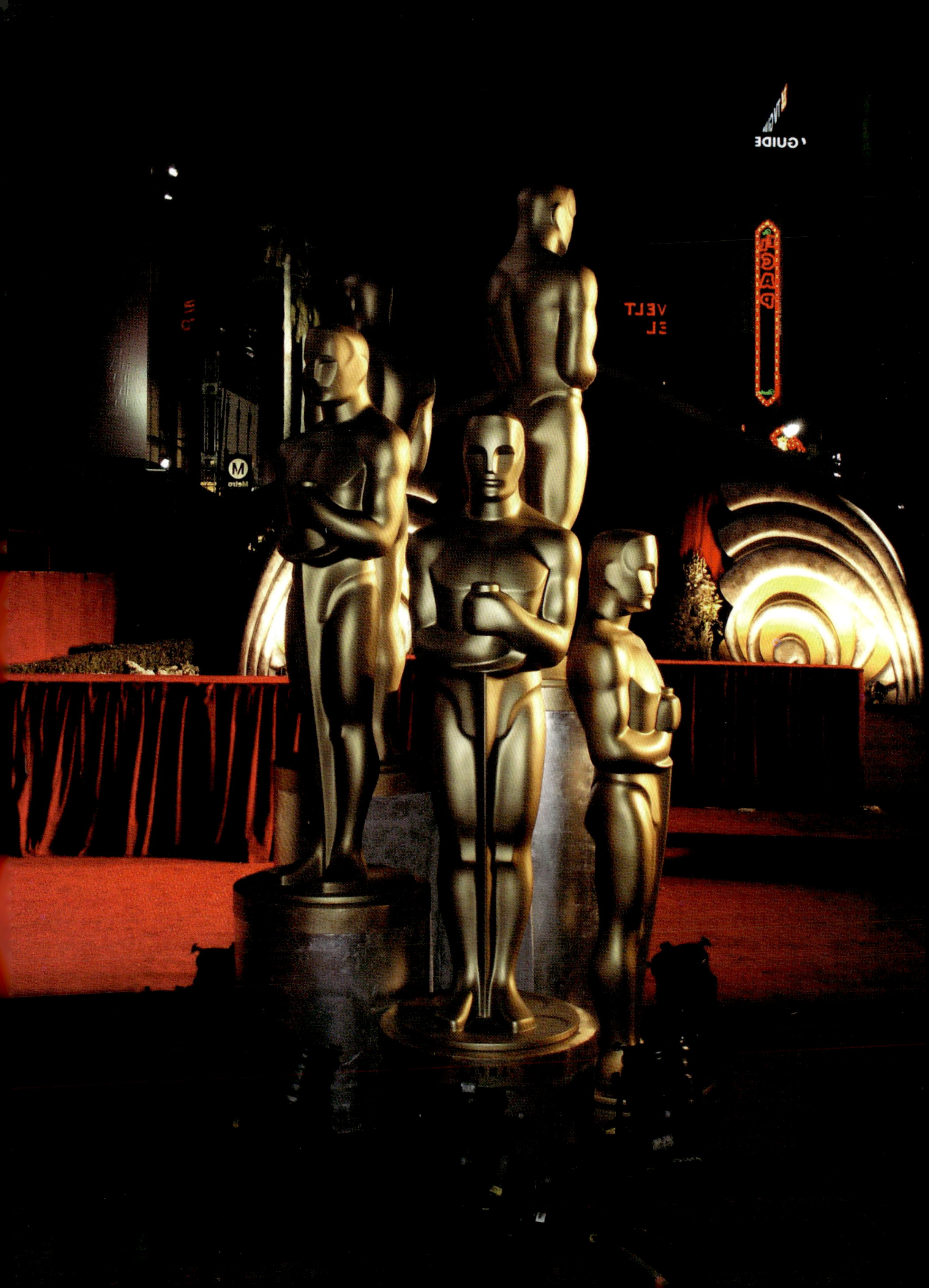

AND THE WINNER IS...
THE GAY OSCARS

THE EARLY YEARS

THE WIZARD OF OZ (1939) – Although nominated for Best Picture back in 1939, this classic, gay-interest movie didn't win. However, some Oscars were awarded to Oz: Special Award to gay icon Judy Garland; Best Original Score (Herbert Stothart); and Best Song for 'Over the Rainbow'. More recently the song claimed the number one spot in the American Film Institute's list of 'The 100 Years of The Greatest Songs'.

MILDRED PIERCE (1945) – An undisputed classic. For sheer, unadulterated star power, Joan Crawford's return to fame, fortune and an Oscar (after being 'let go' by MGM) is unrivalled. The film's appeal with gay film lovers lies with Crawford, a true diva and gay icon, and the fact it's as camp as they come.

1950s

ALL ABOUT EVE (1950) – Joseph Mankiewicz's jaundiced look at the show-biz battle zone of Broadway. Eve was originally written as a lesbian character but all overt references to her sexuality were dropped. Nevertheless, to those in the know, the gay subtext was fairly obvious. George Sanders won an Oscar for his turn as the camp theatre critic, Addison De Witt. As well as the lesbian subtext, the film's appeal amongst the gay community also lies in its star. Bette Davis, like Joan Crawford, was a true gay diva, a 'bitch' in every positive sense of the word.

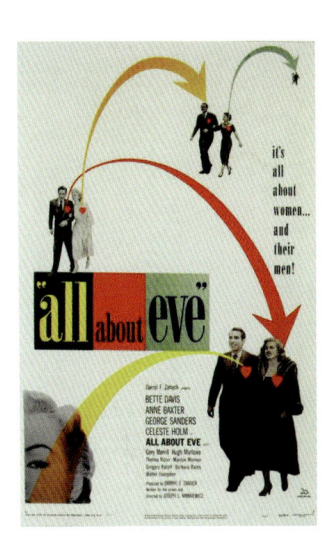

SUDDENLY LAST SUMMER (1959) – One of the big groundbreakers in gay cinema history. In 1959, the Motion Picture Production Code and the Catholic Church granted a special dispensation permitting the film to include the first male homosexual in American film. The word is never mentioned, the character did not speak and his face never appeared. Oscar nominations for stars Elizabeth Taylor and Katherine Hepburn.

1960s

THE SOUND OF MUSIC (1965) – The beloved movie musical has won legions of gay fans over the years, perhaps Maria's transformation being key to the story's enduring popularity. A complete outsider who's been living in a convent and afraid to live in the real world, she is still able to conquer her fears. Back in 1965, the film won Best Director (Robert Wise), Best Music (Irwin Kostal) and Best Picture. Julie Andrews was nominated for Best Actress but did not win.

MIDNIGHT COWBOY (1969) – The first gay-themed Best Picture winner in Oscar history. Also won Best Director for John Schlesinger.

1970s

CABARET (1972) – Won eight Oscars including Best Actress Liza Minnelli and Best Director Bob Fosse. *Cabaret* is a truly inspired version of Christopher Isherwood's 1939 memoirs and bisexual tales of pre-WWII Berlin.

LA CAGE AUX FOLLES (1978) – This camp classic was nominated for three Oscars: Best Director, Screenplay and Costume.

1980s

THE DRESSER (1983) – Tom Courtenay played the highly camp, gay dresser who is infatuated with the ageing, spoilt actor played by Albert Finney. Both received Oscar nominations for Best Actor.

MY BEAUTIFUL LAUNDRETTE (1985) – Best Screenplay nomination for Hanif Kureshi.

1990s

THE CRYING GAME (1992) – Won Best Screenplay (written directly for the screen) for Neil Jordan. Also nominations for Best Picture, Best Actor (Stephen Rea), Best Supporting Actor (Jaye Davidson) and Best Director (Neil Jordan).

PHILADELPHIA (1993) – Won Best Actor (Tom Hanks) and Best Original Song (Bruce Springsteen). It was also nominated for Best Screenplay.

PRISCILLA, QUEEN OF THE DESERT (1994) – The outrageously camp road movie won Best Costume Design.

GODS AND MONSTERS (1998) – Won the Oscar for Best Writing (Screenplay Based on Material from Another Medium) awarded to Bill Condon. Plus nominations for Best Actor (Sir Ian McKellen) and Best Supporting Actress (Lynn Redgrave)

BOYS DON'T CRY (1999) – Best Actress for Hilary Swank. Plus a nomination for Chloe Sevigny in the Best Supporting Actress category.

2000s

THE HOURS (2002) – Nicole Kidman won the Best Actress Oscar for her role as Virginia Woolf. The film also achieved nominations for Best Picture, Editing, Adapted Screenplay and Original Score. Further nominations went to Ed Harris for Best Supporting Actor, Julianne Moore for Best Supporting Actress and Best Director (Stephen Daldry).

FAR FROM HEAVEN (2002) – Nominated for Best Actress (Julianne Moore), Best Original Screenplay (Todd Haynes), Best Original Score (Elmer Bernstein) and Best Cinematography (Edward Lachman)

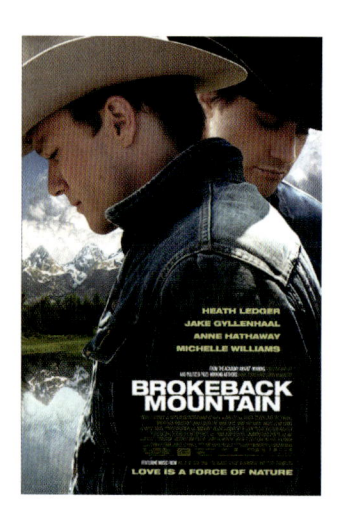

BROKEBACK MOUNTAIN (2005) – Won three Oscars for Best Director (Ang Lee), Best Original Score (Gustavo Santaolalla) and Best Adapted Screenplay (Larry McMurtry and Diana Ossana). Also, nominations for Best Picture, Best Cinematography, Best Actor (Heath Ledger), Best Supporting Actor (Jake Gyllenhaal) and Best Supporting Actress (Michelle Williams).

CAPOTE (2005) – One Oscar win for Best Actor (Philip Seymour Hoffman) plus nominations for Best Picture, Best Director (Bennett Miller), Best Screenplay (Dan Futterman) and Best Supporting Actress (Catherine Keener).

TRANSAMERICA (2005) – Nominated for two Oscars: Best Actress (Felicity Huffman) and Best Original Song (Dolly Parton).

INDEX

A

Adventures of Priscilla, Queen of the Desert, The (1994), 124, 137, 203
AIDS, 9, 14, 21, 60–61, 71, 87, 94–96, 102, 107–108, 114, 116, 118, 121–122, 124, 132–136, 142, 146–147, 159–161, 168, 172, 177, 186
A.K.A (2002), 164
All About Eve (1950), 18, 34–35, 201
Almodovar, Pedro, 97, 129, 170
And the Band Played On (1993), 13, 122, 136–137, 147
Angels in America (2003), 114, 160, 185–186
Anger, Kenneth, 48, 75
Another Country (1984), 98, 116
Another Gay Movie (2006), 154
Araki, Gregg, 122, 130
Australian cinema, 137, 155

B

Basic Instinct (1992), 127
Beautiful Boxer (2003), 166
Beautiful Thing (1995), 11, 123, 139–140, 142–143, 170–171
Bedrooms and Hallways (1998), 10, 114, 129, 138
Beefcake (1998), 130, 153
Bent (1996), 123, 140, 147
Benzina (2001), 163
Bidgood, James, 68, 75–76
Big Eden (2000), 157
Billy's Hollywood Screen Kiss (1998), 129
Birdcage, The (1996), 14, 84, 124, 140, 185

Bisexuality, 8, 77, 112
Blossoming of Maximo Oliveros (2006), 166
Bogarde, Dirk, 47, 52, 60, 68, 73, 75
Bound (1996), 127, 163
Boys Don't Cry (1999), 128, 203
Boys in the Band, The (1970), 8, 13, 67, 71–73
Brando, Marlon, 21, 36, 46, 55–56, 188
Breakfast on Pluto (2005), 15, 178
British cinema, 31, 47, 61–62, 97, 115, 164
Brokeback Mountain (2005), 8, 10, 13, 15, 51, 58–59, 171–173, 176, 178, 187–189, 196–197, 204
Broken Hearts Club, The (2000), 153, 185
Buddies (1985), 96

C

Cabaret (1972), 67, 76–77, 202
Cage aux Folles, La (1978), 70, 84, 124, 202
Callow, Simon, 8, 109, 114, 175, 185–186
Camp characters, 9, 14, 19, 26–27, 30, 34, 69–71, 77–78, 80, 84, 97, 102, 121, 123, 128, 137–138, 141, 147, 166, 168, 170, 175, 198, 201–203
Can't Stop the Music (1980), 93, 101
Canadian cinema, 158
Capote (2005), 13, 15, 172, 191–192, 204
Caravaggio (1972), 33, 86–87, 98, 108–109
Carry On series, 22, 30, 47
Chant d'Amour, Un (1950), 19, 32–33
Children's Hour, The (1936), 20
Children's Hour, The (1963), 46, 48, 54–55
Chinese cinema, 196
Circuit (2002), 161–162
Claire of the Moon (1992), 128
Clift, Montgomery, 20–22, 31, 37, 43
Closet, The (2001), 167
Closeted actors, 14, 28, 52, 104, 115, 136, 158, 160, 174–175, 181, 185–186, 198
Coming out, 13, 28, 47, 69, 103, 122, 148, 167, 175
Cowboys & Angels (2003), 165
Crawford, Joan, 14, 22, 25–26, 30–31, 34, 72, 201
Crisp, Quentin, 68–69, 81–82
Crowley, Mart, 8, 67, 72
Cruising (1980), 13, 68, 72, 93–94, 102
Crying Game, The (1992), 123, 130–132, 203
Curry, Tim, 78–79
Czech cinema, 123–124, 141

D

Davies, Terence, 99, 115
Davis, Bette, 22, 34, 201
Davis, Brad, 97, 105, 115
Dean, James, 13, 21–22, 35, 40, 42–43, 188
Dearden, Basil, 47, 52–53, 60
Death in Venice (1971), 53, 60, 68, 71, 74, 88–89
De Generes, Ellen, 13, 128
Distant Voices, Still Lives (1988), 99, 115
divas, 22
Divine, 30, 69, 77–78, 85–86, 89–91
Dog Day Afternoon (1975), 68
drag queens, 49, 65–66, 89, 122, 137–139
Dresser, The (1983), 97, 202

E

Endgame (2000), 164
Englishman Abroad, An (1985), 98
Everett, Rupert, 19, 62, 116–117, 158, 175, 185, 197

F

Far From Heaven (2002), 146, 159, 184–185, 203
Fassbinder, Rainer Werner, 19, 60, 82, 97, 104–105, 116–118, 140, 146
Fierstein, Harvey, 99, 112–113, 118–119
first love, 139

Fluffer, The (2001), 157, 179–181, 195–196
Forgive and Forget (2000), 164
Fosse, Bob, 67, 76, 202
Foster, Jodie, 175
Fox and his Friends (1975), 82, 118
French cinema, 167
Fried Green Tomatoes (1991), 127, 163
Friedkin, William, 67–68, 72, 93–94, 102
Fry, Stephen, 123

G

Garland, Judy, 11, 14, 22, 27–28, 40–41, 65–66, 201
Gay Brothers, The (1895), 17
Gay Deceivers, The (1969), 50–51
German cinema, 117
Get Real (1998), 123, 142, 170
Glatzer, Richard, 122, 134–135, 179, 181, 195–196
Go Fish (1994), 128
Gods and Monsters (1998), 130, 144–145, 147, 153, 203
Greece, 125
Grief (1993), 121–122, 134–135, 179, 195
Grodecki, Wiktor, 123–124, 141–142
Group, The (1966), 48

H

Hamam (1996), 125
Happy Birthday (2002), 158
Harold and Maude (1971), 70
Harry and Max (2003), 159
Harvey, Jonathan, 11, 139
Hawtrey, Charles, 22, 47
Haynes, Todd, 33, 121, 124, 131, 146, 159, 184–185, 188, 203
Hays Code, 19
Hedwig and the Angry Inch (2001), 158, 176, 183, 198
High Art (1998), 127
Hitchcock, Alfred, 19, 31, 70, 150
Hoffman, Dustin, 51, 58–59, 99, 133
homophobia, 116, 122, 148, 154, 167, 189
Hours, The (2002), 159, 203

Hudson, Rock, 20, 39, 43, 46, 60–61, 95
Hurt, John, 69, 80–82, 94

I

I Love You Phillip Morris (2008), 15, 176
I Now Pronounce You Chuck and Larry (2007), 154–155
incest, 123, 168
Ireland, 132, 165, 173
Iron Ladies (2001), 166
Israel, 167
Italy, 19, 29, 50, 68, 73, 84, 88, 133, 149, 169

J

Jarman, Derek, 33, 68, 75, 82–83, 86–87, 98, 108–109
Johns (1992), 122

K

Kalin, Tom, 32, 121
Kendall, Bobby, 75–76
Killing of Sister George, The (1968), 13, 50, 57
Kureishi, Hanif, 203

L

L.I.E (2001), 15, 156, 181–182
La Bruce, Bruce, 122
Law of Desire (1982), 97
Leather Boys, The (1963), 46, 67
Leaving Metropolis (2002), 158, 165
Lee, Ang, 13, 51, 125, 171–174, 187–189, 196–197, 204
legislation changes, 147 – 148
lesbian Interest, 163
Like It Is (1998), 123, 143–144
Lilies (1996), 125–126
Lola and Billidikid (1998), 122
Longtime Companion (1990), 122, 172
L-Shaped Room (1962), 45, 67
Luster (2002), 158, 185, 197

M

Maedchen in Uniform (1931), 18, 25

Making Love (1982), 13, 94, 104
Mala Noche (1985), 99, 106, 149
Man of No Importance, A (1994), 123
Mankiewicz. Joseph, 23, 34, 37–38, 201
Mathias, Sean, 123, 140–141
Maurice (1987), 98, 110, 114
McKellen, Sir Ian, 10, 130, 136, 140–141, 144, 147–148, 174–175, 203
Midnight Cowboy (1969), 8, 51, 58–59, 62, 133, 202
Midnight Dancers (1994), 125
Mildred Pierce (1945), 30–31, 201
Milk (2008), 15, 151, 177
Mineo, Sal, 21–22, 35, 42–43
Minnelli, Liza, 41, 67, 76–77, 202
Mitchell, John Cameron, 158, 176, 183, 193–194, 198–199
Morrissey, Paul, 49
musicals, 10, 27, 29, 41, 67, 69, 76–77, 79–80, 84, 91, 115, 122, 137, 158, 173, 183, 202
My Beautiful Laundrette (1985), 11, 203
My Hustler (1965), 49
My Own Private Idaho (1991), 99, 106, 121–122, 125, 133–134, 149

N

Naked Civil Servant, The (1975), 68–69, 81, 177
'new queer' cinema, 106, 121, 122, 124, 160

O

O'Brien, Richard, 69, 78, 80
Oldman, Gary, 98, 111, 112
Orphée (1950), 19, 32
Ossessione (1942), 19, 29–30, 88

P

Pacino, Al, 13, 68, 93–94, 102–103, 185–186
Pandora's Box (1928), 18, 24–25
Parting Glances (1986), 14, 96, 108
Pasolini, Pier Paolo, 50

Personal Best (1982), 94–95
Philadelphia (1993), 10, 14, 121–122, 130, 136–137, 174, 188, 203
Philippines, 125, 166
Pink Flamingos (1972), 69, 77–78, 85, 90–91
Pink Narcissus (1978), 68, 75–76
Poison (1991), 14, 33, 121, 131, 146
porn industry, 49, 90, 142, 158, 179–181, 190, 195
Prick Up Your Ears (1987), 98, 111
Priest (1994), 123
Production Code, 19–20, 22–23, 31, 37, 48–51, 73, 202
P.S. Your Cat is Dead! (2002), 43, 153

Q
Queer as Folk (1999), 11, 14, 128, 162
Querelle (1982), 97, 105, 116, 118, 146

R
Rebel Without a Cause (1955), 21, 35, 39, 42
Reflections in a Golden Eye (1967), 46, 56
Reid, Beryl, 56–57
Rocky Horror Picture Show, The (1975), 69, 78–80, 158, 183
Rope (1948), 19, 31

S
Schlesinger, John, 8, 11, 51, 58, 61–62, 67, 133, 202
Sebastiane (1976), 68, 83, 86–87
Sergeant, The (1968), 46, 56
Sherman, Martin, 11, 123, 140, 147
Shortbus (2006), 15, 176, 178, 193–194, 198–199
silent cinema, 17–18, 24, 47, 81, 85, 89
Silkwood (1983), 95
sissies (see also Camp characters), 15, 22, 46–47, 67
Some Like it Hot (1959), 22, 36, 124
Son Frère (2003), 168
Sound of Music, The (1965), 202
South Korea, 166
Spain, 97, 170

Spartacus (1960), 20
Staircase (1969), 46, 50, 58
stereotypes, 15, 50, 57, 118, 127–128, 135, 155, 164, 183
Stonewall riots, 51, 66
Strange Bedfellows (2004), 155
Suddenly Last Summer (1959), 37–38, 202
Sunday, Bloody Sunday (1971), 8, 62
Swoon (1991), 32, 121, 134

T
Taiwan, 125, 196
Taste of Honey, A (1961), 45, 67
Taylor, Elizabeth, 13, 37, 39, 55, 202
Thailand, 166
Thelma & Louise (1991), 126, 163
Therese and Isabelle (1968), 48
To Wong Foo, Thanks for Everything, Julie Newmar (1995), 124, 138–139
Torch Song Trilogy (1988), 99, 112, 118
Transamerica (2005), 15, 173, 190–191, 204
transgender, 65, 99, 156, 166, 174
Trick (1999), 129
Troche, Rose, 10, 114, 129, 138
Turkey, 125

U
Underground cinema, 33, 48–49, 68, 89, 179
Urbania (2000), 156–157

V
Van Sant, Gus, 15, 99, 106, 121, 132–134, 149–151, 177
Victim (1961), 13, 47, 52–54, 60, 177
victims, 46, 67, 96, 197
villains, 45–46, 67
Visconti, Luchino, 11, 29–30, 60, 68, 73–75, 88–89

W
Warhol, Andy, 49, 59, 75, 87, 118
Waters, John, 69, 77, 85, 91, 165
Webb, Clifton, 22, 40, 191
Wedding Banquet, The (1993), 125, 196
Westmoreland, Wash, 179, 195
When Boys Fly (2002), 161–162
Will & Grace, 13–14, 128
Williams, Kenneth, 22, 47
Wizard of Oz, The (1939), 22, 27–29, 40–41, 72, 199, 201
Women, The (1939), 25–26

Y
Yossi & Jagger (2003), 167
You'll Get Over It (2001), 167